HONG KONGED

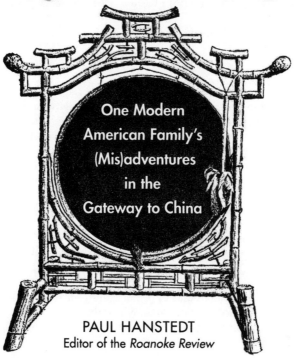

One Modern
American Family's
(Mis)adventures
in the
Gateway to China

PAUL HANSTEDT
Editor of the *Roanoke Review*

AVON, MASSACHUSETTS

Published by
Adams Media, a division of F+W Media, Inc.
57 Littlefield Street, Avon, MA 02322. U.S.A.
www.adamsmedia.com

ISBN 10: 1-4405-4073-X
ISBN 13: 978-1-4405-4073-8
eISBN 10: 1-4405-4105-1
eISBN 13: 978-1-4405-4105-6

Printed in the United States of America.

10 9 8 7 6 5 4 3 2 1

This publication is designed to provide accurate and authoritative information with regard to the subject matter covered. It is sold with the understanding that the publisher is not engaged in rendering legal, accounting, or other professional advice. If legal advice or other expert assistance is required, the services of a competent professional person should be sought.
—From a *Declaration of Principles* jointly adopted by a Committee of the American Bar Association and a Committee of Publishers and Associations

"Help" was previously published as a stand-alone essay in the *Chronicle of Higher Education*, March of 2010; "Grief and the Village" appeared in *Brain, Child: The Magazine for Thinking Mothers*, under the title "What Do You Say?", March of 2011.

Many of the designations used by manufacturers and sellers to distinguish their product are claimed as trademarks. Where those designations appear in this book and Adams Media was aware of a trademark claim, the designations have been printed with initial capital letters.

Interior illustration © 123rf/Violeta Stosic

This book is available at quantity discounts for bulk purchases.
For information, please call 1-800-289-0963.

NOTE TO THE READER

I'd like to think this book passes the Oprah test, that were she somehow to invite me (hint hint) onto her now nonexistent show, she wouldn't nail me to the floor with that look of hers that says I've blown it so badly I'll be lucky if the local paper ever prints my name again, much less my stories. That said, I'm sure someone somewhere will read this book and say, "But that's not how it happened. That's not how I remember it." And that person may be right. These are my words, these are my stories, and I've done my best to recount them in as true and gracious a manner as possible. To the extent that I may have failed, I invite those who feel offended (including Oprah) to join me some evening for a nice glass of wine, a good dinner (likely involving squid), and a chuckle over the wonder that was our year in Asia.

For William, who knows who he is,
Lucinda, who will try anything,
James, who brings joy to our lives,
and Ellen, who keeps it all together.

ACKNOWLEDGMENTS

I wish to thank the Fulbright Organization and Po Chung for making our year in Hong Kong possible. I also wish to thank Roanoke College for allowing me the chance to explore. Thanks as well to my wonderful friends and family, particularly to those who guided us so generously and kindly during our time in Asia and to those at home who read my blogs and encouraged me to keep going. And many thanks to my agent, Coleen O'Shea, for working miracles; my editor, Katie Corcoran Lytle, and copyeditor, Skye Alexander, for making me make sense; and the designer, Frank Rivera, for creating a cover that captures the spirit of the book.

CONTENTS

OUR FAMILY ON THE VERGE OF DESTRUCTION

It's our first night on the junk in Ha Long Bay, and our ship is sinking.

Or at least I think it is. I base this on the fact that, when I creep to the bathroom at midnight, the water outside the porthole seems awfully, well . . . *close.*

Granted, it's not like I have much to compare it to; I hadn't spent much time in that particular restroom during the day. What with the amazing scenery (lush green mountains rising out of the sea), the activities (touring through a local floating village and ducking into caves), and the amazing food plucked fresh from the bay, we'd been pretty busy. Not much time for me to climb down into our family-sized room and take measurements out the bathroom window, eyeballing the exact level of the water outside the porthole.

But even so. The few times I *had* been there during the day, and *had* glanced out that particular window, my sense had been that I was looking more *above* the water than *along* it. Staring out the porthole now, muddled and swaying with sleep, I'm struck by the sound of waves lapping only inches from my face. I squint, peer more closely into the dark: The sky is moonless and clear, sparkling with starlight. Against that, I can see the distinct soft-peaked mountains of the bay, and below that, glowing ripples of water as the tide comes in. Very *close* glowing ripples of water, have I mentioned that?

It probably doesn't help that during dinner Thinh, our Vietnamese guide, had asked us how old we thought the ship was. We glanced around at the red-brown paneling, the latticed windows, the slightly worn floorboards, and guessed anywhere between fifteen and thirty years old.

"Wrong!" he said, grinning. "Only three years old."

"Really," we said. "Are you sure?" He nodded, still smiling. "Only three years old. They built it after the last one sank."

Now he had our attention.

"Sank?" said Bay, the only passenger other than Ellen and me and our three kids.

Thinh nodded. Then, realizing suddenly what we were thinking, waved his hands in front of him. "Oh no, no," he said. "In the harbor. It sank in the harbor. The captain put it in too close. The tide went out, the keel broke, and it sank. There was no one on board."

Even so, an image like that tends to stick, tiptoeing back into your mind in the middle of the night when it's dark and you're tired from a long day of adventure. Going back to bed doesn't help. Curling up next to Ellen, I tell myself not to worry: We'll be fine. The boat is small, yes, and, well, *cheap*. We're in Asia on a Fulbright, after all, so it's not like we can do—or would want to do—a five-star cruise. And Vietnam is a developing country, just getting the hang of this tourist thing. But even so, the company we signed on with got great reviews online. The crew members seem to know their way around the bay, they're a little young maybe, but they've done this hundreds of times. Surely they can keep one tiny boat afloat for three short days.

I listen to my kids, ages nine, six, and three, snoring in the next bed. This reassures me some, and laying my head down on the pillow, I try to sleep.

The only problem is that my pillow—which rests on my mattress, which rests on the bed, which rests on the floor of our cabin, which rests in the lower part of the boat—acts as a sort of megaphone, magnifying all the sounds of everything below me:

the rustle of the sheets, the squeak of the mattress, the scrub of the bedpost on the wooden floor.

And beneath all of that, very quietly and very steadily, this sound: glub, glub, glub.

We're not actually an ugly family, it's just that the boat and the beauty of Ha Long Bay make us look that way.

It may help to know that one of my childhood memories is pulling into a family friend's driveway in Pennsylvania after a long trip from the Midwest. We are there to visit the parish where my father, a minister, used to preach, but as we roll up to the house, all of us, even me at the age of four, notice the surplus of cars in front of the garage. Some of them are police cars, state cruisers, an ominous sign even when it isn't dark and you're not exhausted from traveling all day.

What happens next is more family legend than actual memory. We step into the kitchen of our old family friends, Aunt Cel and Uncle Jim. Jim and a minister friend of theirs step out of a back room. They take my father by the arm, draw him into a corner, and tell him that his parents have been killed in a car wreck.

We learn later that the accident was frighteningly simple. My grandparents were driving along a rural highway in Northern Wisconsin, my grandmother at the wheel, when the right front tire of the car slipped off the pavement and onto the gravel. Struggling to maintain control, my grandmother steered to the left. The tire came free and their big Oldsmobile shot across the yellow line and into the path of an oncoming tanker truck carrying milk.

A milk truck. Think about that. My grandfather, a small-town kid who went from pushing a broom to being town mayor and president of the local bank, was killed instantly. My grandmother was still alive when the emergency people arrived, but died soon after. One minute earlier, the truck would have been a half-mile away. Twenty seconds later, thirty yards past. Either one and I would maybe have a memory of Gus and Marie, rather than just a bunch of photographs of two people whose voices I wouldn't recognize.

I have more memories from that night. Almost as soon as we'd arrived at Cel and Jim's, we climbed into a friend's station wagon—my dad was in no shape to drive—and started the trip back to Wisconsin. My brother and I were in the way-back in kid-sized sleeping bags. I remember those sleeping bags, how they were half the length of regular ones. I thought they were neat.

Anyhow, I must have snoozed most of the drive out, because I couldn't sleep at all going back. And I must have been loud and antsy and asking all the wrong questions, because at one point I remember peering over the way-back and seeing my father twist in his seat, struggling against the headrest as he shouted at me, his voice ragged and wet.

Driving in from the airport to Hanoi, prior to our trip to the bay, we'd peppered our guide with a million questions: Where should we eat? How do we know we're not getting ripped off? How much should a good meal cost? He answered everything we threw at him, even though it was late and the kids were rowdy and he knew we were leaving for the bay the very next day and none of this would earn him a tip. Beyond that, he offered us two pieces of advice. The first was that, as good as the street food may look, we shouldn't eat it. Chances were that our digestive tracts didn't have what they needed to handle it. His second piece of advice?

"Cross the street very carefully."

This sounds like a funny thing to say to two grown people, but once we get into the city itself, we see why he mentioned it: Hanoi driving is insane. *Insane.*

Imagine the worst traffic jam you've ever seen: cars crowding into a single lane from three different directions, drivers honking, fenders inches from bumpers that are centimeters from the wheels of a Mack truck. The streets are so congested that you could walk from one side of the road to the other without touching the pavement.

Now imagine that densely knotted corrosion of vehicles moving at forty miles an hour.

Now add 10,000 motorcycles—this is not an exaggeration—weaving at high speeds through this traffic.

And keep in mind that half of these motorcycles are going the wrong way.

And that a good third of their drivers are texting.

The only things missing from the equation are alcohol, drugs, and a machine gun fitted, Mad Max style, on the top of a rusty Toyota.

Seeing this insanity, we decide that Hanoi is perhaps best enjoyed from the single city block upon which our hotel is located. "Look!" we tell Ha, our guide. "Tons of restaurants! A grocery store! Even a laundry service! Why would we ever want to cross the street?"

He just shakes his head and tells us a trick. "Stay together," he says, "in one big group. And move slowly. And whatever you do, keep walking."

I'd like to say that this is an atypical picture of traffic in Hanoi, but it's not. Insanity. Total Insanity.

We try this and it works. Moving steadily is the key. That way, the motorcycles can anticipate where you'll be and zoom by without actually touching you—even if you can feel the heat from their exhaust pipes.

After a while, it even becomes kind of fun. You start to see the natural breaks in the traffic, momentary lulls where two blocks away a light hasn't yet turned green, or some old lady's been knocked off her bike and everyone has stopped to put the oranges back in her basket.

You might even say that we begin to take the traffic for granted. More than once, we step off the curb without really looking, confident that whoever's out there will keep an eye on us. And they do. We're five people in Hanoi for four days, three of us under the age of ten, and each of us leaves with ten toes, ten fingers, and two eyes.

Only once are we in actual danger. Coming out of our hotel, we begin to cross to a nearby restaurant when we hear a chorus of "Woooaaaahhh!"

Freezing, we looked to our left. Three young men sit astride a white moped that's just come around the corner.

We look at them. They stare at us. Two of them are smoking. All three are grinning. Then they nod and call out, "Sorry!" before roaring back into traffic.

The crazy thing about Ha Long Bay is not that it's unimaginably beautiful: It's not. You can imagine it.

You just can't believe it's real.

Or that you'll ever get to go there.

Made up of karst limestone formations, the bay, legend says, was created by a dragon who came for a visit and loved it so much he stayed, curling up beneath the water so that only the coils of his tail—all 1,960 of them—could be seen. Everywhere you turn, steep rocky hills rise out of the green water, as evocative and forbidding as castles in a gothic novel.

Being on the junk only adds to the effect. Our boat is high and narrow, hewn from rough planks stained deep red, topped with a pair of flapping canvas sails. We chose the smallest boat we could find, and we don't regret it. There are only three cabins, and we occupy two of them. Bay, who's on vacation from a diplomatic job in Kandahar, is in the third and tolerates us and our kids, allowing that we are an improvement, albeit only a slight one, over a war zone.

During the days we climb into sea kayaks and go skimming across the water, exploring quiet coves, limestone caves, and entire villages floating on rafts of Styrofoam. Lunch is served with white linen on a deserted beach.

Yes, it's true: we came halfway around the world to one of the most stunning landscapes on the planet, all so Will could sit on a junk and read a book.

At night we return to the boat for seven-course dinners, which include sea mantis in caramelized onion, barbequed goat (tastier than you'd think), and vegetables and fruits carved into the shapes of exotic waterbirds and miniature replicas of our junk. Our boat has its very own chef, and as much as we love the captain and our guide and the man who makes us Vietnamese coffee every morning with condensed milk at the bottom, the person we really love is our cook, who bears more than a passing resemblance to Johnny Galecki from *The Big Bang Theory*. At the age of twenty-one, he has more talent with a sauté pan than a whole kitchen of Rachael Rays.

That said, it's worth noting that the boat itself is hardly up to code by Western standards. For one thing, the railing along the top only comes up to my son Jamie's waist—and Jamie is only three. Which means the railing only comes up to Lucy's thigh, and Will's knees. Which means falling overboard would take nothing more than, say, stepping left when you should have gone right.

Then, of course, there's that glub, glub, glub noise. Lying awake our first night on the boat, I listen to this sound, two thoughts swirling through my mind: 1) glub, glub, glub is exactly the sound sour milk makes when you pour it down the drain; 2) glub, glub, glub is what the bubble says above a cartoon boat as it disappears beneath the waves.

A few years ago, when we only had two kids, I was lying down for an afternoon nap in Virginia when a horrifying idea came into my head: *If all of us were on one of those huge cruise ships in the Caribbean and it started to sink, could I save my family?*

After a moment of thought, I came up with an obvious solution: We could jump overboard if we had to, Ellen holding onto Lucy (who was then just a baby) while I held onto Will.

But then I thought: *But would we be able to grip onto the kids when we hit the water, or would the impact shake them loose from our arms?*

And then I thought: *Even if we could hold onto them, would a child that small survive hitting water with the velocity you'd build up free-falling four stories from a cruise ship?*

And then I thought: *What the hell is wrong with me?*

Turns out I was suffering from acute anxiety, brought on by an incredibly difficult year at work and too much caffeine. Once I cut back on the coffee and the Dr. Pepper and quit caring about my job, the anxiety diminished. Even so, I spent the better part of a year thinking about my fears and my worries and where they came from and why they wouldn't go away. And it wasn't the first time either.

Ten years ago, back when my elder son was born, a doctor told us that SIDS happened mostly during the first six months.

So, neurotic parent that I am, I spent the first six months of Will's life creeping into his room every eleven minutes to make sure he was still breathing.

When we passed the half-year mark, I expected the fear to go away. But it never did. There was always something to worry about: falling down the stairs, drowning in the swimming pool, getting hit by a car, swallowing a thumbtack.

Consider: My senior year in college I dated a woman named Marsha. The next year, while I was in England, Marsha went to bed one April evening and fell asleep. Around 11:00, a high-school friend knocked on the door and invited her to go out for a drive. She went, and cruising back into town an hour later, their car was hit and Marsha was killed.

She'd been asleep. In bed. How much safer can you get?

I love the movie *The Station Agent*, but in it is a mother who's haunted by the memory of her child who died while playing on the monkey bars. One minute the kid was fine, swinging happily. Then the mother looked away for a second—just one second—and grief became her constant companion. I'm like that mother. Only nothing has happened.

Yet.

Our last stop in Vietnam is Hoi An, a small, historic city on the central coast. It's a wonderful place, though a little touristy. The old town is a rabbit warren of narrow streets and old buildings, most of them housing overpriced (for Vietnam) tourist shops and restaurants. Nevertheless, the town has its charm. You can take a boat to a nearby island filled with woodcarvers, for instance, and on the fourteenth night of the new moon, motorcycles and electric lights are banned from the inner city. Those evenings, as you wander from shop to shop, all you hear are the slap-shuffle of sandals and the occasional murmur of women singing to the *dan bau*, the traditional Vietnamese instrument said to be so beautiful that young girls were forbidden to listen to it.

Our hotel is on the beach. It's a five-star affair, which is sort of embarrassing at first—we're Democrats, after all, and snotty about our relative poverty—but when we lay our heads down on our pillows that first night and hear the surf crashing on the shore, we think, "Well, okay. We can get used to this."

The next morning, the waves aren't really that big but the current is strong. Will and another tourist kid named Jacob jump over the foam, and every few minutes we have to tell them to move to the right, move to the right, move to the right. But they keep getting pulled to the left by both the waves and the undertow. Even the lifeguards—who spend most of their time hanging out in the shade and chatting up bikini-clad hotties—seem worried by the phenomenon. Every fifteen minutes or so they come down to the waterline and gesture with both arms: right, right, right.

The next few days are calmer. The kids, so sunburned they scream every time they step into the shower, spend most of their time in the shade, building sandcastles and catching ghost crabs.

I'm sunburned, too, but I can't stay out of the waves. I'm from Wisconsin, after all. I hadn't seen the ocean until I was twenty-one, and I've only actually had beach holidays twice in my life—this being the second time.

I love the waves. I love diving through them as they crash. I love floating on them as they buoy me up. I love surfing them as they rumble toward the shore. I could do this all day long, for ten days straight, breaking only for the occasional Vietnamese coffee and a shower to get the salt out of my eyes.

Our last morning there, the kids have absolutely no interest in going into the ocean. Which is fine with me. During the night, a front moved in and the swells are huge; standing twenty yards out in knee-deep water, I let the first two or three waves break around me and realize they're actually going over me. And I'm six-foot-three.

Even so, I stay out there. I dive under. I ride over. I body surf, lying face down just as the waves break and letting them glide me to the shore in a churning boil of water and salt and sand.

Every so often, as I come up from a particularly fun ride, I glance toward the beach, wipe the salt from my eyes, and make sure Lucy or Will hasn't tried to follow me out. When I get tired, I get out of the water for a while, sit with the kids under the umbrella, catch my breath. Then I dive back into the crests.

There's no surprise ending here: It's always the last wave that gets you, after all, because only then do you get a clue and get the hell out because it's too dangerous. And as this particular wave—the one that made this point to me that day—comes in, I remember looking up at it and thinking, "Holy crap, this is going to be fun." It's huge, the biggest wave I've seen yet, like something out of a surfing movie.

And it is fun. For the first three seconds. Then the wave takes my 220-pound body and turns me on my head, slamming my neck and shoulder against the bottom like it's a hammer and I'm a twisted, slanted, very stupid nail.

I come up coughing and spitting and wondering if my right arm has been torn off or just broken into a thousand pieces. Struggling toward the shore, I try to move my fingers. I can, but lightning shoots from my wrists to shoulders and down to my toes. I nearly fall over, gasping.

Collapsing onto the sand, I rub my arm and move it, waiting for the pain to go away. But it doesn't. It hurts so bad, I keep thinking I'm about to vomit. And it keeps hurting.

Eventually, Ellen goes for a lifeguard, who finds a doctor, who calls a car and accompanies me into town to the hospital for an X-ray. The pain sticks with me pretty much until the very moment the ER doctor steps into the room, holding the X-ray, and says nothing is broken. Then, suddenly, it's gone.

Before that, though, sitting in that waiting room, filling out the forms, the ER doc asked me what had happened. I told him what I'd been doing, told him how big the wave was, told him how it had turned me over and pounded the back of my head on the ocean floor.

When I was done, he just gazed at me for a long time, wearing that inscrutable, bland expression that Westerners get so often from people in Asia. Looking at him looking at me, I suddenly knew how lucky I was. In that instant, I could imagine my neck snapping as I hit the bottom, could imagine the current tugging me out, helpless, as more and bigger waves crashed down over me. Could imagine Ellen and the kids and those stupid lifeguards not even noticing the disappearance of one very big, very sunburned, very sorry white guy.

I finally fell asleep that night in Ha Long Bay. And the boat didn't sink, of course, and I didn't drown, and none of this is a tale from beyond the grave, though, let's admit it: That'd be pretty cool. The next morning we got up and went kayaking, paddling our boats across a 2,000-foot-deep bay, carrying a nine-year-old who can swim, a six-year-old who can swim but is great at panicking, and a three-year-old who sinks like a rock every time he steps into the water.

Which is pretty stupid, of course. But sometimes you get tired of being worried. And sometimes it just seems out of your control anyhow, so you do it, and don't worry about it—or, more realistically, you do it, worry about it at first, then get used to the idea and give up.

Case in point: When I saw our agenda for the Vietnam trip, my eye was drawn to a tiny passage in the middle of all the details about where we'd go and what we'd see. It said: "Transfer to Hoi An via the cloudy Hai Van Pass."

"Um," I said to Ellen. "This doesn't sound good."

She read it. "I'm sure it's nothing."

"But it's a pass," I said. "Passes are in mountains. And it's cloudy. And clouds are hard to see in. Which means," I continued, following her into the bathroom where she was trying to flee, "that we're driving in the mountains and we can't see. Ergo . . . "

But she was rolling her eyes. I let it drop.

Then, when we're in Hue, our tour guide hands out a binder full of photographs of the city during the Vietnam War. They're fascinating, including shots of buildings and streets that still exist. It makes the war very real.

One picture, though, freezes my heart. It's called "Hai Van Pass." In the background, you see a gritty army truck chugging up a steep mountain road. In the foreground you see, and I'm not making this up, a human skull planted on a stick.

"Um," I say to our guide. "Isn't this where we're going? Like, tomorrow?"

She glances at the picture. "Yes. This is a very beautiful drive."

I point to the skull, which sports one of those conical Vietnamese hats that you still see on women carrying laundry. "But it's been improved, right? The road? It's not so dangerous anymore?"

She looks at the skull, then at me, and then at the skull again. And frowns. "No," she says. "It is the same."

"Isn't that kind of dangerous then?" I ask. "I mean, we've got kids and everything."

"Oh no," she says. Then she gestures toward the blue sky. "If the weather is like this, we will be okay. If not, we'll take the tunnel."

"It's that bad, huh? The pass?"

"When it's raining," she says, "many accidents. But you don't worry."

The next day it's raining. It's just a mist, but as I climb into the van I ask, "So we'll take the tunnel? Because of the rain? Don't want an accident or anything, right?"

She and the driver both lean forward, peer at the sky through the windshield. They don't even consult. "No," she says. "It'll be okay."

When we reach the foot of the mountain, the misting has increased to a drizzle, and I stare longingly at the line of cars and trucks heading toward the tunnel. We, on the other hand, veer to the right and begin to ascend. It doesn't help my nerves any that the driver seems to think the best way to go around hairpin bends is to swerve into the left lane to give himself a better angle on the curve.

Watching the line outside the tunnel below us, I say, "Looks like almost everyone else is going under the mountain."

She nods. "Only tourists go this way," she says. "Tourists and gasoline trucks."

And then she laughs.

And we do too.

Because sometimes it's all you can do.

But then: Our vacation ends, and we make it back to Hong Kong, limbs intact, still more or less sane, all five of us alive. We're exhausted, but we've had fun. Ellen and I are fairly impressed with ourselves. We survived two weeks in a developing country with three kids, the oldest of whom is still afraid to read Harry Potter by himself.

We crawl into bed, exhausted. The next morning we wake up, feed the kids, start the laundry. And we check e-mail. Nothing special there, until we get to a note from our friend Lia. Turns out she broke her wrist ice-skating backward. But that's not the half of it. Not even a tenth. Not even a thousandth.

Lia's mother has a boyfriend named Vic, an affable guy who's a bit deaf but a sweetheart with the grandkids. Vic has a daughter who's Lia's age, who was actually a friend of hers growing up on Long Island. Not a close friend, mind you, but a friend nonetheless. This daughter has a husband, Thomas, and they have a little baby, Samantha, who's only a year old.

They—the daughter and her family—teach at an international school in Africa. During Christmas, they decide to take a vacation, booking rooms at a resort just outside Mt. Kenya National Park. One morning they wake up, they take their showers, they get dressed. They go down to the dining room and have breakfast—toast with marmalade, maybe, and fresh orange juice with slices of pineapple on the rim. The baby eats cornflakes or bits of scrambled egg her mother feeds her with a spoon. One of the serving ladies pauses at the table, laughing at the *mzungu* mommy and her sweet little *mzungu* baby, who laugh back.

Afterward, the family goes for a walk. A guide accompanies them—hotel policy—but he doesn't carry a gun; you're not allowed to so close to a national park where poaching is so prevalent.

For a while they stay out in the open, looking at ants and mushrooms, taking photos of the baby as it squeals in its carrier. Then it starts to rain a little, and they move toward the brush. They come to a bend in the road. The guide peers around. He shouts. They run. Behind them, a mother elephant charges, protecting, it believes, its calf. The mother, Vic's daughter, Lia's friend, Thomas's wife, mother of Samantha, baby Samantha, who's only just one—the mother slips and falls. She is holding the baby.

A milk truck. A wave. A scooter. An elephant. Popeye's ship going glub, glub, glub.

Some things you can't imagine.

And then there are some things that you can.

You just never imagine they'll happen to you.

Part I

Kowlooned

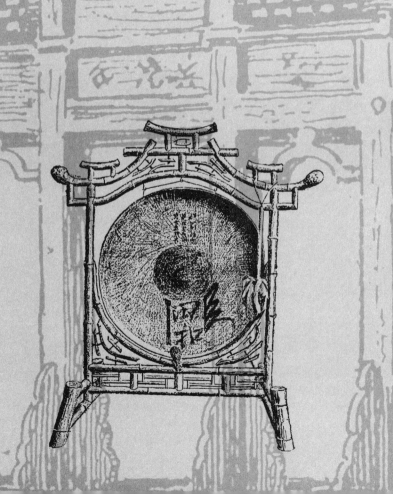

CHAPTER 1

FIRST DAZE

I f you're anything like me—that is to say, ignorant almost to the point of heresy—then you've always assumed that Hong Kong is a city. And certainly, there are city *parts* to Hong Kong— multiple ones, in fact, with tall skyscrapers and busy streets and markets and throngs of pedestrians waiting to board double-decker buses.

As a matter of fact, though, the term "Hong Kong" refers to a "Special Administrative Region" (SAR) of the People's Republic of China. It covers a grand total of 436 square miles, and is made up of three different parts: Hong Kong Island, Kowloon, and the New Territories. The oldest and best known of these, colonized by the British in 1841, is Hong Kong Island. It contains numerous stand-alone villages and towns, as well as one long urbanized area on the northern coast. The focal point of this urban region is "Central," where you'll find Hong Kong's famous trams, Chinese tailors, and *dai pai dongs*—small open restaurants—selling noodle soup and eggs cured in tea.

Across the harbor from the island is Kowloon, occupied by the British in 1861 using some preposterous rationale that basically boiled down to, "We make better cocktails, we've got better guns, and if you don't give us this land, we're going to take it anyway, so there." Kowloon-side is where you'll find Nathan Road, the flower markets of Mong Kok, several night markets, and lots and lots of spas with names like "Water Moon Light Beauty," "Man Paradise," and "Cyberspa"—this last one a concept, I will admit, that simultaneously intrigues and scares the living crap out of me.

The "We've got guns, we drink G&Ts" argument worked so well that in 1898 the British used it again to expand even further inland, creating the New Territories. Of course, "expand" is sort of a misnomer, considering that back then no Brit in his or her right mind had any intention of living in the godforsaken, mosquito-infested hills bordering Mainland China. For one thing, the New Territories were away from all the action in Central. For another thing, they were godforsaken, mosquito-infested hills. Godforsaken, mosquito-infested hills, I might add, in which my family and I lived for a year.

I mention all this because a week after we arrived in Hong Kong, Will, Lucy, Jamie, and I find ourselves huddled beneath an underpass somewhere in Kowloon, hopelessly lost. It's maybe 99 degrees, drizzling rain, and so humid that you can actually feel the pores on your face sucking moisture from the air.

Ellen, meanwhile, is 8,000 miles away, about to go through one of the hardest days of her life.

"Dad," says Lucy, who's just about to turn six. "What are we doing?"

I look around, trying to get my bearings. Traffic flows on all sides, two streets merging to form a triangle of red taxis, BMWs, and green minibuses with numbers like 28K and 107M. No one, we'll soon learn, blows a horn in Hong Kong, so the scene is oddly quiet, only the swish of tires on rain-soaked roads and the occasional rumble as a lorry driver downshifts. To our left stand rows of upscale shops: Rolex, Louis Vuitton, Tiffany. To our right we see mainly construction zones, giant cranes behind walled-off lots.

"I don't know," I tell my daughter.

Have I mentioned we've never been to Hong Kong before? Have I mentioned that this is our first time out of the New Territories? Have I mentioned that I don't have a map?

"I'm hungry," Will says.

Have I mentioned that I forgot to bring food?

It was a simple enough plan: We came to Hong Kong to be in a big city, surrounded by people and traffic and tall buildings. Never mind that by some twist of fate we ended up living in the most rural part of the SAR, a site that made our hometown in a Virginia county of 33,000 look downright hip and swinging by comparison. Never mind that Ellen had to fly back to the United States almost the moment we set down. Now we are in Hong Kong and now we are going to see some tall buildings.

The kids are being pretty good, relatively speaking. I mean, they're jet-lagged, sure. And they're missing their mother, sure. But when I told them my idea, they'd strapped on their sandals and followed me out the door.

Once we are on the MTR, Hong Kong's excellent train system, heading south to the city, Will, who's eight, looks at me and says, "Where are we going again?"

"Kowloon."

"Cow-what?" asks Lucy.

I open my mouth to explain, but Will kicks in again.

"Why are we going there?"

"Just to look around."

"But what are we going to do?" Will's the kind of kid who can't enjoy watermelon because he's so busy picking out the seeds.

"Explore."

"Explore what?"

"Why the ancient Hong Kongers used to sell their eight-year-olds into slavery."

That gets me a look, and then he rises from his seat and moves farther down the train, settling in next to a plump, grandmotherly woman in a red sweatshirt who, I'm sure, he hopes will take him home.

The MTR is one of the best transit systems in the world. Funny thing, though, is that as good as their little wall maps are with their brightly colored lines and their peculiar station names (*Mong Kok?* really?), they don't tell you where all the action is.

"Why are we getting off here?" my son asks when we follow the crowds off the train at maybe the sixth station.

"Because this is Kowloon Tong Station," I answer. "Kowloon is where all the tall buildings are."

"I don't see any tall buildings," says my daughter.

And indeed, as I look at the parts of Kowloon revealing itself in the open-air station, there are no particularly skyscraperly buildings.

"We need to get back on the train," I say.

The next time we get messed up isn't really my fault. I'd been given my map by one of last year's Fulbrighters, and since it had been printed they'd changed some of the lines so that what used to be the end of the East Rail line is now part of another line entirely. What a person is supposed to do is get off the old line, stroll across the platform, and step onto a train shuttling to the new line. I know this because when we push Jamie's stroller off the first train, everybody moves en masse across the platform and onto another train. Plus, a young woman is standing there holding a three-by-four-foot purple sign over her head that reads: "Passengers for the East Tsim Sha Tsui Station embark here."

I freeze. I stare at the map in my hand. I stare at the map on the wall of the station. I stare at the woman holding the sign, at the sign itself, and at the train car full of Chinese people silently watching this very tall, very bald man with three very pasty-white kids, wondering if he is insane, stupid, or both.

Finally, a chime sounds, the doors of the car close, and the train pulls away.

"That was our train, wasn't it." It's less a question than a statement. Who knew an eight-year-old could sound so mournful?

"Yes," I say. I feel a tightening in my gut, but I can't tell if it is hunger or the first pangs of panic. "But don't worry. There'll be another one in"—I glance up at the digital arrival board—"thirty-seven minutes."

We're not idiots. We knew that living abroad would be hard, especially with three little kids. We knew there'd be fatigue and arguments and petty bickering over where to eat and what to eat and whose turn it was to stay with the napping toddler instead of wandering through antique markets and bakeries overflowing with Chinese *bao*—fresh steamed buns—and egg tarts.

Nonetheless, when we found out we'd be spending a year in Hong Kong as part of a special Fulbright program working with general education, what we pictured were sparkling skyscrapers; green Star Ferries chugging across the harbor; quaint if dirty *dai pai dongs* where we could slurp noodles next to university students, Filipino helpers, and elderly Chinese women dressed in—well, whatever it is elderly women in Hong Kong dress in.

And we pictured our children there, too, not necessarily eating what we ate, but seeing what we saw and experiencing what we experienced. Both my wife and I lived abroad when we were young, and felt that all the clichés applied: Our lives had been broadened, our eyes had been opened, we saw the world—and the United States—from a fuller, more nuanced perspective. We relished the opportunity to bestow these gifts on our children, to provide them—at a very young age—with a sense of what the world has to offer, and of just how easy it is to go out there and explore.

Then our first morning here, I hooked up our laptop using an ethernet cable that our new neighbor Colin had brought over. Anita, Colin's wife and my boss for the year, was in the next room with the housing staff, taking care of a few last-minute repairs to our flat. Ellen was talking to Anita and keeping an eye on the kids, who'd been up since three, five, and six, respectively.

I clicked into my e-mail, intending to drop a note to the grandparents, letting them know we were fine. Halfway down the page, a note from Ellen's brother caught my eye. The subject line read, "Dad."

Uh-oh, I thought. Ellen's dad, Merlyn, had been ill for some time, fighting Parkinson's and a nasty staph infection that had deteriorated his spine. Twice, he'd been pretty much declared dead, his wife in the hospital room holding his hand while Ellen and her brother sat in the lobby phoning funeral homes. Both times, though, he'd come back, and we'd almost assumed that he'd outlive us all.

Figuring it was another close call, I clicked on the e-mail. Immediately the words "airline" and "died" caught my eye—as in, "I don't know if the airline told you, but Dad died last night." I read more closely, struggling to focus. He'd been resting in his chair by the lamp when Arline, my mother-in-law, urged him to get up, get a little exercise or a snack. He'd tried, rising and reaching for his walker, but then had crumbled, half on the chair, one knee on the floor. Arline, small but strong, tried to coax and lift him back onto the recliner, but it soon became clear that something wasn't right, that one of his arms wasn't working, that he couldn't quite control his muscles. Lowering him to the floor, she went to call the EMTs. By the time they arrived, he was gone.

I turned my head and stared into the hall. Colin looked at me. "What's wrong?" he said.

I just stared, mouth open.

"What's wrong?" he said again, half-smiling, uncomfortable.

I stood, walked into the hall, and called for Ellen. She was busy telling the kids not to stab each other with the steak knives they'd found in a drawer, and didn't hear me. I called again. This time she came, and I hugged her.

I'd like to tell you it was a warm hug, a reassuring hug, a good hug. But it wasn't. We're not a couple prone to public displays of affection—we're Midwesterners, after all, and Lutherans to boot—and when I suddenly put my arms around her in front of people we'd just met and tried to get her to look at me, she squirmed and pushed away. I said something, vague and apologetic and mournful, and she looked at me—and then looked at me again. And then she got it.

Scrambling away, she went to the computer, clawed at the keyboard, deactivating the screensaver. I turned to Colin, about to explain, and then I heard her laugh.

"Oh Jesus," she said, her voice cracking. "He was getting up for ice cream."

Because we have plenty of time before we catch the next train, I take the kids up the escalator and ask a uniformed man where to get off to see tall buildings.

"Where you want to go?" he asks.

Nowhere, I tell him. Anywhere. Just someplace with skyscrapers, bustling crowds, lots of neon. I glance at my watch. It's nearly noon, a dangerous time for a family full of hypoglycemic children. "And some restaurants," I add.

He looks at me carefully, then down at the children, obviously checking for signs of abuse. Then he names a station, one stop farther along, where, he says, there will be tall buildings.

When we get off the train we are faced with nine possible exits. Tired, hungry, sweaty, and worried that Jamie's two-year-old bladder is being pushed to the limit, I pick one at random. I can't say I'm surprised when we emerge to a mostly empty street with no tall buildings, no restaurants, and guardrails ensuring that the only way to cross the road is to go back down the stairs we've just come up and take an underground sidewalk. Which we do, me hefting Jamie still in his stroller because it's easier than carrying the thing with one hand and helping him down the stairs with the other.

Coming up on the other side, we're forced to go right, strolling along in the drizzle that arrived almost as soon as we left our flat in Tai Po. Eventually we reach the busy intersection where

Salisbury meets Nathan Road, the heartbeat of Kowloon-side, with more tailors, teahouses, and massage parlors than anyone can count. Not to mention restaurants.

Only we can't get across. Concrete barriers have been erected all along the intersection, making sure dumb *"gweilos"* (Cantonese for sweaty pale people) and their hungry kids don't make a mad dash across one of Hong Kong's busiest intersections. I look around, wondering if there's another underground walkway, and spot something that makes my heart tick.

"Look!" I say, pointing. They turn. "Water!"

"Dad," says Lucy, who's begun gnawing her thumb. "We're hungry."

"What do you say, Will? Want to see Victoria Harbour, one of the biggest seaports in the world?"

He just glares.

So we trudge on. Eventually we reach a corner, not too far from the water, with a clock tower and dozens of buses and taxis going in and out. It's now 12:43. I'm sticky with sweat, my head light from lack of food. All pretense of being a super dad, or even a passable dad, are gone. I drop a few choice words that my kids have heard more and more since their grandpa died, and turn to my eldest.

"Straight, or to the right?"

He looks at me. "Huh?"

"Straight or to the right. Where do you think we'll find food?"

He looks at me again. Then he considers the options. His sister, who is now gently licking her baby brother's fat hand, watches him carefully.

"Straight," he says.

"Straight it is." And on we go.

Now I know what you're thinking: What a brilliant father. What a profound man. What better way to raise children, to expand their horizons, develop their sense of self and their place in the universe than by allowing them to make decisions that shape their interactions with the world?

Well, okay. Maybe a little. But what was actually going through my head was: "You think you're so smart, you little bugger, why don't you make a few decisions and see what it's like to fail?"

And for a while we do fail. Canton Road, where we now are, is filled mainly with upscale shops and fancy hotels, the kind that don't want big, sweaty men and their small, sweaty kids ruining their leather upholstery. We stumble on, searching for someplace, anyplace, to eat.

Well, okay: not really *anyplace*. Because eventually we find our way to a glass-plated restaurant front. Inside, dozens of Hong Kongers cluster around linen-draped tables, black-tied waiters and waitresses edging past carrying trays laden with tea and bamboo steam baskets. Just inside the front door is a glass booth. And hanging at eye level in that booth are—what? chickens? duck? geese? All cooked, all a clay brown, all . . . with their heads on.

I glance at the kids. Lucy's and Jamie's cheeks are bright red, their noses and necks shiny from the heat. Will, more his mother's son, looks pale, almost sick. He never could stand sweating. I look back at the restaurant.

"What do you think?" I say.

Lucy twists her mouth to one side. Will draws a deep breath. Jamie leans his head against the side of his stroller and sighs.

"Um," says Will. And Lucy nods.

I glance at my watch. Almost 1:15. In less than five hours, my wife will rise in Minnesota to prepare for her father's funeral. Meanwhile, we'll be in Hong Kong still looking for a place to eat. I turn the stroller and lead the kids up the street.

They say that grief is often associated with guilt. I mention this because for me, Merlyn's death brought with it layers of anxiety. There was the fact that I couldn't be there at the funeral; Ellen and I had decided—rightly, I think—that turning the kids around after seventeen hours on a plane and a change of twelve time zones was just a bad idea. And there was the fact that Merlyn and I weren't exactly close. This was largely my fault. Particularly in recent years, I'd kept my distance from him. It's hard to say why this was, but perhaps I saw in him parts of myself that made me uncomfortable. Both of us were deeply passionate about things we cared about, to the point of assuming we were always right. Both of us, though articulate, could sometimes be socially awkward. Both of us thought there was only one way to load the dishwasher, and that no one else on the planet knew the secret.

On top of all this, though, was another layer of guilt, maybe related, maybe not, maybe just brought out by all the other crappy feelings. I worried that coming here might just have ruined my kids' lives.

Okay, maybe not *ruined*—but severely dented, keyed on both sides, with a broken side-view mirror thrown in for good measure. They'd lived a pretty Mayberry life up until this time, you see. We come from a town of roughly 8,000 people in central Virginia that sports two highly ranked colleges, cobblestone streets, a historic downtown, and relatively easy access to moonshine—which, if not necessarily good for the kids, at the very least makes for more relaxed parenting. Summer evenings in our hometown are spent at the public pool at the top of a hill where a 360-degree vista provides views of the Blue Ridge Mountains and the kids can splash until sunset with friends they've had since they were born. Life is easy there. Incredibly easy.

When we found out we were going to Hong Kong, we made a big deal out of it when we told the kids. "Look!" we said, flashing Internet pictures of Star Ferries, red-sailed junks, lantern festivals, and dragon dances. "Look where we get to go! Isn't it great? Aren't we lucky?"

It was anything but a soft pitch, particularly for two people who would feel guilty selling water to a billionaire who'd just strolled out of the desert. We're just not sales types. At the same time, though, we didn't want to debate our decision, didn't want to discuss with the kids the pluses and minuses of being away for a year, of taking them away from their friends and the only place they'd really ever known. Going was the right thing to do, we knew that. We were certain of it. Positive. Absolutely.

Really.

All of which has exactly what to do with wandering around Kowloon, looking for something to eat that doesn't still have its head attached?

Well, absolutely nothing. And everything.

Consider: We're still standing beneath that overpass on Canton Road. The rain is still drizzling down, the traffic is still sluicing by. It's well after 1:30, and I've just decided that now is the time to teach my kids dumpster diving, when Lucy says, "What about in there?"

She's pointing to a squat building wedged between a parking garage and what looks like an upscale sporting goods store. I'd noticed it before but had ignored it, assuming it was just another hotel with a restaurant we couldn't afford. Straining now to see behind the mirrored glass, I catch a glimpse of an escalator, of multicolored storefronts. It's a mall. Pulling the kids to the nearest zebra crossing, we wait for the light to change, then cross the street. We walk up to the building, push through the doors, and look around. Even from the ground level we can see the food court on the third floor. I look at the kids. "What do you think?"

They nod, glassy-eyed and salivating.

We take the escalator up and stop at the first place we see. It's Thai, and relatively normal to our still westernized eyes. I order chicken with rice for the kids and a bowl of beef noodle soup for myself. The chicken ends up being on the bone, chopped by a huge cleaver so that the marrow is exposed in all its gritty, bloody glory, but by now we don't care. Grabbing the trays, I follow the kids as they push the stroller through the dining area, looking for a table. We find a two-top in a corner and huddle around it. My daughter, who's more adventurous than her older brother, takes her chopsticks and pulls off a piece of the chicken, which— I now realize—is cold and steamed and looks almost raw. She pops it in her mouth and chews.

"Delicious," she says.

"What's this?" Will says, pointing a spoon at something on their tray.

"Soup."

"Yeah, but what's in it?"

I lean over Jamie, who's on my lap fisting noodles into his mouth. I can't tell what's in the kid's bowl. It looks like chicken broth, but what are those two square things at the bottom?

"I don't know. Celery?"

"It looks too big for celery."

"You got me."

Then my son, who would eat nothing but bologna-and-cheese sandwiches every meal for the rest of his life if you let him, takes a sip of the soup. "It's good," he says.

Mine isn't really, but I don't care. It has protein and it's warm and after half a bowl I start to feel the layers of worry slide off. Ellen will be fine, I know. I want to be with her, of course, but she'll survive this just as well without me as she would were I there.

And we'll figure out Hong Kong. We'll figure out the trains, the crazy pedestrian patterns, where to find a good Kentucky Fried Chicken when we really, desperately need one.

And the kids will survive. Yes, it'll be hard at times, but speaking as a man who's seen his kids fall off their bikes more than once then get right back on, if their spirits are half as flexible as their bones, they'll be fine. We'll all be fine.

Arguably the most striking skyline in the world, even if that big building in the middle does look like a nose-hair shaver.

Once we've finished, we hit the restroom and pee and don't even get freaked out when the man tending the stalls yells at Lucy for some reason we can't understand, but that seems to have something to do with the solid platinum tiles surrounding the sink or with Elvis having shaved there once.

We're heading back toward the escalators when Lucy points out two small flights of stairs. "I want to go there."

I stop. "Why?"

"Just because."

I hesitate. I don't see the point, myself—who wants to spend all day in a mall?—but then, Will's decision found us a place to eat, so what the hell.

"Okay," I say.

We go up. It's a hotel lobby. The kids are on their way back down in an instant, and I'm about to join them when I glance out the door and notice a few small tables with umbrellas on a terrace. I call the kids back (they nearly crush an old lady with a wide black hat as they sprint up), and the four of us step back into the August heat.

And it's amazing. We're up maybe five stories above the water. Below us are ferries and waves and boats of all sizes. And across from us—holy crap, across from us is one of the most amazing sights I've ever seen in my life: Hong Kong Island rising up out of the harbor, tall brown mountains looming behind silver skyscrapers, row upon row of narrow apartment buildings staggering up the hillsides in pink and red and orange. The air is clear and the sun, now out, flashes off the entire scene.

Back in March, I was on a treadmill when a program came on that named the top ten skylines in the world. They mentioned Seattle, Kuala Lumpur, Toronto, Tokyo. Singapore got a mention, and so did New York. I kept waiting and waiting for Hong Kong and then suddenly it appeared: It was number one. Now I see why. There's steel and glass and neon and water and earth and sky. And all around on both sides, stretching off into the distance of the bay, are rounded greenish-brown mountains rising from the South China Sea. It is so beautiful—so shocking, so different from anything I've ever seen—that I laugh.

"Look!" says Lucy.

"I know," I grin, feeling like the best dad in the world. "Isn't it amazing?"

"A pigeon!" she says. And then both she and Will crowd around some poor gray bird nearly dead from heat stroke and take 128 pictures of it with their digital cameras.

But never mind. It—all of it: the harbor, the buildings, the sky, the heat, even the damn pigeon—is awesome. It's wonderful. It's so cool it takes the air from my lungs. We're here. Really here. We're in Hong Kong.

I didn't have the heart to tell the kids that we actually have pigeons in Virginia . . .

CHAPTER 2

THERE WILL BE SWEAT

Not long before we left for Hong Kong, Ellen and I made the decision that because there were only three bedrooms in our new flat, Lucy and Will would have to share.

"But I want my own room!" Will said.

"We know," I began—

"I need someplace to read!" he urged. This is the boy, after all, who loves to read so much that his grandmother once apologized for not taking more photographs of him, saying, "But there are only so many pictures you can take of a boy reading a book."

"I know you like to read," I said.

Then Lucy piped in. "I want to room with Jamie!"

"You can't," Ellen told her.

"Yeah," said Will. "Lucy and Jamie should room together."

"Jamie wakes up too early," Ellen said. "If Lucy doesn't get her sleep, she's—"

"I won't mind!"

"She won't mind!" Will said.

"—cranky all day," Ellen finished.

Ellen and her brother had shared a room when they were little, and for some reason she thought that was a keen recipe for a long-lasting sibling relationship. I wouldn't know, because my brother and I had separate bedrooms and spent most of our childhood using each other for BB gun practice.

"I wake up early," Will said, and in his voice you could just hear his determination to rise at 4:00 A.M. for the next three weeks running. And Will? When he's determined, you can rest assured he will do it.

"You do sometimes," said Ellen. "But you're also old enough to know how to be quiet. We know you won't wake your sister up, even if you do get up earlier than she does."

Will glanced at Lucy, and you could almost see the little cartoon thought balloon over his head with the words "Oh yeah?" inked inside.

But we stuck to our guns. And he stuck to his. The night we arrived in Hong Kong, grimy and aching from twenty hours on a jet with a crappy American airline that charges you for drinks and makes you keep your window shades down even though it might mean you don't see the sun for twenty-four hours—that very night, Will strolled into the flat, scoped out the two smallest rooms, and tossed his stuff into the room with only one bed.

Of my three kids, the hardest to write about is Will.

I don't know why this is. Maybe because he's more like Ellen, so different from me that he scares me sometimes. Back when he had just turned four, I remember going to his preschool Christmas party. All the other kids stood up and sang silly songs about Santa losing his reindeer and Jolly Old St. Nick. Will knew these songs, I know he did, because he sang them at home. But that morning he refused to get up with the rest of the kids. He just sat on the floor by himself, in his black turtleneck and brown corduroys. Watching. It just about broke my heart.

"He's lonely," I said to Ellen that night after showing her the video I'd taken. "He doesn't know how to socialize."

"He's fine," said Ellen, who'd spent many a moment in her life standing on the sidelines. "He knows what he wants. He made a decision and he'll be okay."

"But he looked so sad," I said.

"That's just because you don't like being by yourself," Ellen responded. "You're sort of pathetic that way."

I am not pathetic, and I have 441 Facebook friends who will back me up on that. Implicit in her comments, though, is the idea that Will is a breed I don't quite understand. And that's true enough.

Then again, maybe writing about Will is hard for me because he's the first of my children, the first one I held after he was born, feeling the knobs of his spine like tiny peas and thinking: *Oh my God. He's alive. And he's mine.* And then I felt my heart bend in a way it had never bent before.

Or it could be because, of all my children, he's the one for whom I was most scared as we packed up our lives, said good-bye to our friends, and drove away from the only house he'd ever known.

It's not so much that he's fragile. More like brittle. Will likes what he likes, knows what he likes, and doesn't apologize for not liking anything else. Lucy has seventeen different favorite foods, but Will likes only two meals: bologna-and-cheese sandwiches and chicken fajitas. Nothing more. Nothing less. And believe me, if you make him fajitas, you'd better have the right kind of tortilla, or you'll be reaching for the cold cuts.

And it's not just food. Will is like this about everything. He has a highly tuned sense of right and wrong and is keenly aware of any injustice in the universe, particularly—some might even say exclusively—if it's injustice toward him.

In short, he's an eight-year-old boy.

When Will moved all of his stuff into the single room that first night in the Hong Kong flat, I did what any father who'd been up for the better part of thirty-six hours and was now facing the pressures of a new job in a country he'd never been in before would have done: wept like a small child and begged Ellen to wake me up in a year.

After which, I marched into "Will's" room and moved his suitcase and the six *A–Z Mysteries* books we'd allowed him to bring down the hall. He followed, too tired to complain. The next few days, though, he made his dissatisfaction clear.

After Ellen returned to the States for her father's funeral, I had to take the kids everywhere—grocery shopping, getting household items, stopping at the personnel office to pick up insurance forms. This would have been rough under any circumstances, but when you're jet-lagged and in a completely new non-western country—and you're half-mourning, half-dying inside for your wife—it's misery. Absolute, complete, crappy, bugger-all misery.

Hey! Look! Will's reading! What a shock! This is in Bali, toward the end of the trip, and frankly, I can't blame him: what a beautiful spot to sit and read.

In the midst of all this, Will was astoundingly—indeed, almost admirably—passive-aggressive. He walked ten feet behind Lucy and me at all times. While Lucy and I struggled to get the stroller past a heavy glass door—there are very few automatic doors in HK—Will stood aside, hands in his pockets, looking sullen and distracted.

Fortunately for him, I'm nothing if not calm, particularly when stressed, so when he behaved this way all I did was scream as loud as I could, "Can't you see that Lucy and I are trying to get Jamie through the door? Did it ever occur to you to help?"

And he just looked at me, face mildly startled, but frankly more bland than anything, as if to say, "Maybe if I had my own room, you and I could work a little something out."

Ninety percent of the time for 90 percent of kids, the yelling and screaming would lead to nothing but a stand-off. And to be honest, Will and I both stayed the course for a while: He kept walking slowly, hands in his pockets, and I kept feeling anger swell in my chest, competing with the exhaustion and the heat and the sense that maybe, just maybe, coming to Hong Kong was the stupidest thing I'd ever done.

But then something changed. After about a week, I suddenly realized Will was walking beside me when I pushed the stroller, his hand on one of the handles. And when Ellen got back, he explicitly asked her if he could push Jamie. And he did.

And there were other things: a week after Ellen's return, we headed down to Tsim Sha Tsui, the southernmost tip of Kowloon, and ended up at the Spring Deer, a restaurant we later discovered was one of the most famous in Hong Kong for its Peking duck. We ordered almost at random, only ensuring that at least one dish had chicken in it to keep the kids happy. I'm not going to pretend that Will ate the dried, pickled cabbage— he didn't even look at it—but he drank some tea and ate some chicken and then some broccoli and some rice and then more chicken. Afterward, when he and I were in the restroom, I asked him how his dinner was.

"Great!" he said. And my son is not one for exclamation points, in speech or otherwise.

I nearly peed on my shoe. "Really?"

I mean, this is the boy of a thousand explanations for why he shouldn't be asked to eat his food: It's too soft, too hard, too mushy, too slippery, too salty, too vinegary, too gucky, too murky, too sludgy, too potato-y, too grimy, too slurpy, too granola-y. You can put double chocolate chocolate chip ice cream in front of him, and if for some perverse reason he decides he doesn't want it, he will assure you it tastes "funny."

"Really?" I said that night at the Spring Deer, reminding myself to tell the management they might need to mop the men's room floor.

"Great," he said again.

He's even added a few more dishes to his repertoire. He will eat sweet-and-sour pork anywhere, anytime, under any conditions. He likes barbequed pork, too, and won't turn away Peking duck. One night we took a taxi down to Tai Mei Tuk, a little beachfront village two miles down from my host campus, and he interrupted us as we began to order some boring chicken-patty dish for him.

"I want the chicken wings with lemongrass," he told the waitress. He'd found them on the menu himself. And when he got them, he ate them with chopsticks.

Chicken wings. With chopsticks. The boy with one thousand faces for food he doesn't like.

Now I really *have* seen everything.

When cognitive neuroscientists talk about the brain in relation to age, they often discuss its plasticity. Young brains have high neuroplasticity, meaning the physical properties of the brain can shift and expand and change and grow relatively easily. Older brains, on the other hand, have less plasticity, making it harder for them to adapt to new situations. The near-complete absence of neuroplasticity is, some argue, one of the reasons for Alzheimer's. This is why so many doctors encourage the elderly to try new things, learn new languages, pick up new hobbies—new adventures mean new learning and new learning keeps the brain supple.

I mention this because before our year in Hong Kong, I was pretty sure Will was about to enter the *Guinness Book of World Records* as the youngest-known case of early onset Alzheimer's—he was just that inflexible.

I no longer fear this, for one very simple reason: sweat. You see, above and beyond everything else, my older son hates to sweat. If it's hot outside, it doesn't matter what's going on—tree climbing, Frisbee throwing, the resuscitation of a fully grown, previously frozen woolly mammoth—Will is inside, lost in a book. Before starting archery that fall, the only sport he liked was swimming, because—duh—you don't sweat in water.

But early in October, my son Will did a 3.5K run for no other reason than that his gym teacher convinced him—convinced the whole school, for that matter—that it would be fun. Ellen thinks this man is David Koresh, but I think he's a genius. Anyone who can get little kids to thrill in using their muscles, in stretching out their flexible, pain-free legs and sprinting across the school field in 90-degree heat and 86-percent humidity—that person is a genius.

This particular race was at 8:30 on a Sunday morning on Hong Kong Island, a good hour's drive from where we live. And that's assuming we had a car. Which we didn't. So getting there required taking a taxi across town and catching a bus, which meant rising at 6:00 A.M. on—have I mentioned this?—a *Sunday*.

So naturally, good parents that we are, Ellen and I spent most of Saturday trying to talk the kids out of it. I mean, we love the little buggers, but we're not idiots. It'll be hot, we told them. It's on a mountain. You'll have to get up early. You'll sweat. You'll probably lose, and people will laugh at you.

None of it worked. So we set the alarm for 6:00, got up, slapped some water on our faces, and got a taxi that took us to the bus that drove us to the island that held the mountain that swallowed the cat that ate the rat that chased the spider.

We got there at 8:00, the haze still lifting from the South China Sea, revealing oil tankers and the occasional fishing boat coming in from a long night. We were startled to find that it was a city-wide race, with kids of all ages and plenty of women too, most of whom actually had serious running shoes and did serious stretches that made them look like they were serious about what they were doing.

"You sure?" we said to the kids.

Lucy grinned. Will looked pale, glancing at all the people, at the uniforms and the numbers they pinned to your shirt—and nodded. Just once. Quickly.

"You sure?" I said, a little more gently. He nodded again.

So we helped them pin the numbers to their chests. We found a place in the pack behind the starting line for them. And then we stood back and looked at our two kids, our two, rather small, children, we now realized, surrounded by a group of what looked like pretty serious runners for a race we'd thought would be just a bunch of goofy school kids running around the top of a mountain early on a Sunday morning, stopping to stare at a pair of butterflies, maybe, or ladybugs warming their wings in the sun.

And then the gun went off, and the pack surged forward, and Will and his sister disappeared in the crowd as it rounded the first bend and began the initial, long climb up the eastern side of the peak.

And Will ran the darn thing. The whole thing.

He hated it, of course. I mean, he's not an idiot. It was hot out there, and a long run, and some of it was uphill, and what the *hell,* it's a Sunday after all; he should've been curled up in bed reading some novel about magical bats or flying machines that do battle with giant bugs shaped like squids.

But he did it. The whole thing.

Afterward, when someone mentioned the next race in November, Will looked doubtful. Later, when it was mentioned again and Lucy said she was definitely going, Will said he'd probably pass. Looking at his face, you could just see him picturing himself lying on the little couch in our living room, the one right under the air conditioner, actively not perspiring.

After the race: The look on Will's face pretty much says it all.

As October wore on, though, he started to talk more and more about the November race. One day, he even announced that he and two of his friends had signed up for some weird obstacle course challenge where you run some, swim some, climb a rope some, and kill a baby alligator with nothing but a pound of raisins and a copy of *Goodnight Moon*.

Sometimes I'm not even sure I'm talking to the same boy. Running races? Obstacle courses? Sweating?

Then, on some rainy Sunday when I'm buried in work and he's finished his Mandarin homework and Jamie's asleep and Lucy is in the kitchen seeing just how crazy she can make her mom, Will will drift over to where I'm sitting on the couch, tapping at my laptop, and curl up next to me, book in hand, losing himself completely in its pages. And I'll lean into him a little, still typing, and he'll press back and maybe put his head against my arm, all without looking up, and—sweat or no—I'll think, *Oh my God. He's mine. My little boy.*

CHAPTER 3

EATING OUT

Twenty years ago when I was in Africa, I spent an entire weekend consuming nothing but bananas and beer. This may sound fun, but it was not: because of a misunderstanding involving their visa, both of the women I was with had been ejected from Tanzania with "No Re-Entry" stamped in their passports. Further, because one of them had been robbed of all her money, Malawi, the country we were trying to enter, refused to let her out of the six-mile wide no-man's land separating the two countries. Eventually the problem was solved, but not before the banks closed for the weekend, which left us penniless until Monday morning. Feeling sorry for us, the border guards talked a trucker and his wife into giving us a ride to the capital. Unfortunately, the tractor trailer was hauling a load of iron over the Malawi mountains, so it took the better part of two days to reach Lilongwe. Meantime, the trucker's wife saw fit to keep us fed on bananas. And the trucker's assistant saw fit to buy us an endless supply of beer.

It was fifteen years before I would eat another banana. I still don't like beer.

Once I left Africa, I spent a month traveling around England with my friend Pete before starting a year abroad at Durham University. This is back in the 1980s, you have to understand, when the licensing laws in the United Kingdom were stricter: Most shops closed at 5:30, and all shops were closed on Sundays. Thus, if you were in a remote village in Scotland and it was 5:32 on a Saturday evening, you'd better be well stocked with food, because it'd be another thirty-eight hours and twenty-eight minutes before you could get any more.

As you might imagine, this made a six-foot-three kid who'd gone to Africa weighing 168 pounds and left nine weeks later weighing 130 just a little bit nervous. One evening in a hostel on the Isle of Skye, Pete came into our room holding his toothbrush and a towel and did a double take.

"What's that?"

I looked up from the book I was reading. "Stephen King."

Pete pointed. "No. That. Is that a stuffed animal?"

I glanced down. "No."

He leaned closer. "Is that a *muffin?*"

"A scone, actually."

"Why are you holding it like that?"

"Like what?"

"Like that. Like—are you taking that muffin to bed with you?"

"Be quiet," I said, "or you'll hurt her feelings. You make it sound like I'm using her."

All of which is a roundabout way of saying that being in Hong Kong made me nervous, food-wise. Part of it was simply Africa/England residue. Part of it was the complication of traveling with kids: As you know, Will, my oldest, whom I love dearly, gets itchy when you feed him anything more adventurous than bologna and cheese—and that damn well better be mild cheddar, pal. Lucy, my middle child, is more of a risk taker, but even she has her limits; she's not a big fan of say, anything that has fish in it, or the letter "f," for that matter. And Jamie—he's two and just likes to be contrary.

But part of it is that, well, people in Hong Kong eat funny stuff. Soon after Ellen got back from her dad's funeral, we were on the top floor of the Tai Po wet market, where the food stalls are located. We were at a noodle stand, looking entirely confused, when a young lady in black jeans and a purple sweater came up and, in perfect English, offered to help us. We handed her a menu and she started to translate.

The dish in the foreground is marinated jellyfish; behind it is stuffed duck. Doesn't Will look thrilled?

"This," she said, moving her finger down the menu, "is the wonton soup. And here is the fish ball soup, a Hong Kong specialty." Flipping the menu over, she continued. "This is pork soup, and the shrimps, and then, these are—are various kinds of, you know, internal meats."

The key word here—strike that, the key letter—is the "s" at the end of meat. We're not just talking kidneys here, people. Or even tripe. We're talking everything. *Everything.* Lungs. Spleen. Thorax. You name it, it's in your soup.

On an intellectual level, of course, I know my resistance is stupid. After all, we're not just talking about Hong Kong, we're talking an entire continent that finds bladder soup tasty.

Too, I've always admired my Icelandic friends who talk about how they eat the whole sheep: guts, lungs, cheeks, brains, eyeballs. I mean, it makes sense, doesn't it? If you're going to kill an animal, you might as well eat the whole thing? Granted, as much as I've always admired people who think this way, I've usually shown my respect from a distance, the same way I admire, say, bomb-disposal experts, or harmonica players.

Deepening the contradiction is the fact that one of my favorite restaurants—the Red Hen, in Lexington, Virginia, arguably one of the best restaurants on the East Coast—essentially practices whole animal philosophy. On any given night, an order of lamb might lead to a presentation involving neck, liver, heart, and loin. I've had this dish, and found it delicious. Why do I like it in my hometown, but get light-headed and fuzzy-stomached when it's placed before me in a foreign country?

I'm sure there are lots of explanations, beyond the fact that I'm a huge coward. The heat doesn't help: It's hard to feel comfortable trying new things when your brains seem to be leaking down your back into your underwear. Then, too, there's the low blood sugar issue: If I'm not in a restaurant, seated, and within six minutes of being fed no more than four hours after the last time I ate, nothing—not filet mignon, not rack of lamb with mint sauce, not my grandma's homemade doughnuts—*nothing* looks good. That at least one of my kids is similarly hypoglycemic doesn't help matters.

Then there are the intangibles. Consider, for example, our trip to the top-floor food court the other day. We were there plenty early, so no blood sugar problems. The place is clean in a rustic kind of way—seventy-five feet long, it contains three rows of shallow booths selling noodle bowls, stir-fries, fried bread, sesame buns, eggs and toast, and pretty much anything else you can imagine. And the food looked—and smelled—*good*. All around us kids and grandmas and dads and moms were seated at cheap round card tables, slurping bowls of noodles with wonderful green vegetables.

The plan had been to check out the market and get back to our flat in time for PB&J sandwiches and a nap for Jamie, but Ellen and I couldn't take our eyes off those big steaming bowls of noodles and broth. So finally we broke down and got two Hong Kong specialties: wonton soup and fish ball soup.

Now I want to tell you straight out that neither of these is quite what it seems. The wonton soup, though similar to the version you'd get in, say Springfield, Illinois, is actually pretty different. For one thing, it has a much fishier taste. For another, this fishy taste comes from a huge roll of dried fish skin floating beside those lovely wontons. And for the record? This huge piece of fish skin looks exactly like what it is, including the odd scale sticking to its side.

The fish ball soup, on the other hand, isn't nearly as disgusting as you might think. First of all, no matter what you might be thinking, no, the main ingredients are not fish testicles. Second, though this soup also contains a thick, fatty roll of fish skin, strangely, the soup does not taste particularly fishy. The fish balls themselves, made of densely compacted fish meat, taste more like rice than anything, and fill you up nicely. I can provide no better evidence to the appeals of this soup than the fact that Will gobbled it up.

Go figure.

Jamie was another story. One issue with wonton soup in a real Chinese restaurant is that the noodles are incredibly long, and thus difficult to stuff into a two-year-old's mouth. And the wonton dumplings are big, somewhere on the upside of ping-pong balls—also difficult for toddler stuffing. The simple answer, of course, is to cut both noodles and dumplings into kid-friendly sizes. But, oops, you're in Hong Kong, where the only utensils available are chopsticks and these thick porcelain spoons with triangular handles. That the Chinese somehow manage to make eating with these implements actually look graceful— dipping the spoon into the soup and using it to suspend noodles closer to their mouths while eating with the chopsticks—is a testimony to both their elegance and their perseverance.

I am neither elegant nor persevering. I take one chopstick in each hand and half-saw, half-crush the wontons into two pieces. This works, but only after sloshing a third of the broth onto the table. Next, I take the big fat baby spoon and try to trap a few noodles between the spoon and the edge of the bowl, effectively slicing them. This works also, but only until I release the pressure from the spoon, at which time the freshly cut noodles sink to the bottom of the bowl. No worries. I reach in with my fingers and fish the damn things out. I put them in the spoon-bowl. I bring the bowl to Jamie's mouth.

"Too hot," he says.

"No," I tell him. "It's not hot. Daddy just stuck his fingers in, didn't you see?"

"Dirty," he says.

"No, Daddy's fingers are very clean. He licks them all the time."

But his jaws stay clenched.

I put the noodles back, scoop up some of the chopped wonton.

"Too hot," he says.

No, I explain, it's not too hot. To show him, I stick some of the dumpling in my mouth. It's amazing: ground pork, shrimp, green onions, all saturated with salty chicken broth. I want to eat the whole bowl right then. But there's only one spoon.

"Come on, Jamie," I say. "Daddy's hungry. Open up."

"Too ho—" he begins again, but I'm too fast. The moment his lips part, in goes the dumpling.

"Aaaaaagh!" he screams. "Aaaaaagh! Too hot!"

My wife looks at me. So do a couple at the next table, whose one-year-old is contentedly eating his noodles in that elegant bowl-spoon/chopstick way.

"It's not too hot," I say to my wife. "I tasted it myself. It's fine."

"Too hot!" Jamie hollers. "Too hot!" His mouth is wide open, his lower jaw hanging down. Soggy, partially chewed, sloppily cut wonton is pouring over his lower lip. He looks for all the world like a demon from a Japanese horror film, come back from the grave to haunt the owners of the noodle hut where he choked to death.

"It's not too hot," I say to the couple at the next table. "I blew on it. He's just a fussy eater."

"He doesn't like the texture," Ellen says.

"Aaaaaagh!" says Jamie, his jaw unhinged. His eyes are frantic, skittering back and forth between his mother and me.

"How can you say that?" I ask my wife. "All he's saying is 'Too hot.' Where do you get texture from that?"

"Wontons have a weird texture," she says. "Gluey. With lumps."

"Aaaaaagh!" says Jamie. He's starting to sound like he's gargling. The whole of his tongue is coated with thick rice noodle and what looks like half-digested beef.

"Get it out," Ellen says.

"How?"

Jamie expresses his opinion of wonton soup.

Good question. There are no napkins anywhere. There's not even a tablecloth, the corner of which Jamie might spit into unobtrusively. The bowl of soup has barely been touched, so if he spits there, it's a complete loss. The only option is to have him hack into my hand, which means that I'll be stuck with a fistful of meat and noodle with nothing but my shorts to use as a towel. I love my children, but I'm not about to spend the rest of the day with shrimp stuck to my pants.

"Too hot," Jamie moans, plaintively.

So I do what any good father would do when faced with a contrary child and a rapidly cooling bowl of absolutely amazing wonton soup: I grab a bottle of water, stick it in his mouth, and pour some in. Then I clamp his jaw shut and force him to swallow. Which he does, instantly.

Then he looks at me. I look at him. He looks at Ellen. She looks back, then glances at the other two kids, who are staring at us. The couple at the next table watches all five of us, wondering if we're related maybe to Paris Hilton. Then I look back at Jamie.

"Was that good?" I ask.

"Yummy," he says. "Good. More."

CHAPTER 4

KNOWING

R emember starting kindergarten?
     Me neither.

How about starting kindergarten eight days after moving to a new country?

No?

On a new continent?

In a different hemisphere?

Or try this one: starting kindergarten eight days after moving to a new country, then having your sixth birthday three days later?

Or starting kindergarten and being the only kid in your class with blond hair. A week after your grandfather died. And your mom's been gone. And your dad's been a total stress case. And you're away from your two best friends—whom you've known since before you could talk. And you're not able to walk to the school that you walked to with your brother five days a week, for three years, always assuming that you'd be going there as well. And having to take not one, but two buses. And having to run down a hill to catch the first of those buses in 90-percent humidity and 95-degree heat. And having seven-eighths of your classmates speak a different language?

No?

Really?

Wimp.

The first thing we did when we found out we were going to spend a year in Hong Kong was start looking for an English-speaking school for the kids.

Turns out we were already too late.

For most international schools in Hong Kong, applications are due early in December. Acceptance letters come at the beginning of February. Receive your Fulbright in mid-February and have a pair of school-aged children? One word: Homeschooling.

Now, Ellen was very excited at the prospect of having her first extended leave from any job, anywhere, at any time in her life. Ellen was excited about spending a year exploring the streets and neighborhoods of Hong Kong. Ellen was excited about expanding our children's horizons by taking them to a completely different place.

Ellen was not excited about homeschooling.

"It'll be fun," I told her. "Think of how much time you'll get to spend with the kids. Think of the impact you'll have on their lives."

"Think," she said, "of how difficult it will be to contact your divorce lawyer while you're in Hong Kong and the kids and I are in Virginia. With—" she added pointedly, "free public schooling."

Frantic, we Googled "Tai Po and international schools," "Tai Po and English schools," and just plain "Tai Po and schools."

Four came up. We e-mailed all of them. Two never replied. One of the other two was full and had an extensive waiting list. The last said they still had room, and that if we'd like to talk with them on the phone about the possibility of our kids enrolling, they'd be happy to give us a call.

Excuse me?

Logic dictates, of course, that if every good school in Hong Kong is booked up with a waiting list that stretches into the hundreds, then the one school that is *not* booked up and does *not* have a waiting list—and, indeed, is willing to make an expensive international call just to get you to consider their place—probably sucks. And if that is in fact the case, then any logical person can have only one response: "Sign 'em up!"

Ellen ignored me, scrolling through the website of the Other School, the one that had returned our e-mail but had the monster wannabe list. "I think we should wait," she said.

"Why? They've got space. They're desperate enough to call us. It would be un-American not to take advantage of the situation."

It didn't help that when I e-mailed one of my soon-to-be colleagues in Hong Kong and mentioned the two schools we were considering, her response was to rave about the Other School (her daughter was enrolled there, and had been since birth) and to say of the Small School with spaces, simply, "They don't have the best academic reputation."

"Sign 'em up!" I said.

"If they fall behind," Ellen replied, "they'll never catch up. You know how this town is. Do you want your children to be tracked as 'special' for the rest of their lives?"

"I do if it saves me tens of thousands of dollars."

"That's Hong Kong money, you idiot. In U.S. dollars it's maybe twenty bucks."

Making everything tougher was that we were 8,000 miles from both institutions. Here you are, trying to decide where your blood of blood and flesh of flesh will spend most of their waking hours, and you can't even go look at the place, much less talk to the teachers and make sure their idea of pedagogy doesn't involve hickory.

Needless to say, we did what any good, doting, American helicopter parents would do: We acted like complete idiots.

We e-mailed what few HK contacts we had three or four times a week for weeks on end. We e-mailed any friends they had who knew anything about either of the schools. We e-mailed their friends' friends, and their colleagues' friends, and their friends' colleagues. We e-mailed people we didn't even know, but whose names appeared when we did a Google search of the neighborhood surrounding the schools. Some replied. Some didn't. Some filed restraining orders.

We talked to the principal of the school that had space. I thought he seemed very knowledgeable, very nice. "Too nice," Ellen—who was clearly angling for the Other School—said. "You never heard of John Wayne Gacy?"

We managed, through wrangling and pure luck, to get Lucy moved up from 207 on the waiting list at the competitive school to number three, which made her chances pretty good. Will, though, sat tight at number forty. As insane as we were, we at least had sense enough not to consider sending our kids to two different institutions. It seemed the least we could do, given that we were already upending their lives.

In the end, we didn't have much choice. The kids either went to the Small School or I went to Hong Kong looking for a new wife.

It helped that my friend Susan, who was in Hong Kong the year before us on a Fulbright, visited the Small School and came back with a solid report. The neighborhood was nice, she said, via Skype. You could hear birds and the kids would like that, particularly with the usual standard chaos that is Hong Kong. The buildings were clean and well taken care of. The principal was friendly, the teachers very professional. All in all, she said, it was a very nice place.

"Nice?" I said. Nice was a word that girls always used with me in college to explain why I probably wouldn't be having sex with them anytime soon.

Susan shrugged and gave a little smile. She'd done her part, visited the place, given it the most accurate assessment she could—no small matter given her strong background in education and pedagogy.

I must have had trouble keeping the disappointment out of my voice, because Gary, Susan's husband, spoke up.

"Can I say something?"

Gary was a banker who'd quit his lucrative career so that his wife could take a one-year position in a really cool place and their kids could experience an extraordinary culture. You have to like a guy like that.

He came into view on the screen. He's a big guy, like me, only less flabby and whiny. And his eyes gleam with this weird light that someone once told me was something called, "common sense," a trait that eludes many academics.

"Listen," he said. "Nice or whatever, I don't know. It was a normal school, exactly the kind of school we all went to when we were kids—and we all turned out just fine. It was clean. It was quiet. The teachers cared about the students. Hong Kong is a crazy place, and a little peace and quiet can go a long way. If my kids were a little younger and I had to do it all over again, I'd love to send them to this school."

All of which, I have to admit, struck a chord. Sure we were excited about giving our kids the best international education they could receive; sure we like the idea of them being at some huge, swarming, prestigious Hong Kong school with fancy uniforms and a coat of arms. But what Gary said made sense. We were already putting Will and Lucy in an extreme environment. They would already be surrounded by major changes, not just the chaos of one of the biggest cities in the world, but the chaos of a new language, different smells, different foods, a different quality of light just walking down the street every morning. There was something to be said for providing them with a small haven in the midst of this storm.

I exchanged a few more words with Gary and Susan, tossed around an idea or two about the move and setting up a bank account, and then signed off. Going downstairs, I found Ellen in the dining room, helping Will with some homework. I told her what Gary had said. It didn't take long to make a decision. Firing up her computer, we sent the principal of the smaller school an e-mail: "Sign them up."

Valerie and Chris, our upstairs neighbors in Hong Kong who came to be our best friends and some of Lucy's biggest fans, have a magnet on their fridge: "All I want is a warm bed, a kind word, and unlimited power."

I mention this because it describes Lucy perfectly, especially during our first week in Hong Kong while Ellen was back in the States. I'd be in the kitchen trying to figure out how to turn the gas on when I'd hear, "Wi-i-i-ll! Stop it!" Lucy's voice would rise and fall and then rise again, screeching as though her older brother were pulling off two of her limbs. I'd hustle into the living room, only to find Will lying on the couch with a book.

"What's going on?" I'd holler, because I was tired, and stressed, and sad, and in a new country, and an idiot.

"He was looking at me!" Lucy would say.

"I was not," Will would reply, and from the tone of his voice I could tell that he had been, but only just, and that even that had been enough to set his sister off.

Or I'd hear, "Jamie, don't do that!" And I'd rush into her room expecting to see Jamie standing there holding her teddy bear in one hand and a knife in the other—only to see him waving a tissue paper in the air as though it were a butterfly.

"Who do you think you are?" I'd hiss at Lucy, thinking of the rice burning on the stove, or of the e-mails I hadn't yet replied to, or of the 400 faculty members I'd never met but whom I was supposed to convince to embrace general education in ten months. "You're not in charge of him! Leave him alone. What is wrong with you?"

Well, duh.

Maybe the only real insight I've ever had in my life is that people need to feel like they have the power—even on a small scale—to reshape their world. That this exists in the visual and literary arts is obvious. Storywriters often retell tales in such a way that they're able to make sense of otherwise meaningless events. Painters, similarly, can reconfigure the world they're representing on their canvases in order to achieve some pleasurable end for themselves: erasing the signs of aging in someone they love, for example, or deleting an ugly concrete silo in an otherwise naturalistic landscape, or making the king and his wife look like vain idiots.

But my theory extends beyond that. My friend Andrea has a sister-in-law who repaints her living room two or three times a year. I get this. Bad day at the office? Change your world, assert your existence in the universe by choosing salmon over teal. A colleague in biology has a half-dozen tattoos. I get this, too—even though it makes me wince like the coward I am. I've had students who buy junky old cars, gut them, strip them, and turn them into showroom pieces resplendent in chrome and high gloss. All of this fits my theory, as does gardening, rearranging one's bedroom, body-piercing, getting a new hairdo and—sadly—eating disorders.

My point here is obvious. The minute we decided to come to Hong Kong, Lucy's life went completely out of her control. And not in the good, gosh, I just won a trillion dollars kind of way. Consequently, she was now casting about for some way to regain that control, asserting herself whenever and wherever she could. And because I wasn't about to let my six-year-old get any (more) tattoos, she spent most of her time telling everyone in the family what to do.

Which is fair enough.

Even if it is a pain in the ass . . .

The good news—or at least we thought—was that she loved school. On the Friday at the end of her first week, she came into the flat holding up a mimeographed sheet of paper. "Look!" she said. "Homework!"

It was Mandarin, and her first real homework after three years of seeing her brother and her older friends doing it. While

Will curled up on the couch with a book, calculating that he had sixty hours before his own math and writing and Mandarin were due, Lucy sat down at the dining room table and did hers immediately.

Lucy with her first ever homework. This does not look like a kid who hates school.

And as if that wasn't enough, the minute she was done she laid the paper on the floor, got out her camera, knelt on the parquet, and took a picture.

Now all of this is a rather long, rambling, only vaguely humorous preface to "Curriculum Night" at our kids' school, the HK equivalent of what in the States we call "Harass the Teacher with Stupid and/or Obvious Questions Night." This took place on the last Friday of September, so after a dinner of spaghetti and French bread (hey, it can't be fish ball soup every night, right?), we left the kids with a babysitter and took a cab across town to the International School.

The evening started off well enough. The principal, a man who impressed us as much in person as he had over the phone, gave a small speech. We were introduced to the various teachers, all of whom seemed nice. We watched a short, digitized film about the school and the kids, designed especially to make us feel all warm and fuzzy about sending our kids there. And there were amazing chocolate-banana cakes at the refreshment table. All in all, not bad.

After the school-wide presentation, Ellen and I split up to meet with Will's and Lucy's teachers. In Lucy's classroom, Ms. Kee reviewed the kindergarten's curriculum, then clicked on the computer and flashed a couple pictures from the class website on the screen. There was the teacher sitting on a chair in the comfy corner, reciting numbers and nouns and talking about eating your vegetables and holding hands when crossing the street. There were her cute little students, gathered around her like so many baby rabbits, all broad-faced and smiling, eyes bright, chubby little hands waving in the air.

Except Lucy. Who looked like she's just drunk a quart of antifreeze. And then sat on a waffle iron. A *hot* waffle iron.

No biggie, I thought. Maybe she was having a bad day. Or even a bad hour. I was still clinging to that image of Lucy in my head, her kneeling on the floor of our flat, photographing her first-ever homework. She *loved* school. You could see it in her eyes as she rattled on night after night about learning Putonghua, about playing football during recess, about the funny things her teacher said that day. Just that afternoon, two seconds after I walked in the door, she was tugging at my briefcase, showing me a worksheet she'd done that day, unscrambling "-at" words and spelling them in the right order. She then went through the list, sounding out "cat," "sat," "bat," and even "flat." The only two she got mixed up were "hat" and "that," and the hell if I was going to correct her.

So no biggie, I thought. Just a bad hour, maybe indigestion from a bad apple or too much heat. Thirty minutes and good bowel movement and she'd be back to her usual perky self.

Only she wasn't. Every picture showed the same thing: all those chubby little bunnies, looking little and chubby and bunnyish and engaged and learning and all-American despite being from places like Finland and Malaysia. And then there was Lucy, forearms on her knees, face somewhere between grim and discouraged. Watching this, I felt mildly faint and sick to my stomach.

Still I didn't panic. I knew my little girl. She was full of spirit and goofiness and piss and vinegar and salt and humor. This is a kid whose favorite dish is Pad Thai, who learned to swim when she was barely three, and who charmed my Hong Kong work colleagues the first time they met her by requesting the head off the baked chicken we'd been served for lunch.

Lucy nibbling on a pigeon head. Just in case you thought I was kidding.

Once the orientation ended, I approached the teacher and handed her the contact sheet she'd asked everyone to fill out. "So how's it going?" I said.

Even then, I suppose, I expected assurances. "She's doing fine," her teacher would say. Or at worst, "Well, she started off a bit rough, but she's coming along."

What I got, though, was a dip of the eyes as Lucy's teacher brushed the cake crumbs from my completed form and said, "Actually, I wanted to talk to you about that."

"Oh?" I squeaked, my heart sliding down my chest to somewhere between my stomach, my liver, and whatever it is that allows us to get up in the morning and go forward with the assumption that the world is a good and just place.

"She seems . . ." Lucy's teacher bit her lip, choosing her words. This was a woman, I should add, I trusted entirely as a professional. Though twenty-seven at the most, she was a natural in the classroom—firm but caring, funny but able to communicate ideas in a way the kids could understand. She'd only been at the school for two years, but already they'd made her their curriculum director.

"She seems so serious," is what she finally came up with. "I don't think I've seen her smile once in the classroom."

My chin must have hit the floor. Lucy? The girl Will once said was funnier than the entire cast of Chicken Little put together? The kid my dad says makes you grin just by walking into the room?

Then Ms. Kee met my eye. "What's she like at home?"

I stuttered. "A—she's—a goofball. An absolute nut job."

Now it was her turn to stare. "Really?" She gestured toward the bulletin board, where all the kids had hung pictures of their families with strands of yarn drawing a line to their home countries. Lucy's photo showed all of us at the Virginia Military Institute on the Fourth of July. We're sprawled on the grass, just having finished a dinner of barbequed chicken and coleslaw. Will's doing cross-eyes and Jamie's sprawled in his mother's lap, holding a slice of pizza as big as his face. Lucy is behind Ellen, two fingers over her own head, giving herself bunny ears and grinning insanely.

"When Lucy brought this picture in," her teacher said, "I thought, 'I've never seen this person before.' "

If it's possible to break a sinking heart, that's basically what happened at this moment. Ms. Kee and I talked for a few more minutes, me asking questions, waiting for answers that would reassure me, her growing increasingly puzzled by the disparity between Lucy at home and Lucy at school and saying very little—through no fault of her own—that could actually make me feel better.

Eventually I thanked her profusely and stumbled out into the wrenching hot Hong Kong night, the sound of bugs and tree frogs rattling my ears, the smell of jasmine or some other night blossom almost suffocating me. Kids were running around on the Astroturf playground, shouting in the humid dark, waiting for their parents. Taking a seat on one of the benches along the wall, I tried to get my head around all of this.

Lucy was happy at home, I knew that. And she was happy about school, too—I knew that, and had pictures to back me up. Nothing like this had ever happened back in Virginia; on the contrary, her preschool teachers had always said she was the perfect student, obedient but funny, goofy but the first to sit on the floor at the appropriate time and be quiet for the teacher. What was going on?

There were, of course, the obvious answers. She'd just started school. Her grandfather had just died. Her mom had been gone for a long time. The food was kind of bland, often tempered only by lots and lots of soy sauce. It was so hot we had to take baths every evening or the kids would develop scabby red sores on their legs. Old ladies kept touching her blond hair when we were riding the subway, or standing in line at the grocery store, or basically doing anything out in public.

But still. This wasn't like Lucy. I couldn't picture the kid I knew sitting in a classroom, with a teacher she loved, being miserable.

Years ago my older brother struggled some with alcoholism (he's now been sober for twenty-five years). One day, midway through his junior year of college, he arrived at my parents' doorstep and announced he was dropping out. My father told him that was fine on one condition: that he go to see a counselor.

So my brother did, choosing my dad's old friend, a folk musician guru psychologist with the genre-appropriate name of Dave Ardapple. Dave and my brother closeted themselves in his office for an hour, then emerged. As my brother headed to the bathroom, Dave took my father's hand, looked him straight in the eyes, and said, "Bruce, you're son's an alcoholic."

My father didn't hear him.

Or more accurately, my father *heard* him, but his brain refused to register the information. It was just too big, too terrifying, for my father to take in. In his second decade as a Lutheran minister, my father had seen what alcoholism meant, had witnessed abused wives and children, had seen broken marriages, knew a man who'd actually managed to drink himself to death at the age of thirty-two. To learn that his son—*his* son, his first boy—might be headed down that path was simply more than my father could process, mentally or emotionally.

I understand this completely. And I mention this story now because, while listing all the reasons why Lucy might be unhappy, I left out one major, glaring possibility: that we'd messed up, big time, by coming to Hong Kong.

Think about it: This wasn't some abstraction we were talking about here, some theoretical child living a theoretical year in a theoretical land. This was my kid. And that was one hell of a big decision we made, pulling her and her brothers out of the only reality they'd ever known, the only friends they'd ever had, taking them to a place so hot that even the mosquitoes promise to be nice if only we let them stay in the air conditioning. And a year is a long time for a kid. I mean, twelve months is only 1/44th of my life, barely a blink. For Lucy, though? Twelve months equals 1/6th of her total time on Earth, roughly the equivalent of seven years for me.

I was glad Ellen was still in with Will's teacher, and that it was dark. I needed time to let my thoughts settle down. Maybe it was just the heat, or the long week, or the fact that, now six weeks into our time in Asia, some of the glossy excitement was starting to wear off. But the thought of my little girl—the goofy kid whose idea of a "fruit salad" is blue Jell-O stuffed with figs, oranges, strawberries, coconut, and M&M's—the thought of her sitting alone in a classroom for five days a week for eight more months being morbidly unhappy was overwhelming.

Leaning back, I looked out over the field. Mr. Blain, the PE teacher, a tall, stooped Scot with glasses, was playing Kick the Can with maybe ten of the kids. An empty water jug stood in the middle of the field, barely visible in the pale glow from the streetlights surrounding the schoolyard. The teacher patrolled the edges of the Astroturf, his long arms dangling, his polo shirt soaked with sweat, ducking his head, trying to spot the kids.

They skittered along just out of his sight, hiding behind hedges and beneath playground equipment, oversized geckos in bright clothes and bare feet. One, a small boy in a yellow shirt, seemed particularly adept at slipping below his gym teacher's sightline and sprinting toward the jug without getting caught. Twice while I watched, he flew across the pavement and onto the turf, speeding to the water bottle and sending it spinning into the air with a swift *Pfooft!*—all before Mr. Blain could catch him.

What I didn't know then was that, two days later, this little boy would run in that 3.5K race around the peak of Hong Kong Island, and that he would come in fourth for his age group and gender. And I didn't know that my kids would also insist on running this race, never mind that it was at some ungodly hour on a Sunday. Nor did I know that Lucy would run faster than either this boy in yellow or her brother, placing second in her group. This despite wearing sparkly purple basketball shoes that were flat-soled and definitely not designed for sprinting 2.25 miles around the top of a mountain in 90-degree heat.

Lucy with her class on her birthday. We bought the Bugs Bunny cake, thinking it was a tradition for parents to bring elaborate cakes for their kids' birthdays. It was not.

I know my little girl. I know her probably better than any of my children. Will, as I've said, is too much like Ellen and still a mystery to me. And Jamie—well, Jamie's a toddler and border-line insane.

But Lucy? I get her, see in her the energy and joy and passion and jealousy and hunger I felt when I was a child. There's no other way to say it: She's my little girl.

That said, the terrifying thing is that there's plenty I don't know—and a lot of it has nothing to do with Hong Kong. I don't know when she'll fall in love for the first time. I don't know when she'll first get her heart broken, or how she'll respond. I don't know what she'll choose to do for a career, or where she'll decide to live, or what kind of mother she'll be, or if she'll be one at all. I don't know if she'll struggle with alcoholism or anorexia or an inappropriate affection for boy bands. I don't know if she'll ever achieve her wish of dying her ash-blond hair black, or if she'll wear too much makeup or get good grades in school. I don't know where she'll see her most beautiful sunset, or what music will make her close her eyes and sigh, or what book she'll read and want to carry with her for the rest of her life. I don't know when she'll die or how—though I do know I'd better not still be around for it, or there is no God and that's all there is to it.

And I don't know what she feels like when she's there in that kindergarten classroom and her teacher is talking about nouns and verbs and two-plus-two and holding hands while going to the library—or why the little girl who makes everyone laugh just by being who she is doesn't smile as she sits there listening.

CHAPTER 5

CLEVER DUCKS

When Ellen came home and said she'd bought three tickets to sail on a junk—one of those red-sailed Chinese boats they're always showing on *The Price is Right* when the grand prize is an all-expenses-paid trip for two to the Orient—I said, "That's great. You and the kids should enjoy it."

"I'm not going," she responded. "You are."

I stared at her. "Me? But I'm the one who barfs on a riding lawnmower. There's no way I'm getting on some rickety old ship and hurling in front of strangers."

But apparently there was. See, Jamie was too little to go on the cruise, and Hong Kong seems to have a rule prohibiting two-year-olds from wandering around by themselves. So someone had to stay on the dock. And according to Ellen, that someone wouldn't be me.

"I can ride the junk another time," she said, "when my mom's here. Or when Jamie turns three and the Junk Nazis lighten up."

"But—" I began, ready to explain again about my propensity to empty my stomach every time our car went over a speed bump.

"You'll be okay," she said, and patted me on the shoulder in that way she does that makes me feel like I'm eight years old. "You can wear a raincoat. They're easy to hose off."

When we get to Kowloon on Saturday, the water looks like a typhoon just came through. Victoria Harbour isn't big, maybe a quarter mile across, but nevertheless it sees 250 oceangoing ships a day pass through its narrow confines. All the wake from all those boats bounces back and forth between the banks, and in no time at all the water gets not just choppy, but jagged, with twenty-four-foot swells causing six or seven shipwrecks a week. Men who have been sailing for fifty years cling to masts and scream like little girls.

We stroll along the harbor promenade for a while, trying to stay in the shade. There's a mall down there, and a great museum with amazing exhibits of calligraphy and pottery, and I'd give pretty much anything to spend the afternoon gazing at landscapes and underglazed blue ceramics. Around one o'clock, we head to a spot near the ferry terminal where our ship, the *Duk Ling*, (funny, right?) will meet us.

The *Duk Ling*. Besides being a clever pun in English, *duk ling* is Cantonese for "clever ducks."

It doesn't help that when the junk rounds the bend in the harbor, it's pitching front to back so dramatically that not only are there times when I get a complete view of the cabin roof, there are times when I swear I'm looking straight *down* the main mast. I am not making this up. I wish I were.

I glance at Ellen, suddenly certain I should have taken her advice and worn that raincoat. She just waves and smiles, and strolls off with the one child that, I now realize, she truly loves. Clearly, the other two are about to sink to the bottom of the harbor along with their spewing father.

We climb onboard. The *Duk Ling* itself is gorgeous. Maybe forty feet long, she sports a high rear deck and three sails, the tallest of which rises out of a long canopied area that provides shade for tourists on the center deck. Lucy and Will head immediately to the poop deck despite my insistence that this is entirely the wrong scatological reference for this particular venture. I follow, feeling the tilt and rock of the boat beneath me—this despite the fact that we're still moored—then crawl past an old couple smiling and holding hands, obviously thrilled that their dream of a double suicide will finally be fulfilled. Vaguely remembering something about keeping a low center of gravity on boats, I crawl across the deck and join Will and Lucy at the back railing.

"Careful," I croak. "There are sharks in these waters."

"Dad," says Will, turning it into a three-syllable word. "No there's not. All the pollution killed them years ago." He's entirely right, of course. To save money, the Hong Kong government only treats its sewage at the lowest of the three recommended levels, meaning the harbor itself is essentially an open cesspool—which is good to know, in case it's hot and you're considering a quick dip.

"Even so," I say to the kids. I curl up in a corner, my back to the water, having heard once that if you pretend the ocean isn't there, eventually it'll take the hint and go away. A bell rings, somebody somewhere throws a rope to the guys on the boat, there's a grinding and shredding of wood and metal, someone screams—and we're off.

And then a funny thing happens. I feel the wind. I mean, I *really* feel the wind. Maybe it's just because I'm covered in sweat. Or maybe it's that, for the first time since arriving in Asia, I'm not surrounded by either mountains or buildings—or in the case of Hong Kong Island, mountains *and* buildings. I feel a cool breeze across my forehead, tugging at my shirt and whistling gently past my ears.

Amid the chatter of Cantonese, three men in blue shirts come up onto the deck. Ropes creak, canvas snaps, and three thick red sails sewn around bamboo battens are hoisted into the air. They crack and buck. In the cabin beside us, a barefoot old man wearing a striped shirt turns a wooden wheel. The junk cuts a line into the harbor, past a steaming green-and-white Star Ferry and through a gap between a police cruiser and a rusted buoy. Beside me, Lucy and Will chatter, pointing to a red-and-yellow tour boat floating by. I hear the slap of the wake behind us. The sun is warm, but not hot, and the breeze blows steadily, cooling everything off.

It's wonderful. I mean, really wonderful. I've sailed only once before, on a little rowboat-sized thing on a lake near my hometown. We were the guests of one of my dad's parishioners, and he kept screaming at my brother and me to move this way or that across the rough-hewn bottom of the boat. Needless to say, the only impressions that experience made on me were that: a) sailors need to drink less coffee, and b) sailing can give you slivers.

Now, though, I find myself leaning against the dark-stained railing of a boat that was built in 1955 and used for years by real fisherman as a real fishing boat catching real fish. The trim of the cabin is coarse beneath dozens of coats of varnish. The floor of the main deck is untreated wood, scraped raw by years of salt and wind and water, so that only the seams and nail holes are dark; the rest is a worn gray color like the sides of a barn.

The ride is relatively smooth. Sure, there are some bumps up and down, but very few. The guy steering is leaning back in his small cabin, one foot up on a post. A thick strand of what looks like clothesline secures the wheel. Every so often he lifts the rope, turns the wheel 10 degrees, then reconnects the line one notch further along. The junk adjusts accordingly, and we shift slightly to the left.

It's lame to say, I know, but it's peaceful out here. In the middle of one of the busiest deep-water harbors in the middle of one of the busiest cities in the world, I feel perfectly calm. And so do the kids. Will was a little worried that he might get green around the gills, but now he's standing by the rear mast— I'm sure it has an official name, but I'm from America's dairy land, for Pete's sake—looking out over the water and tugging on a rope like somehow he's controlling this whole venture. Lucy, of course, loves every minute of it, taking 10,000 pictures of the junk, the sails, passing ships, the waves, old shoes bobbing on the water.

Do you get the impression that Will also fell in love with junks?

And me? I'm loving it too. In recent weeks I've been busy with my job, stuck in my office working on PowerPoints about learning outcomes or departmental briefings. When I'm not stuck in the office, I'm stuck in meetings discussing quality assurance, or stuck on the couch in our living room writing. In addition, a part of me had begun to think I'd pretty much discovered everything there was to know about Hong Kong. Which is naïve, I know, but seriously, how many neighborhoods can you visit with tall buildings? How many malls can you stroll through filled with shops whose names you recognize from glancing through the fashion section of the newspaper, but whose wares you can't possibly afford? How many quaint markets and kitschy souvenir shops and spas can you visit before it all starts to blur together?

Now, though, I'm on a real junk, cutting across the harbor with my blonde-haired girl and my blue-eyed boy, with the sun on my closed lids and the wind blowing what's left of my hair. We sail southeast toward the convention center—a modern, space-shippy looking thing reminiscent of the Sydney Opera House done on the cheap—then curve north past the old airport runway and a bunch of new developments going up in Hung Hom. I can see Hong Kong Polytechnic, where my friend Hedley works and to which, more importantly, Jackie Chan gave a bucket-load of money so a building here could be named after his wife. Then we turn again, sailing southwest toward the island and the main ferry docks near Central.

That night, after the tour ends, we get dumplings on the Island and visit an art show that is seriously fantastic. After all of that, and after we put the kids to bed, I go online and Google "Chinese Junks" and learn that these ships have been around since 220 B.C.E., that their design is considered one of the most efficient and easy to use in the history of sailing, that some junks in the 1400s were as large as 390 feet long, and that the sails are red to please the big dragon in the sky so that he won't make typhoons.

I read about how, in 1938, some guy named E. Allen Petersen sailed a junk from Shanghai to the States, fleeing the Japanese with his wife and two others. And about how, in 1955, six young men from Taiwan took a junk and sailed all the way to San Francisco, learning how to handle the old ship along the way, gliding under the Golden Gate Bridge on a mist-shrouded day. And I learn that they did this just because they could, and because they wanted to.

And I get it. Man, I get it.

CHAPTER 6

HELP

When we first got our housing in Hong Kong, one of my soon-to-be colleagues e-mailed me a copy of the floor plan.

"Holy crap," I said to Ellen. "You could land an airplane in there."

Seriously, we'd been expecting a "typical" Hong Kong housing experience, a euphemism for five people crammed into a room designed to store wicker furniture.

The floor plan, though, showed a spacious flat with a large kitchen, separate dining and living room areas, and not one, not two, but—

"Hey!" I hollered to Ellen, even though she was standing right behind me. "There are four bedrooms. Now we won't have to fight over who has to share!"

"That's the study," she said. (Did I mention our airport has a study?)

"No." I pointed. She leaned in.

"Huh," she said.

"See the bed?"

"Yeah, but look: no windows."

"There's a bathroom right beside it."

She used the mouse to zoom in. "Is that a washer and dryer?"

I wrote an e-mail to my colleague, asking if it was a bedroom, and if so, would it be a good place for Jamie to sleep?

"Those are servants' quarters," she wrote back. "I just use it for storing suitcases."

Turns out she's about the only one using that room for storage. Some basic Internet research shows that roughly 10 percent of Hong Kong households have a real live human being stuffed away into a closet somewhere—and that rises to 30 percent if there are kids in the home. We never actually went door to door and took a survey ("Excuse me, but do you traffic in human flesh?") but we felt pretty sure that a good half of the academics in our building had "help." As someone who's generally proud of his career choice, I have to admit: those numbers disappoint me. Because "closet" is by no means an exaggeration: There were no windows. No air conditioning. And a bathroom with a showerhead in the corner, so that you can bathe while sitting on the toilet—something I've always longed to do, preferably with a laminated copy of *Maxim* or *Cooking Light*. I'm not fussy.

There are several reasons why so many Hong Kongers have domestic helpers of this sort. For one thing, a lot of HK families are dual income, meaning someone's got to take care of the kids, feed the dog, and mop the floors. Then there's the fact that, well, in Hong Kong at least, help is cheap. Really cheap.

Consider: For a one-time fee of HK $9,600 and a mere HK $3,580 a month, you, too, can have someone who cooks all your food, does all your dishes, takes the kids across town to school, picks them up again and takes them to ballet lessons and English lessons and piano lessons. That person will do your laundry, water your plants, shop for groceries, polish your silver spoon until it's so light and shiny you barely notice it's in your mouth. All for about $500 U.S. a month. I've bought furniture that costs more.

At least once a week when we first arrived, someone who'd just found out we have three kids would ask if we were going to hire a helper. "No!" we'd say with a snort. "What are you, crazy?"

We didn't actually say that, of course. Though frankly, that's what we were thinking. I'd like to say this is because we're in some way morally superior, but it's more complicated than that. Truth be told, we're just not domestic helper types. Ellen's Midwestern, Lutheran, Scandinavian-American brand of martyrdom is so ingrained she won't even take aspirin to cure a headache; I can hardly see her paying somebody else to pick up her dirty socks. Which is probably just as well, because my guess is if we brought a helper into our home, within a matter of weeks I'd have hired five or six hundred of them and formed my own army. Nine months, and you'd find me marching on Beijing, demanding human rights for all, and more of those woman soldiers in mini-skirts and white go-go boots.

So, when someone asked us if we were going to hire a helper, we just shook our heads and changed the subject, or explained that we were only there for a year, or that Ellen wasn't working, so there wasn't a need.

Back when I was in grad school, I remember taking a multicultural literature class and having a discussion about the white man's burden.

"We're so arrogant," one of my classmates said. "We go into these countries and think we're helping people, but really we're making their lives worse."

I should have kept my mouth shut, of course, but when have I ever done that? I absolutely got her point—I mean, really, is there a part of the world we *haven't* screwed up?—but I was also starting to see a peculiar theory-geek *laissez-faire* going on with some of my classmates, a sort of, "Whatever we do we're damned to oppress, so we should just shut up and sit on our hands." Actually, it might have been the professor who said that, or maybe the dean, or my mom, but someone said it and several people nodded in agreement.

Anyhow, stupid straight white dude that I was, I raised my hand and talked about my stint in Africa a decade earlier, how one of the projects we'd worked on was digging a well outside a village so that the women wouldn't have to walk five miles each way to and from a sometimes dry creek, carrying fifteen-gallon jugs on their backs. Wasn't that a good thing? I asked.

Whoever it was I was debating looked awfully smug and white and grad-studenty in her carefully faded jeans and pseudo-Indian scarf. "But how do you know," she murmured, "that for those women that ten-mile walk wasn't the best part of their day, because they didn't have to cook or tend to children, and they could talk to their friends or be alone with their thoughts?"

"Because they told me," I said. I might as well have added, "When we were having cappuccino and trading scone recipes," it was that big a lie.

But she had me. I didn't know. And this was annoying. Because seriously, what good is being an American if you can't go into some minimally developed country and throw your weight around? And worse, what good is being an American if you can't even go and get all judgmental, pointing fingers and telling folks they should act like this or that and don't they know they shouldn't make their wives walk ten miles carrying water?

In the end, the worst thing about all this was that I'm not sure I left the class with any clear answers about how to act in a situation like the one with the well, or now, with the helpers. Which is fair enough—education isn't meant to give us the answers, just give us the line to lasso the fish with, or whatever. But even so, tell a mildly insecure, navel-gazing academic type (I was getting a PhD in Victorian literature after all) that the best thing to do in any situation is question your own judgment and motives, and what you get is a *severely* insecure, navel-gazing academic type who can't figure out whether to go forward or backward and who ends up metaphorically standing in the metaphorical corner of the not-so-metaphorical ethical ballroom of life.

Hong Kong "helpers" on their day off.

All of which is a pretty roundabout way of saying what's probably obvious: We didn't know how to respond to the people who employed these helpers. On the one hand, it was none of our damn business. On the other hand, these were our friends, and we were around them and their helpers a lot—sometimes in fact, we interacted more with the helpers than their bosses. If Ellen or I went to the market on a weekday morning, we weren't surrounded by mothers in pearls and heels, but the Philippine and Indonesian women who make up 98 percent of the hired help in Hong Kong. Sometimes on Sundays we'd go into the city center and find ourselves in the midst of thousands upon thousands of helpers, camped out on blankets in parks and shady walkways, playing cards and sharing food out of Tupperware containers with their friends. The noise was unreal, cacophonous, like flocks of geese arguing politics.

Then you have to consider the fact that, relative to some countries, Hong Kong treats these women very well. The

Malaysians, for instance, only recently have passed laws that standardize helper salaries, provide helpers a day off each week, and forbid employers from holding helpers' passports. These are laws that have existed in Hong Kong for years. And a good thing, I might add.

Ellen makes the point that we have helpers in the States, too, only instead of having one person to do everything, we farm it out to several parties. One lady comes in twice a month to scrub the floors and Clorox our toilet, and another pair of women take care of our kids. Of course, we pay these folks more than $500 a month—but we don't give them health insurance, something that's covered for helpers in HK.

And there's the fact that, by hiring women from incredibly poor countries, Hong Kong employers are helping to spread the wealth around. When I first wrote this piece and published it in a magazine in my field, several people went online and pointed out that by employing women from the Philippines, Hong Kongers improve the prospects of not only those women, but their extended families and friends—and indeed, the entire Filipino economy. Some of these folks actually went so far as to criticize me for questioning the practice: "Can't you see we're *helping* these women?"

Fair enough. But then I'd step into what we called our "suitcase room" and think, *Holy Jesus, it's hot in here.* And my mind would run a clip of what it must be like lying in that pitch black room at night—no AC, no window, no breeze, no chirp of crickets, just you, lying on your back in the dark trying not to sweat, trying to sleep, knowing you have to get up before everyone else the next morning. How bad must your life be that you look at sleeping in 3,000-degree heat, getting up at dawn to iron someone else's shirts, only getting two weeks a year to fly home and see your family—God, only getting to be with your *children* fourteen days out of 365—how bad must your life be for you to consider these conditions as an improvement?

Lucy at the bird market, kind of being the center of attention. Again.

I mentioned this to my friend Stuart one day. Stuart's a Canadian and a smart guy who's lived all over the world. He and his wife are two of the most generous people I know.

"I'm not sure," he said, after I'd spent twenty minutes looking for a metaphor to describe those tiny rooms, finally settling on "dead baby whale, without all the goo." "Abigail's already told us that she won't be renewing. It's too bad, too, because she's great."

"What's she going to do?"

"Go back to the Philippines. They have a couple kids there, little ones. Her husband's a foreign worker, too, in Saudi Arabia, and she only gets to see him and the kids once a year, when we fly her back. They've been doing this for years, saving money to build a house."

"A house? Really?"

He nodded his head. "Abigail quit an office job to come work for us. She can make as much here in four months as she can in the Philippines in a year. That means everything she earns the next eight months goes straight into the bank. Coming here makes sense."

A few nights later, we were invited to Stuart's for dinner. It was the first time I'd eaten in someone's home where the food was prepared by a person other than the host. This makes for awkward moments—who do you compliment if you like the pie?—but all in all it was a nice evening.

Stuart and his wife have a bunch of kids, so we gathered all of theirs and all of ours around the coffee table and cut up their hotdogs and poured their ketchup before gathering around the bigger table for pork chops and Szechuan vege-tables. Occasionally Ellen or I checked on the brood to make sure they were getting something in their bellies besides apple juice. After our food was on the table, we only noticed Abigail once, peeking out of the laundry room to see if it was time to clear the dishes.

Eventually, Jamie let us know that he wasn't going to eat his hot dog, subtly making his point by spitting bits of masticated meat onto his plate, the floor, and our hosts' cat. I grabbed an extra chop, cut it up, and put a few pieces on his plate. I fed him a little and he ate, chewing carefully, so I drifted back to my seat. Every few minutes or so, though, I went back to the coffee table, speared a few more pieces, and shoved them in his mouth.

Then I got distracted. I don't know, it might have been the spicy vegetables, the wine, the double-chocolate chocolate mousse they served for dessert. Anyway, when I finally got back to Jamie, Abigail was sitting on the floor beside him, forking bits of pork into his mouth. She'd cleaned up all the dishes but his, and I assumed she was feeding him so that she could finish up and start in the kitchen.

"That's very nice of you," I said, "but you don't have to do that." Jamie was taking the food from her happily, like a baby bird, leaning forward to receive her fork.

"It's okay," she said. "I like it."

And then she wiped one cheek with the back of her hand.

And then, of course, I understood that she was crying.

CHAPTER 7

A DAY AT THE
BITCH, BITCH, BITCH

We're in the taxi on the way to the beach when Will pinches Lucy on the arm.

"Oww!" she howls.

"Will!" I say. "What are you doing?"

"She pinched me first!"

I turn to Lucy, which isn't easy in the back of a tiny green taxi with a two-year-old on your lap. "Lucy, did you pinch him?"

"But he hit me!"

"Will! What on earth?"

"She had her hand on my bottom!"

"Lucy!" At this point, Ellen kicks in from the front seat, where she's been frantically paging through the English-Cantonese dictionary so that she can tell the driver exactly where we want to go. "What have we told you about touching people there?"

"But you and Dad—" she begins.

I interrupt. "If you guys are going to behave like this, we're going to turn this taxi around and go straight back home. Then you can both sit in your room all day while your mom and I go do fun things."

"What about Jamie?" Lucy asks.

"He can do fun things too."

"But he pinches."

"And touches bottoms," says Will.

"You guys!" I almost roar, but not quite. The taxi driver gives me a look—opaque, yet judgmental—in the rearview mirror. "If I have to say this one more time . . ."

And I leave it at that. Which is a joke, of course. Because in the fifty minutes we've been en route to Sai Kung—fifteen on the bus, thirty on a train, and the rest in this taxi—I've already said this six times. On the bus it was about them fighting over the front seat; on the train it was about them using the support pole like a pair of strippers, swinging their legs as they spun from top to bottom. In fact, we've been doing a lot of threatening lately. Back in the States, our kids were the ones teachers gushed about, the perfect little angels who never committed a wrong. And if they were perhaps a little less than perfect when they were with us, at least we'd gotten to the point that, when I took them to church, I could leave the glue gun at home.

Since we'd moved to Hong Kong, though, those kids seemed to have disappeared. Just a few days before, Ellen and Lucy came home from Lucy's after-school activity (baking), and Lucy was sent straight to her room for the rest of the day. This is not something we do often—in fact, in the nine years we've had kids, I can only remember it happening twice, and once it was for me. But apparently Lucy had spent most of the journey home doing exactly the opposite of what her mother had asked her to do. In Virginia, this isn't such a big deal. Our town is so small that the biggest danger is tripping over a sleeping dog. In Hong Kong, though, the consequences for not paying attention can be devastating. Earlier in the month, in the middle of a busy MTR station in Central district, Lucy had hauled out her Octopus card—Hong Kong's multiuse travel pass, good for anything from train fares to liquor purchases—and went through the turnstiles by herself while we were busy getting Jamie out of his stroller. Five more feet and she would have been down the escalator and I don't know how we would have found her again. And she did this despite the approximately 2,478,592 times we've told her, "When we're in a crowd, stick with us." We've even said, "Damn it."

For the rest of the taxi ride, the kids are pretty good, less because they want to be than because I've sandwiched myself between them, making a point of throwing an elbow or two as I do so, because yes, I learned my parenting skills from Charles Barkley.

When we get to Sai Kung, it's a delight. A small harbor nests in the low hills of eastern Hong Kong, filled with blindingly white yachts, houseboats shaped like junks, and at least one dragon boat, narrow and twenty feet long, with nine pairs of rowers on each side, stroking in sync to a broad-faced drum struck by a coxswain.

The ferry is old and wide, squat in the water, with a tin roof over the open rear deck. Its baritone engine chugs out faint blue clouds of diesel smoke, but the effect is more nostalgic than gagging. Like so much of the mass transportation in Hong Kong, the ferry's benches and trim are of dark, glossy pine. Cruising past the yachts and around a sandy promontory, we reach the beach in a matter of minutes.

Hong Kong has maybe two dozen beaches, ranging from the trendy to the isolated to the white and sandy. Unfortunately for us, many are on the south side of Hong Kong Island, meaning it'd take us a full two hours to get there, and then a full two hours to get back, leaving maybe eleven minutes of actual sand time, during which we'd undoubtedly have to take the kids to the bathroom.

Never mind. Trio Beach is lovely. There's a two-story shower house with changing rooms, a snack bar, and a place to rent umbrellas. There's a picturesque walkway along the back of a nice clean beach of white sand. The swimming area is huge, edged by a rock outcropping on one side, and two white rafts float on the blue-green water.

The afternoon is great. The water's cool and relatively clear by Hong Kong standards, the beach dropping off quickly so that you can swim to the two rafts, which we do, finding ourselves a little surprised by just how far away they are, how choppy the water is, how difficult it is to swim trying to keep a two-year-old made of concrete afloat beside you. After we return, we collect sea glass. We gather shells. We trap tiny crabs. I spend as much time as I can underwater, completely submerged and not feeling sweaty for the first time in two months. Will has his goggles with him and he floats face down, picking up anything that shines. At the end of the day, he's actually paler than when we arrived.

So the day is splendid: There's a breeze, the few other people on the beach are nice, the water feels good. We even go upstairs to the snack bar to get some ice cream.

Which is, of course, where the spaghetti hits the fan.

I don't know what I was thinking, buying them a Fanta. There's so much wrong with that phrase—"a Fanta." The "a" for one thing: Why would I buy one soda for two kids? Then there's the fact that we're not really sugar-drink people. For most of their lives, our kids were under the impression that Sprite and Coca-Cola were alcoholic beverages, and that kids should stay away from them whenever possible. (I'm not sure where, exactly, they got this impression, though I suspect it was from me, and that I was savoring a Coke at the time.) Then, last spring, some idiot at some party somewhere gave them a root beer. From then on, every time we went to the grocery store, the gas station, a restaurant, anyplace that had a vending machine— even to the health food store where the only sodas they carry are made from tree roots and yellowish, pulpy berries imported from Bolivia—in short, anytime we went *anywhere*, it was all about the root beer.

And we gave in, of course. Because we're kind parents. With no spines. Who like large dental bills and kids with brown teeth.

Anyhow, there we are at the refreshment kiosk at Trio Beach. Because it's the end of the season, all the ice cream has run out and not been restocked. No problem. We're *gweilos*, of course, so one form of fat is as good as another. I buy two bags of chips and an orange Fanta for Will and Lucy to share.

And then it begins.

"Will! I didn't get any!"

"You had it for ten seconds."

"No I didn't!"

"Well, eight then. It's my turn." Will has just touched his mouth to the straw when Lucy jerks the can away. "Hey!"

"That was ten. I counted."

"You can't count!"

To which Lucy responds by planting her lips around the straw and attempting to inhale an entire can of orange soda in one gulp.

"Lucy!" Will shouts.

"Will!" Lucy screams back.

"Aaaaaaaaaaaaaaaagh!"

Doesn't matter what language you say it in: sugar-water is still sugar-water.

In an instant, the can is out of their hands and arching through the air. *Whump!* It hits the inside of a nearby trashcan and falls, bottom up, leaking sugary neon orange over a discarded copy of the *South China Morning Post*.

They both look at me. So do the two Chinese couples at the tables near the balcony, their assortment of small children sitting quietly beside them.

"What'd you do that for?" Will asks.

I hiss, "Because murder is illegal!"

They look at me, not quite sure how to respond. Tapping each child on the shoulder, I urge them down the stairs, back to the sand. Ellen gives me a questioning look. I just shake my head. I'm angry, of course, but also embarrassed—for my kids, for myself, for my race. I think about that taxi driver, his eyes in the rearview mirror. I think about the driver of the bus, who glanced back when Lucy started to weep because Will could see the *whole* screen for the rear-mounted camera, whereas she could see only 98/100ths. I think about the people on the train who didn't so much stare as Will and Lucy did their Demi Moore impressions as they actively avoided looking our direction.

Now, of course, it's entirely possible you're reading this and thinking, "Oh puh-lease! Surely you care less about the opinions of strangers than you do about your own children?"

No. Not really.

Ellen and I have both lived abroad before. We're both aware of the way America and Americans are perceived—sometimes justly, sometimes not—as loud and clueless and pushy and socially inept—and that's just our politicians. Neither Ellen nor I want to reinforce that impression, and we don't want our kids to either. We don't wave flags every chance we get, we don't complain when we're served pigs knuckles instead of hot dogs (essentially the same thing, give or take a chemical or two), we don't thump our chests and talk loudly or insist on making casual conversation with people who just want to be left alone. If anything, we actually take a fair bit of pleasure in behaving in such a way that we're actually able to stuff all those negative stereotypes of Americans back in people's faces. (Except, of course, for the one about being passive aggressive.)

And remember, too, where we live. In the village of Tai Po, only twenty minutes from China's border, we're usually the only white folks at the market or in the park or waiting for the train or sitting on the bus or eating curried fish balls or using the public toilet. And when the only *gweilos* in the toilet include two boys having an, um, "swordfight," then we've got a problem.

That said, as someone gently reminded me the other day when I was whining about one or another of the little buggers, it's all about how you frame it. Is your daughter hyper, or just full of love and excitement? Is your elder son rigid, or just very comfortable with who he is and what his limits are? Is your toddler linguistically impaired, or just "creative" with his pronunciations?

And when you reconsider this particular moment, this particular day, from another angle, what you have is two kids who like each other and trust each other and are excited about going to the beach and express all this by—how else?—punching each other in the arms.

But I have to tell you: That sort of re-angling is good and easy when you're having a nice cup of coffee in your nice comfy home in Topeka or Toledo or Raphine, Virginia, with your favorite books on the shelves and your cat and your plants and everything else you've accumulated in the past nine years snug and safe around you. It's something else entirely when you're 8,000 miles from that home and sometimes just going to the grocery store to buy pork chops requires more mental and emotional energy than you can muster.

Fortunately for us, there are moments like the following: At 4:00 we start to pack up our stuff to leave the beach. The rest of the afternoon has gone fine, no more screaming fits or punching or hitting or acting like a baby (and the kids were fine, too). But now it's cooling off and the skin on our faces feels tight from all that saltwater and sun. After showers and changes of clothes, we call the ferry and ride back to Sai Kung. Once there, we walk around for a bit, checking out the restaurant options, finally settling on Thai, something everyone likes. Sure enough, Will finds a chicken dish and orders it. Lucy gets her usual Pad Thai. We pick out something for ourselves and for Jamie, and settle in for nice quiet meal.

Which we have, for about ten minutes, until a family of five walks in. They're Chinese, at least ethnically, but the two older kids—who could be twins, around six or seven—speak fluent North American English. They take the table behind us, and immediately the ruckus starts.

BAM!

"Nathan!"

"It didn't break," a small, bold voice says.

My back is to their table, but I manage to catch a glimpse of a dinner plate lying on the tiled patio.

"How many times," his mother says, "do I have to tell you not to play with your dishes?"

"You never told me that."

"Yes, I—you know I—you know you shouldn't play with stuff like that. Leave it on the table."

"But Mom," he says, and I can hear his sister snigger, "you never told me that."

"Nathan," his mother begins, and then her voice fades, and we lose track of the conversation.

Eventually the food comes, and we're chewing happily, quietly dazed by a day in the sun, when we hear: "Get down from there!"

Will is staring over my shoulder, eyes wide, so I start to sneak a look just as the father says, "Sit down in your seat! You know you're not supposed to—" and I turn around and think *Holy crap: That kid is standing on the table.*

"—stand on the table!" his father finishes.

Which isn't entirely accurate. Because actually, the toddler is *walking*. On the table. With his feet. On the table. Past the butter dish. Toward the saltshaker. He couldn't have been more than two, but even so—*on* the table.

"Thomas," says his mother, "get down from there this minute!"

I glance at Ellen and she raises her eyebrows. I'm feeling a little smug, I have to admit. After all, *my* little angels are sitting quietly in their seats munching on their noodles and chicken and watching the drama unfold. True, they just spent seven hours in the hot sun, running, swimming, diving, swimming, running. They couldn't be more lethargic if I'd dunked their heads in a vat of Nyquil. But even so, *they're not walking on the table!*

We finish our dinner, get the bill, and begin shuttling the kids to and from the restroom, one at a time, before the long journey home. I'm just squeezing the leftovers into my backpack, when I hear a loud *POP!* followed by the tinkle of glass over pavement. Behind me erupts a storm of shouting, swearing, and crying.

"What happened?" I say to Ellen, who's just strolled in and must have seen the whole thing.

She grips my arm above the elbow and shoves the backpack into my hands. "He threw a glass over the balcony," she hisses in my ear.

"Who—? What—?" I start to turn to get a better look, but Ellen pushes Jamie and me out of our chairs and in a moment all five of us are on the street. Behind us we hear scolding and arguing and a baby crying and two smaller voices assigning blame.

Ellen's grinning. And I am too, I realize. I know we shouldn't feel pleasure at other people's misery, particularly when it involves kids, not to mention our own blatant hypocrisy. But I don't care. I'm smiling so hard my face hurts.

We hail a cab and pretty soon we're buzzing off toward Ma On Shan and the train station. I'm in the backseat again, and

Lucy and Will are sitting dazed and exhausted beside me. On my lap, Jamie's already almost asleep. The harbor is fading off into the distance on our right as the taxi picks up speed and a cool breeze drifts through the window.

Will and Lucy sleeping in the back of a taxi after one of our all-day rambles. Ellen is beside them in this photo, so there was no pinching involved.

"Hey," I say to Will and Lucy.

I want them to notice the deep violet sky, the crescent moon rising over the water. I want them to feel what I'm feeling right now—a sort of calm, buzzed contentment.

"Hey," I say again.

But neither of them notices, their eyelids dropping, their bodies slack.

"Hey," I say for the third time. "You guys." I reach over and grab a bit of Lucy's arm. And give it a pinch.

CHAPTER 8

JOY

As a writer, I try to avoid big words like "Hope" and "Love" and "Patriotism." These are vague terms, empty words that mean so many things to so many people and have been used so many times that they are practically useless. I mention this because I want you to know I don't take it lightly when I say that, most Fridays as I push Jamie away from the drop-off spot in downtown Tai Po where Lucy and Will catch their shuttle bus to the International School, I feel joy.

Pure damn unadulterated joy.

Seriously. My step is light, my head is clear, and there's something in my chest that seems to rise and expand, loosening my muscles, making my whole body feel at ease.

Why, you ask? Why do I feel this way?

Follow along, and I'll show you.

After waving goodbye to Will and Lucy (Lucy always waves back; Will never does), I turn Jamie's umbrella stroller in the direction of the train station. After about a five-minute walk past a secondary school where kids stand in formation behind a chain-link fence, shouting in unison as their principal speaks, we're there.

Jamie looks up at me and says, "Lollipop?"

"Yes," I nod, and push him toward the 7-Eleven near the open-air entrance to the station.

It's testimony to the frequency of these Friday trips that the women behind the counter know and recognize us.

"You like a lollipop?" they say to Jamie, their faces split into grins, their voices chipper in baby talk.

Normally Jamie's shy with people he doesn't know too well—being blond and small, with round blue eyes in Asia will do that to you. But he gives these women a small grin before taking his candy back to the stroller and hiding his face in his shirt. I grab a Coke and pay for everything with my Octopus card. Then Jamie and I stroll into the station, go up the escalator, and climb on board the MTR.

Some of Hong Kong's wonderful, super skinny trolleys. Over the course of the year, Jamie and I must have spent forty hours just riding around on these things.

The MTR, I have to admit, is part of the pleasure of the day. For one thing, it's pure Hong Kong: clean, efficient, and convenient. For another thing, there are TVs onboard. The TV in our flat doesn't work very well, so even if Jamie and I can't understand a word they're saying on the MTR, we enjoy watching. Our favorite part is the commercials. The one for a bank (we think) with a woman who looks like Audrey Tautou helping an old lady and then missing her bus (what this has to do with banking is beyond me). Or the one for tea that tries to imitate an old-style melodrama, a mustachioed villain in a Tang dynasty costume attacking a helpless damsel with a painted face, only to be stymied by a swordsman who slays the foe and pours tea for the swooning lady.

And we enjoy, too, the view out the window: Tolo Harbour passing by, blue-black and choppy against the permanently green mountains of the New Territories; the science park with its deliberately off-kilter architecture and sculptures that look like alien spaceships. Just after Sha Tin we pass under a range of mountains and into Kowloon, the lower part of the peninsula that, for years, marked the outer boundary of civilization in Hong Kong. Here the landscape consists of narrow apartment blocks, prickly with balconies and hovering over gray streets and busy markets. We pass light buses (Hong Kong's version of a mini-bus) and red taxis, and whiz by shopping malls and street vendors selling thousand-year-eggs preserved in ash and lime, soya chickens with the heads still attached, thin potato cakes spiced with green onions.

We could get off at Kowloon Tong and take the Central Line straight to the Island, but instead we keep our seats and continue on to Hung Hom, where we get off, take a bridge across lines of cars and buses waiting to enter the tunnel under the harbor, and stroll across the campus of Hong Kong Polytechnic. Crossing Chatham Road, we roll into Tsim Sha Tsui.

TST is—at the risk of sounding redundant—joyous.

Newer than the Central district on the Island, TST is less touristy and thus, ironically, more Hong Kongy. Many of the streets are curved and meandering and buried in steep valleys between fifteen- and twenty-story buildings, giving the neighborhood a maze-like feeling. There's a mildewy air to the place—indeed, most of the stucco buildings are powdered black with the stuff—and air conditioners hum everywhere, dripping on you as you stroll along the sidewalks. Wandering, Jamie and I pass Korean barbeque restaurants, shuttered nightclubs, bakeries selling buns stuffed with pork floss, noisy breakfast joints where the Chinese are slurping congee, a gruel-like soup made with rice. There are plenty of "spas" here, most of them still closed (after all, prostitutes need their sleep, too), and everywhere hang neon signs in the shape of a foot, advertising pedicures and massages.

Some days we don't even bother crossing the harbor, choosing instead to stay Kowloonside. There's a brilliant Hong Kong history museum right next to Hong Kong Poly, and Jamie and I have spent a couple nice mornings there, learning about the opium wars, the Japanese occupation during World War II, and the riots in the 1950s when the housing system broke down and tens of thousands of Hong Kongers resorted to living in shacks on the sides of mountains.

Closer to the harbor are a science museum and an art museum. Hong Kong is not known for its support of the arts—it's too busy with banking and shopping. That said, it was at this art museum that I first fell in love with traditional Chinese underglaze blue pottery with its scenes of bald-headed children playing ball in gardens full of weeping willows. And it was at this museum that I first came to understand traditional Chinese landscape watercolors. The first time I saw these works, I felt bored and vaguely miffed: all those mountains, all those blank spaces, no colors, just boring black paint. Turns out that blank space, those mountains, those repetitive brush strokes are part of the point, creating a meditative landscape that's supposed to soothe the soul, calm your mind, make you a better, more focused, more reflective human being. Who knew?

On this particular day, though, we're headed to Central, so after a quick stop at my favorite tea shop to pick up some oolong, we continue our stroll toward Nathan Road, the main artery of the peninsula, filled with glass-fronted shops selling jewelry and expensive cameras. Walking down Nathan, I make eye contact with a half-dozen handsome young Indian men in their shirtsleeves. All of them work for tailors. Were I not with Jamie, most of them would try and hand me cards as I shouldered past, asking me if I needed a tailor, if I wanted a suit, if I needed some shirts.

Across Nathan is Hong Kong's biggest mosque, a massive white structure with a huge central dome and turret towers at each corner. Behind it is Kowloon Park, one of the overlooked treasures of the city. Jamie and I have spent hours at a time there, wandering in the sculpture garden, playing chase through the maze, gazing at the flamingos and various ducks in the pond. It has an aviary, with parrots the size of chickens and rhinoceros hornbills, crazy-looking toucan-type birds with strange horns on the tops of their bills like inverted beaks. Two of these once decided to perform the sort of couples act I usually associate with Amsterdam, and I ended up pulling Jamie away less because of the sex than because of the violence with which the male mounted the female, standing his turkey-sized drumsticks on her wings so that she couldn't flee.

Jamie playing in Kowloon Park. I'm not sure if this was before or after the lady at the noodle shop spoiled him rotten.

We stroll along the southern edge of the park, down Canton road with its Gucci and Tiffany and Louis Vuitton, toward the docks where we catch the Star Ferry.

It's hard to know why the Star Ferry has had such a lasting appeal—but it has. Founded in the 1880s by a businessman with the poetic name of Dorabjee Naorojee Mithaiwala, the ferry system began with a single steamboat, the *Morning Star*. The Star Ferry Company itself was formed in 1898 by an Englishman, and the fleet developed its present-day look over the next several decades; long and wide, sitting low in the water, with a green lower and white upper deck, the ferries still have the power to make you feel like you've stepped back into Hong Kong circa 1937. The insides of the boats only strengthen this sense: pine paneling lines the walls and gunwales, stained dark brown with a patina. Seating consists of long wooden benches with metal backs that are reversible. Heading south to Hong Kong Island, the backs rest on the north side of the benches; when it's time to return to the mainland, passengers simply swing the supports on wide bolts and hinges so they can face forward. In the middle of both the upper and lower cabins is the ferry's huge smokestack, big around as a VW Bug. The whole ship smells vaguely of wood and turpentine and diesel, which sounds nasty, I know, but in this situation only adds to the charm.

And then, of course, there's the view. Bobbing across Victoria Harbour, Jamie and I have maybe the best vantage points on the world's most famous skyline: the International Finance Center is right in front of us, its silver-and-glass profile flashing beneath sunny skies, making it look like the world's biggest, bluest, nose-hair razor. Farther to the east squats the convention center, a glowing white rip-off of Sydney's opera house. Between it and the IFC is a mishmash of skyscrapers and apartment buildings, some glamorous and imaginative, some more functional, some older and businesslike, some clearly designed to make this or that architect a household name. Hong Kong's population keeps growing, almost doubling in size from four million in 1970 to seven million in 2010. Consequently, Victoria Harbour has shrunk: Nearly 40 percent of the water has been "reclaimed" since 1900. To the left of where we'll eventually dock is a construction site the size of twenty football fields, in which the foundations are being poured for yet another layer of skyscrapers and apartment buildings. Part of what being rich in Hong Kong means is seeing your $10-million view of the harbor disappear every dozen years as new construction rises in front of you. Much more of this, and a person will be able to walk from Central to Kowloon.

Today the sun is warm and the sky is blue. Tiny sampans putt by, and in the distance you can see ships and cargo tankers. Off to the right, toward Lantau Island, are moored boats too big to enter the harbor, including, at the time, the USS *George Washington*, a nuclear class aircraft carrier.

Jamie sits on my lap as we enjoy the gentle bob of the ferry. He chatters away, and I nod and say, "Uh-huh," and "Really?" at the appropriate moments. Which isn't easy, I have to admit. Before we left the United States, Jamie's speech was so delayed that I squeezed a consultation with a speech therapist into our final days of packing up back in Virginia. She came by, sat and talked with him for a while, and didn't seem particularly fazed by what she heard.

"How much does he understand?" she asked me.

"Pretty much everything."

"Complex sentences?"

"Yes."

"And he can follow your instructions?"

I nodded, stroked Jamie's hair as he played with some blocks.

"Huh," the therapist said. Then she got his attention and asked him to repeat a number of words for her. He did fine with apple, bike, and agoraphobia, and she started to pack up her things.

Then Jamie looked at me and said, "Mope sumgul afid durmphop."

So I got up. "Sure."

The therapist, a no-nonsense sort of woman in her early fifties, gave me a look. "What did he say?"

"More raisins and peanuts."

Her face folded in on itself. "Oh my."

Needless to say, being in a foreign country hasn't helped Jamie any. Cantonese is a notoriously difficult language, involving—depending on how you count—eight to ten different tones, as opposed to Mandarin, which only has four.

Making it worse, many Cantonese words involve sounds foreign to the American palate, for example, the *ng* sound as in *ngoi,* the all-purpose word that means, depending on the situation, "Excuse me," "Thank you," or "I'm sorry." In Cantonese, this sound is pronounced like the last part of "SingiNG," "runniNG," or, perhaps most appropriately, "GaggiNG" with the neck tightening, the rear roof of the mouth coming down to the root of the tongue. This is not a part of the tongue, I'll point out, that's meant to be used for speaking. And this sound comes at the *beginning* of many Cantonese words—think, NGaggiNG. That anyone in this region is capable of speaking more than four words a minute is astounding to me.

Faced with these complications to his already peculiar approach to language, Jamie, it appears, has decided to stick to his guns and pronounce things *his* way and on *his* terms, leaving Ellen and me to nod and smile in our uncomprehending way as he, for all we know, asks us if we'd like him to burn the house down, or feed his sister to a very large snake.

After ten minutes, the Star Ferry pulls alongside a two-story pier. One of the crew on the boat tosses a thick rope with a loop on the end toward a man on shore, who catches it with a hook and circles it over one of the moorings. We climb off, our legs slightly wobbly, and stroll along the elevated walkways toward Central, the heart of Hong Kong. Central has a very different feel than Kowloon. For one thing, there are more white people—bankers and tourists and Australians on shopping jags. For another, these people—and their Chinese and Hongkong-ese counterparts—are generally richer. Central—and the nearby Admiralty district—are places where money matters, where it's not enough just to look good, you have to have the right labels—on your clothes, on your handbag, on your glasses and your watch and your shoes. Central is the sort of place where you learn fairly quickly that there's a difference between a *nice* suit and a *good* suit, that there's some immeasurable but inarguable distinction separating a cheap, go-to-your-local-barbershop-or-hairdresser haircut from a $150 (U.S.) haircut by a stylist named Raven whose sex is indeterminate but who, you are assured, is the barber of choice for all the latest Canto-pop stars who are not currently in rehab.

Not that the Island doesn't have its charms. It does. There are wonderful tailors here, men who frown and grump over you as they measure your shoulders and eye your fat American waist-line that will cost them another half-bolt of material. When you come in for your initial fitting they will ignore you for ten min-utes as you stand by the door and they dodge around the room, waiting on other customers and calculating figures and flipping through any one of the thousands of sample books piled elbow-high on the counter beside the cash register. And then, just when you've decided that they hate you and you're about to run out of the place crying, they drape you in an amazing inexpensive, custom-made suit, and stand back and pinch their lips to keep from smiling because they've just made you look that good. And you feel immensely loved.

Across from my favorite tailor is my favorite noodle shop in all of Hong Kong, a hole in the wall, so small the only reason I can find it is because the headwaiter has green hair that can be seen from the street. The restaurant itself has a row of narrow, two-person booths along each wall, and small round tables made for three people (but that usually seat six) running up the middle of the room. Near the back is a cooler stocked with 6-ounce glass bottles of Coca-Cola, and to the left of that is a restroom that wouldn't pass even the most lax of American inspections, even if the inspector was legally blind, noseless, and inclined to take bribes. But it doesn't matter, because the noodles and dumplings are made at the front of the restaurant, in a small glass booth, by an elderly man who is clearly a magician.

Dumplings in Hong Kong are, of course, as common as toast and marmalade in England or burgers and fries in the United States. Every restaurant has them, and every restaurant makes them almost exactly the same way, with pork, shrimp, and a rice-flour wrapper. What makes the dumplings at this particular restaurant—I'd tell you the name, but there's no sign outside; just look for the man with the green hair—so good is a mystery. Perhaps it's the broth, rich and salty with small crunchy rings of scallions floating inside. Maybe it's the tsui sum—greens with hoisin sauce—that is served alongside. Maybe it's just the freshness of the ingredients, the shrimp caught and ground that very morning, the rice-flour wrappers made on site rather than bought frozen.

It doesn't really matter why: We dig in. Or rather, the grownups do (Ellen is with us now, having stayed behind to get some exercise before taking a bus straight from Tai Po). Jamie likes dumplings fine, but prefers peanut butter and jelly, so I've slipped him a sandwich after ordering dumplings for Ellen and me. The waiters here don't mind—this is the one place in Central where he gets special treatment, the woman behind the cash register coming out every twelve seconds to make sure he has everything he needs, to plead with him to smile, to ask if he likes his sandwich, to say "Hello! Hello!"

Central holds other charms, too. Toward the western end you can find small shops selling bamboo cooking steamers and Chinese drugstores aromatic with ginger, star anise, and dried fungi. The Western Market is generally overrated, but if you climb to the second floor your eyes will be dazzled by a dozen shops exploding with bolts of brightly colored material. And once you've done that, there's a dessert shop downstairs and a German bakery where you can buy thick hearty breads, just like in the motherland.

Jamie tolerates all of this—the tea shops, the museums, the tailors—well enough. We've learned to keep an eye out for playgrounds, which seem to be everywhere in Hong Kong, tucked away at the ends of long alleys, or hidden behind massive banks. One of the best of these is in Wan Chai district, an area once known for its brothels and bargirls—think: *The World of Suzie Wong*—and still sporting more than its fair share of "spas" and Thai "massage" parlors (who knows? Maybe they're for real?). Since the takeover by China in 1997, though, and the subsequent withdrawal of the American fleet, Wan Chai is better known for its wine bars and cheesy "strip" clubs where more often than not the women dance fully clothed—not that I'm bitter or anything.

Anyhow, Wan Chai also has a great little park, secreted away in a corner next to a middle school, and while I sit under the shade trees and try mightily to stop sweating, Jamie climbs the various ladders and slides down the various slides, and works off all that frustration at being cooped up in a stroller for so long.

The other great thing about Central, as far as Jamie and I are concerned, is the tram. Running from one end of the island to the other, the tram system features distinctive double-decker cars so narrow that the upper carriage can only hold three seats across.

Like the Star Ferry, it's difficult to say exactly why the trams are so appealing. Part of it, here again, is historical: The tram system is 130 years old and the cars look it, with their low, wood-framed windows and pine beams. The seats are formed plastic dating back at least to the 1950s.

And part of the appeal of the trams may be their egalitarianism: Ride on any given day and you'll be seated next to a Filipino helper working for $500 a month, a honeymooning couple from Australia, a Hong Kong grandmother wearing silk brocade and a jade bracelet, and a fresh-out-of-college investment-banker clutching his briefcase to his moderately tasteful tie.

Jamie loves the trams. More than once, we've gotten on them not because we had anywhere to go but because we just wanted to (they only cost $2 HK, about thirty cents, U.S.). We always climb to the top level, always squeeze our way to the front, always take the foremost seats when they come open, and always ride as long as we can.

The city looks different from one story up: less crowded, more orderly, the ebb and flow of traffic and pedestrians and red taxis somehow making more sense from up here. And you see things up high that you don't from the street level: apartment windows with laundry strung outside, flowerboxes, tucked-away restaurants serving coffee from silver electric pots. More than once while riding on the trams, I've noticed a new market or shop or avenue and thought, *Man, I have to explore that!*—only to realize a minute later that it was a place I'd been to before but had never seen quite this way.

Today, after visiting my tailor and having noodles at our favorite dumpling shop, Ellen heads off to run errands before going to get Will and Lucy from school. Jamie and I end up returning across the harbor and strolling into Kowloon Park, where we stop for a quick ramble on the climbing castle. Heading north, we roll into the Jordon area, full of computer stores, restaurants, small street markets, and office buildings. We wander.

Jamie falls asleep, as I knew he would. I love it when he sleeps— not because he's a pain in the butt when he's awake, because he's not, but because it makes me feel like I'm a good father, like I'm protecting him, like he knows that he's safe with me.

I find a small market that I couldn't direct you to if you paid me a million dollars, and pick up a couple cheap T-shirts to wear while working out. Next I wander into an old-fashioned Chinese department store, just to see what it's like. The lower floors are just like any big-city American store, teak paneling covering the walls, the aisles crowded with metal racks displaying sale-priced

shirts and blouses, polite and watchful sales personnel who seem
at once humble and eminently qualified to help you pick out a
Mother's Day gift or a new tie for your aunt's wedding.

Upstairs things change. The top floor, for instance, is full
of traditional Chinese herbs, which make it smell like a cross
between a candy store and an Indian spice market. On the third
floor are traditional Chinese home accessories, everything from
delicate porcelain figurines to Buddhist and Taoist gods made of
hardened sap to calligraphy scrolls to jade carvings costing tens of
thousands of dollars. Will and I have been searching for a chess
set for his friend Cameron back home, but the ones for sale here
are made of cheap plastic, so I head back into the busy streets.

My bowl of noodles already seems ages ago, so I grab a pas-
try and milk tea (strong, condensed tea packed with sugar and
stirred into, um, milk) from a small stand and keep moving.
Pretty soon I think I'm lost, but then I recognize an MTR station and realize I'm actually not far from Hong Kong Poly and
the East Rail line that will take us back to Tai Po. I take a right,
holding my tea with one hand and using the other to push the
stroller through narrow curving streets.

Our days out aren't always this perfect. There was the time,
for instance, when the stroller collapsed as we rolled across the
Poly campus, the consequence of a lost wing nut. A nearby jani-
tor, who'd seen the whole thing, offered us electrical tape to hold
the bolt in place, and we forged on, readjusting the tape every
half hour or so as the tackiness wore off.

And there's the time Jamie fell asleep when we were exploring Sheung Shui, a village not far from the Chinese border. I
made it all the way down to Will's and Lucy's school without dis-
turbing him, but then, just as we were leaving the playground, I
inadvertently tipped the stroller forward, dumping him face-first
onto the concrete. He bawled, of course. And he wet his pants.
And well he should have: He'd gone from a deep, comforting
sleep to having half his face scraped off. I carried him, bloody,
wet, stinking of urine, down the hill as fast as I could, Will and

Lucy behind me hauling the stroller as I tried to flag down a taxi, any taxi, please goddamn it, just a taxi to get us back to our flat so Mommy could make it all better.

Today though, Jamie remains asleep and I manage to keep him more or less upright in his stroller. We roll past dimly lit shops and soon-to-be opened nightclubs receiving cases of Tsingtao and Canada Dry. Eventually we emerge on Chatham Road, cross, and make our way back through the Poly campus toward Hung Hom station. Low dark clouds are looming, and by the time the train rumbles north toward Tai Po, drops of rain streak the windows.

I don't care. I have my sleeping boy. I have my other two kids already at home, likely sipping cocoa and doing their homework. I have Ellen, who loves, beyond words, these three children, and who tolerates me. And I have this entire, massive city spread out in front of me, ready to be explored.

CHAPTER 9

MY SO-CALLED WIFE

B ack in the early 1990s when I was in grad school and mullets were still vaguely cool, there was an essay making the rounds called "I Want a Wife." Written by Judy Brady (then Judy Syfers) and published in a 1971 edition of *MS.* magazine, it detailed the narrator's encounter with a male friend who was newly divorced and was now looking for a new spouse.

"As I thought about him while I was ironing one evening, it suddenly occurred to me that I, too, would like to have a wife." Brady goes on to detail all the reasons why she feels this way:

- "I want a wife to make sure my children eat properly and are kept clean."
- "I want a wife who will plan the menus, do the necessary grocery shopping, prepare the meals, serve them pleasantly, and then do the cleaning up while I do my studying."
- "When I meet people at school that I like and want to entertain, I want a wife who will have the house clean, will prepare a special meal, serve it to me and my friends, and not interrupt when I talk about things that interest me and my friends."
- "I want . . . a wife who makes love passionately and eagerly when I feel like it, a wife who makes sure that I am satisfied. And of course, I want a wife who will not demand sexual attention when I am not in the mood for it."

- "I want a wife who will remain sexually faithful to me so that I do not have to clutter up my intellectual life with jealousies. And I want a wife who understands that my sexual needs may entail more than strict adherence to monogamy. I must, after all, be able to relate to people as fully as possible."

Reading this in a class in grad school way back when, I remember having three responses, in no particular order:

- What kind of jerk was this woman married to? "Not interrupt when I'm talking to my friends"? "Relate to people as fully as possible"? *Really?*
- There are men who are occasionally not in the mood for sex?
- Man, I am so getting ripped off.

Because, you see, if what Brady outlined in this document was what a wife did, then I didn't have one. Sure, I was *married,* and before that, in a long-term relationship. But a "wife" as Brady defines it? Nope.

Lest you think I'm complaining, let me make it clear that I'm not. I like Ellen. She's nice to me, usually, even when other people aren't. And she's funny. And smarter than hell. And she tolerates my humor, and my writing, and my occasionally going to church, and my playing the accordion. She doesn't mind that my favorite game with the kids is "Let's pretend I'm throwing up down the back of your shirt," or that on occasion I get home after the kids have gone to bed, that I like fruit-scented soaps (I'm a sucker for anything that smells of grapefruit), or that every once in a while I indulge in a Dr. Pepper even though caffeine can make me a wee bit testy.

In short, I'm not an idiot. I know when I climb into bed at the end of the day and Ellen reaches over and touches my hand, it's a good thing—even if she does snore on occasion.

But a "wife"?

Not really. For years now, I've been the one who cooks dinner every night. Not only does Ellen not iron, she doesn't even know where we keep the damn thing. And we pretty much swap duties with the kids—I'm a great putter-to-sleeper; she's better with the boo-boos and Band-Aids and that whole patience thing.

Then there are the household chores. I cook, even when I (swoon!) come home from a hard day at the office, and really just want to put my feet up with a brandy old Manhattan or whatever you call it. Ellen's the laundry person. And although this may seem unfair—one is creative and can be used to charm visitors, the other involves scrubbing barf out of underpants (don't ask me how it got there), the fact is that these are the tasks we've come to do—not because we don't have a choice, but because we both like control. I like to make sure we have good food to eat ("good" being defined as anything involving olive oil, sugar, red peppers, or some combination of the three) and Ellen likes to make sure that there are no stains, anywhere—*anywhere*—on the kids' clothes.

More importantly, when it comes to gender and professional roles, Ellen and I both agree that jobs are significant well beyond their fiscal benefits—so much so, in fact, that we participate daily in a tri-city commute, leaving our home in central Virginia with Ellen heading seventy miles to Charlottesville and me driving fifty miles in the other direction to Salem.

A few years back, we went to a financial planner, figuring that two people with advanced degrees and good jobs probably shouldn't have to be living on PB&J for the last twelve days of each month. He took a look at our finances, our lifestyles, and our expenditures, and when we finally sat down to talk the first thing he did was turn to Ellen and say, "You do know that between child care and your commute, you're pretty much breaking even on your job?"

Why the financial planner didn't say this to me, I don't know, except that maybe my commute is twenty minutes shorter each way and I make $7 a year more than Ellen. Or maybe it's because I'm, you know, a guy. Regardless, we'd seen this coming, so we gave the stock answer we've given for years when people pointed out that, um, maybe the two of you commuting a combined 250 miles a day isn't the best way to live life.

The answer is this: Jobs are about a lot more than money, you misogynist bastards.

And we believe this. I have an English friend, a woman named Anna, who earned a degree with high honors in literature from Durham University, and then went to Royal Military Academy Sandhurst and became a commissioned officer, who not once but twice won her regiment's marksmanship award. Eventually, she and her husband decided to have kids, so once she got pregnant she resigned her commission. His next placement was in Brussels. As they were being given a tour of the base, the commander turned to Anna and said, "You really must meet my wife."

Anna's response, God bless her, was, "Why?"

Think about it: Most of us, in today's world, don't live in the same neighborhoods we grew up in, where everybody knew who we were, knew what we stood for, knew what we valued and why. Instead, we move around, we drift, constantly encountering new folks who don't know where we come from, figuratively or literally. And when they meet us, they clasp our hands, look us in the eye, and ask, not, "What do you believe?" or "Who are your parents?" but "What do you do for a living?"

Our jobs have always been a major part of defining who we are. Ellen and I are literary people, we're people who work with words and books and ideas. We're people who fight the "good fight" in an increasingly materialistic world full of things that entertain for eleven seconds, but provide no real substance (travelogues, for instance). In the face of a culture that seems to relish stupid (think road rage, deep-fried turkeys, and designer fingernails), Ellen and I are people who relish ideas, who care about the abstract, who value aesthetics and nuances and a little thing called the brain. Our values are reflected in our jobs. What we do for a living matters—or at least that's what we like to believe.

Why do I mention all this now?

Because, living in Hong Kong, for the first time in my life, I had a "wife."

When the opportunity for a Fulbright came up, the first thing Ellen did was go to her boss and check on the possibility of taking a leave of absence. We'd been together for twenty years and never in that time—excluding maternity leave—had she taken an extended break from both school and work. The thought of a year "off" for her, even with a toddler at home, seemed extraordinary to both of us. Think of all the opportunities, we said to each other. Think of you and Jamie wandering the city and exploring and learning the language and bartering with shopkeepers and buying fresh vegetables and squid and coming home and making a delicious supper. Think of how much reading you'll get done, all the quiet evenings on the couch with a book, after twenty years of dutiful labor over the computer every night. Think of . . . well, you get the idea.

It didn't work out that way, of course. The first day I went off to work and the kids had gone off to school, I came home at 5:15 to find the flat in chaos. Jamie was screaming at the top of his lungs, Lucy was complaining about her brother, Will was hiding in a book emerging only to punch his sister on the arm every eleven seconds or so. Ellen was in the kitchen, her hair down, her face sweaty, her eyes slightly dazed. On the counter sat three half-chopped eggplants and a Styrofoam packet of pork chops, frost still glistening on the clear wrap.

"Hi," I said.

"We're ordering pizza," she replied.

There's a reason most people at my host university have "helpers." To get Will and Lucy to school, Ellen had to leave the flat at 7:45, nudging and urging and spanking the kids down a half-mile hill in the hot sun. At the bottom, if she was lucky, there'd be a Number 26 light bus waiting, and she'd climb on it, dragging the stroller and Jamie behind her as Will and Lucy fought about who got to sit right beside the door and who had to sit with Mommy. Twenty minutes later, they'd be in old Tai Po. Ellen would pull the stop cord and they'd get out and wait in the direct morning sun for a shuttle bus to come and take the kids the last two miles up the hill to their school. Then Ellen and Jamie would go to the market, wandering through three floors crowded with Filipino and Malaysian servants, looking for the cheapest pomelo (a type of citrus fruit) and tofu that is really tofu, rather than a fishcake disguised as tofu—not that we'd ever made that mistake, mind you.

Then they'd leave the market, stopping at the little Park 'n' Shop near the playground to get the orange juice that everyone likes. Once that was done, they'd catch the 26 back to campus, walk the length of the university, and take the elevator back to the eighth floor. In the flat, Jamie would play with the Legos a neighbor loaned us, while Ellen prepped a load of laundry and threw it into our impossibly small clothes washer. Once the laundry was good and going, Jamie would make a point of peeing in his pants and all over the carpet that a kind neighbor loaned us. Ellen would strip him down, wash him, and put him in clean underpants—into which he'd promptly poop.

So Ellen would strip him down again, wash his underpants, wipe him off, put him in clean clothes, then take the load of laundry out and hang it on a rack on the terrace as the sun beat down on the red brick, creating sauna temperatures in the low 110s.

Back inside, Ellen would pull Jamie away from the knife drawer where he'd been looking for something shiny, then make them both a nutritious lunch of peanut butter and whatever stale bread we had lying around. By one o'clock, he'd go down for a nap and she'd do the dishes, water the plants, put in another load of laundry, and maybe sneak in half an hour or so on the computer, answering e-mails, paying bills, uploading pictures to the family blog.

That is, of course, assuming that Jamie slept. Because sometimes he didn't. Which was okay, if all he did was lie in bed and sing quietly to himself. Other times, though, it wasn't okay, because what he'd do was toss and turn and say "Mommy" over and over again, sometimes varying it with "MOOOOOOMM-MMMMMMMYYYYYYYYY!!!!!!!" just to keep things interesting. I don't know for a fact, but I'm guessing that if you only have half an hour a day free from directly supervising children and you're trying to use that time to catch up on a few tasks or just to catch your breath, that having someone lying in the next room screaming your name throughout your precious thirty minutes is pretty annoying.

Ellen and the kids taking pictures of a bug. This is one of the reasons they love her.

Other times, Jamie was so exhausted that he collapsed into a deep, deep sleep. Which meant that at 2:30, when Ellen needed to return to the drop-off spot to collect Will and Lucy, she had to go into Jamie's room and drag him out of whatever dark region of the brain he'd entered. As often as not, this resulted in him sobbing uncontrollably, exhausted and confused and just a little angry. So Ellen would toss him in the stroller, stick a bag of peanuts in his hand, and sprint down the hill to catch the 26. She'd meet Will and Lucy, take the bus back to the college, walk through the campus and up the hill and back to the flat. Then she'd give the kids snacks, get them going on their homework, and start to make dinner.

Which is a whole other dimension of work. To begin with, ever try going grocery shopping without a car? Ever try getting on a waiting bus with a stroller, a large toddler, and six bags of groceries? Ever try pushing said stroller with said large three-year-old and said groceries across a college campus?

Then there was the actual cooking. First, we only had three pans: a two-quart saucepan, a frying pan without a lid, and a nonstick wok that steadily lost its nonstick ("Don't worry," we told the kids, "those black flakes are pepper"). On the days we cooked with the wok, the frying pan would double as a lid. On the days we used the frying pan, the wok served as lid. On days we needed both at the same time, whatever it was we were cooking dried up like an old sponge that had been stuck behind the toaster for a month.

Second, there's the fact that Ellen is not a natural cook. This is not to say that she's a bad cook. She's not. Her Pad Thai is about as good as any I've ever had, and she makes killer empanadas. It's just that she has no real desire to cook. For me, cooking has always been a way to kill time so that I don't have to do my schoolwork. I also like it because it's probably the most concrete thing I do. When I cook a dish, it's real, it's physical, I can see it and taste it and smell it and feel a sense of accomplishment. Sure, it disappears when you eat it, but the students I teach disappear whether I eat them or not.

For Ellen, though, cooking is less a relief than a chore. When she lived alone in Charlottesville and New York, she ordered out

Chinese and made it last three days. Or she'd whip up something exotic, like a microwaved potato with—gasp!—frozen corn on it.

Now, though, she had three kids to feed and a husband who hates corn. So around 5:15, I'd stroll in, refreshed and happy from a fulfilling day at work, complete with a three-martini lunch, and see Ellen in the kitchen, slicing eggplants, boiling rice, and picking "pepper" out of the diced chicken.

Okay, so I'm lying about the three martinis. But that might as well have been the case. Or more accurately, I felt as though it might as well have been. Because even if my day was low to moderately sucky—and those days happen, even in an exotic locale full of dim sum and interesting work—at least I got to spend it with adults.

I tried to help, of course. Many Tuesday and Thursday mornings I'd take the kids to school so that Ellen could go for a swim. If I could get away late in the afternoon, I'd pick the kids up as well, so Jamie could sleep a bit longer and Ellen would have a bit more time to herself. And I'd make supper on occasion and do a load of laundry when I got the chance, and I'd do the dishes when Ellen held a gun to my head. But let's face it, folks: This wasn't really what either of us had hoped for. Part of the problem was just that Jamie was the wrong age. A little younger, he'd have slept in the stroller and the two of them could have wandered the city all day. A little older, he'd have been in school. We talked seriously about taking him down to the bird market and trading him for a budgie, but after mentioning this to some native Hong Kongers, we discovered it was actually illegal.

Hong Kong. God. So many rules.

And then, of course, there's the fact that Ellen's father had died while we were en route. Even had she not chosen to attend the funeral of one of the three people she'd known her whole life in a double jet-lagged stupor of surprised grief, this would have been a pretty big blow. And although she made a point of Skyping with her mother and brother regularly, and e-mailed them often, that's not the same as being able to pick up the phone every evening, curl up on the couch in the back room, and just talk and listen and remember.

How does one grieve a big Norwegian man with a pink face, silver-gray hair, and a Germany-trained grasp of theology while living in a country full of palm trees, markets smelling of jasmine and raw meat, and millions of people with black hair speaking a language you hadn't heard until just months ago and still can't understand?

I'll be frank: Sometimes I get angry at the universe. I mean, there's funny—even funny in a melancholy, dark kind of way—and then there's just plain cruel. And this was definitely just plain cruel.

This all sounds very negative, and though all of it is true, it's only half of the truth.

The other half includes the fact that the longer we were in Hong Kong, the easier our life became. Some of this was simply getting used to the ins and outs of a new place. We learned, for instance, that you can order groceries online in Tai Po, and that if you purchase more than HK $500 (about U.S. $70), they'll deliver said groceries to your door.

We've also figured out that there's a Wellcome (yes, that's how it's spelled) or a Park 'n' Shop on pretty much every city block in Hong Kong. So if ever you run out of toilet paper or mango juice or those sour lime gummy worms your husband is addicted to, all you need to do is step off the MTR, walk 300 feet in any direction, and step into the first grocery store you find.

The cooking also seemed to get easier. Ellen discovered online a few reasonable recipes, figured out some nice stir-fry sauces, and found a way to magically cook the chicken while keeping the eggplant nice and crisp. We found some nice fresh noodles at the Tai Po market and some good pork meatballs at a (I'm not making this up) meatball store nearby, so Ellen started making a lovely noodle soup. I don't know that she ever began to love cooking the way that I do, but at least she developed a sense of humor about it, assigning herself the nickname "Spice Whisperer."

It helped that Jamie eventually got to the point that he didn't need a nap every day. Check that: He *needed* one, but if he didn't get it, it wasn't the end of the world. That meant if Ellen was out and about, say, getting visas for our trip to mainland China, afterward she and the little guy could stroll around Central for a couple hours, ducking into antique shops and checking out temples and museums.

Once, in mid-November, I came home and found Ellen in the kitchen, putting away groceries.

"Smell my hair," she said.

"Only if you smell mine first."

She gave me that look that said I'd be eating baloney for dinner if I didn't shut up. So I smelled her hair. The warm, dry scent of incense hung about her.

"You've been to a temple."

Apparently she and her mom—who was visiting at the time— had been looking at the Man Mo temple in Tai Po with Jamie, not far from the market, when suddenly the place was flooded with hoards of people carrying plates of food. Apparently it was the birthday of one of the goddesses, and everyone was celebrating by offering fruit and burning clusters of incense. Afterward, there was a meal of vegetarian stew and rice, and Ellen and her mother were invited to stay. They did. And it was nice.

The other thing that gives me comfort is this: In 2002, I stopped in Reykjavik on the way back from England and discovered that our two Icelandic friends had divorced. Back in the States, I landed in Baltimore, got in my car, and drove the three hours to our home in rural Virginia. Ellen was already in bed. I crawled in next to her, said hello, then put my head on the pillow.

Then I sat up. "Iva and Ingo divorced," I said.

"Oh no," Ellen murmured.

My head hit the pillow again. I was just drifting off, when Ellen sat up. "That's it."

I could barely get my mouth to work. "That's what?"

"Every couple we knew in grad school is now divorced."

And it was true. All of them. Except us. And as our friend Gordon has pointed out so very eloquently, we're something of a dark horse.

We're just not a very affectionate couple. We don't hold hands in public. We don't celebrate Valentine's Day. Significant anniversaries have been rescued from the fingers of death when one of us has written the date on a check and said, "Oh yeah, that's right. What's it been, fifteen years?"

And we bicker. We're pretty good at it, too, and have been known to take our show on the road, creating tension at dinner parties and causing small children to run and hide their stuffed animals. I don't know why we do it, but we do. We agree about so many things: politics, food, movies, childrearing (duct tape is a must). In fact, we don't really disagree about anything. But we're both strong-willed people and neither of us has perfect emotional management—I let my feelings out too soon and Ellen holds hers in for too long.

Our bickering can be especially prevalent when we're traveling. I have very distinct memories of mornings in Chester or afternoons in Lyon when both of us were clenched-mouthed and furrow-browed. This isn't surprising, of course. You're tired when you're traveling. And both of you have agendas, not always the same. And there's the pressure—you've been dreaming of this trip for months, with idealized visions of the two of you munching caviar and sipping *kir royale* in some cafe in northern France dancing through your head as you trudge through a rainy Monday morning in Ohio or Wisconsin or Virginia.

Certainly, we had high expectations for this trip. And certainly, not every aspect of our year was ideal. We bickered some, occasionally, and even regularly. But overall, it just wasn't that bad. Yes, we might be tired. Yes, we were busy. But overall, we managed to keep things pretty good. On occasion we could even be affectionate, as though being 8,000 miles from everyone we know made it okay to hold hands walking down the street.

But was Ellen the perfect "wife," as Brady defines it?

No.

Thank god.

Because I don't know anyone who wants a partner like that, probably not even Brady herself.

And me? I'm not stupid. I know I'm lucky.

And then there's this: Early in December, I'm with Jamie at the market and we come across the Man Mo temple. This is Ellen's favorite, a small, tucked-away place surrounded by highrise flats and bicycle shops. I've never been there myself, so I heft Jamie onto my hip and go through the red gates. It's dark inside. Large coils of incense hang from the ceiling, dozens of them, their ends gray and smoking. Below them are trays rigged to catch the falling ash. Sometimes they do; sometimes they don't. The floor is dusty with powder.

Incense coils in Man Mo temple on Hong Kong Island.

Three or four altars are spread throughout the small rooms; on each rests a golden statue. Offerings of fruit and wine lie on the altars, and candles burn next to bouquets of flowers. I don't know anything about Buddhism at the time—I'd only been in a temple once before. But I love the way it all combines to make my senses buzz—the colors, the tastes, the smells, the stillness.

Jamie leans over in my arms, presses his lips against my ear, and whispers, "We in a temple?"

"Uh-huh," I answer.

"We be quiet?" His voice is hoarse and sibilant.

I nod.

He's silent a minute, then says, "People praying?"

None of which means anything, on the face of it. But what it tells me is that he's been in enough temples, enough times, in his mother's arms, that he knows what's going on and how to behave. And if I felt pretty miserable at the thought of Ellen chopping onions every night (something I enjoy, but she doesn't), I feel pretty good when I think about her and our little blondie standing in a temple, his cheek against hers, his breath tickling her hair. I don't know much about grieving and I don't know much about religion, and I'm 98 percent sure nothing can take away the pain of losing your father. But I'm equally sure that to the extent that anything can make us feel better, it involves a little boy with blue eyes pressing warm against your body and whispering in your ear as incense rises and ash falls in this one silent place in the whole world.

CHAPTER 10

THE BIRTHDAY PARTY

O ur kids hadn't been at their school two months when we
started hearing the rumors. I was lying in bed with Will
one night, asking him about his favorite part of the day. I do this
because Will is definitely a glass-half-empty kind of guy, and if
you just ask him how his day was, you'll get a list of grievances
half a mile long.

That particular night, he paused a moment, then said,
"Nothing. Because of Leyton."

It took me a minute to figure out that Leyton was a person.

"What about Leyton?"

"He's always kicking me," Will said. And then he went on to
deliver a list of perceived slights by this character Leyton, who
apparently found it funny to step on the back of Will's shoe as he
was getting off the bus, or to bang him in the shins when they
were playing soccer during recess.

Later, I mentioned this to Ellen and she seemed surprised
as well. Neither of us had ever heard of Leyton. The next
night, I asked Will about him again and got the same catalogue
of grievances.

"Did you tell your teacher?" I asked.

"Uh-huh," he said.

"And?"

"She just said to try to ignore it."

"Did you try asking him to stop?" asked Ellen from the next
bed, where she'd been cuddling with Lucy.

"I told him it hurt," Will said.

"Did that help?"

Will gave a groan that said, clear as day, *Of course not.*

"Did you try kicking him back?" I asked.

"Paul," Ellen said.

"Hey," I responded. "What's he supposed to do, spend all year with bruised shins? The teachers aren't helping."

"That's not the answer," Ellen said.

"Yes it is," I whispered in Will's ear. "Give him a good shot right in the butt."

The next night, I had another thought. "What does Leyton do after he kicks you?"

Will sighed. "He laughs."

"A mean laugh?"

There was a pause, then Will said, "Not really." Another pause. "More like he thinks it's funny and I'm supposed to laugh too."

Ah. Memories of third grade came back, when I had such a massive crush on Laura Rich that I did the only thing an eight-year-old boy could do: hit her with a stick.

"Maybe he wants to be your friend," I said to Will.

Even in the dark, I could feel him staring at me like I was insane.

"Seriously," I said. "Try being nice to him. Play with him. See what happens."

That was the first clue. The second came when we met with Will's teacher for our annual conference. "Will's one of the best behaved students in his class," she told us. "I sometimes worry that he doesn't get enough attention. You know, because of the other boys."

We must have looked at her blankly, because she frowned, then went on. "Not that they're that bad, mind you. Not bad enough that I qualify for assistance," she continued under her breath.

Ellen leaned forward. "I'm not quite sure we follow."

The kids outside the Temple of Heaven in Beijing. They're holding Chinese hacky sacks with feathers. Not sure why Lucy is standing like a superhero.

Will's teacher sighed. "Take Thomas, for instance. He's very smart. *Very* smart. And most of the time he can control his temper. But say the wrong thing or catch him in the wrong mood, and *WHOOMP!* Next thing you know he's ripped off all his clothes and he's trying to bite anyone he can get his teeth on."

Twenty minutes later we were in Lucy's classroom, meeting with her teacher, when she named one of Will's classmates. "And I'm sure you've heard about Trevor."

Ellen and I glanced at each other. We were still reeling from the story of Thomas the naked cannibal.

"Um . . ." I said. "Not really."

And she went on to tell us about how Trevor's mom was sick with cancer. We'd heard about this, about how she'd had to fly back to Malaysia for treatment, about how Trevor had missed a few weeks of school. Lucy's teacher, though, gave us some new details—like how, for instance, Trevor spent his time goading the girls on the playground into attacking him. Which doesn't sound like much, I know, but according to the teacher it could get pretty intense, Trevor taunting the girls into a frenzy.

"It's nothing raunchy," Lucy's teacher told us. "It just gets rough sometimes. Trevor's very smart. We all understand he's going through something difficult here. But we keep an eye on him."

Everything fell into place when Ellen bumped into Leyton's mom one day at a PTA meeting. In recent weeks, Will had stopped talking about being bruised, and had even mentioned Leyton's name in the context of having fun at recess.

Ellen mentioned the latter to Leyton's mother, who looked slightly pained. "I hope he's behaving?" she asked.

Of course, Ellen said. And then Leyton's mother went on to explain how this was Leyton's third school in four years, how it was the only one he liked—scratch that: the only one he didn't have fits about going to.

When Ellen reported all this to me that evening, we spent a minute or two staring at the kitchen floor, trying to figure out what was going on. It didn't take long before everything clicked: Leyton, Thomas, Trevor, the small class size, the high male-to-female ratio, the repeated comments we'd heard from parents about how they'd chosen this school because the academics weren't so cutthroat.

"Wow," Ellen broke the silence. "We're sending our kids to a school for troubled boys."

Not really, of course. So far as we know, no one's pulling switchblades over dodge ball or selling crack next to the water fountain. We've yet to learn of rubber bits in their mouths and electrodes to their temples or a secret "time-out" room from which students reappear, pasty and thin, six days later.

More accurately, it's a school that attracts kids who aren't very happy elsewhere in the ultra-competitive Hong Kong educational system. Schooling in HK is more or less based on the

British system, with two monster exams (taken at the ages of roughly sixteen and eighteen) that determine whether or not kids will advance and receive further education. This creates a lot of pressure of course; as a result, Hong Kong is thick with trendy "cram" schools—evening programs run by what the *South China Morning Post* calls, "charismatic figures with trendy names," who charge hundreds of dollars with no guarantee of results. Additionally, primary schools are under a lot of pressure to prepare kids for their later work.

Will and Jamie painting Chinese characters in Xi'an. I love how perfect Will's characters are. Jamie's are, um, perfect too, in a different kind of way . . .

The International School, our little private school in Tai Po, was something of an exception to this rule, taking a more laid-back approach. Even so, the academics at our kids' school are tougher than any school we've encountered in the States—Will regularly came home with four sheets of complex multiplication or division problems, in addition to English, Putonghua, and the rest. But it's nothing compared to some private schools in HK that'll kick out a third-grader for failing to delineate pi to the fifteenth decimal.

All of this caused us to start being hyper-vigilant—or paranoid, if you prefer. If Lucy was in a particularly barometric mood one day, I'd gently ask if anyone had touched her someplace he shouldn't have. To which she'd respond by giving me a weird look before running to ask her mother if Daddy had consumed too much caffeine again. If Will came home and mentioned that one of the boys—Trevor, it turned out—had pulled up pornography on the classroom computer, we were quick to assign it to the nature of the school, rather than to the nature of nine-year-old boys with access to a computer.

And when Will came home, two weeks before his birthday, and declared that he wanted to invite a bunch of boys over for a party, Ellen and I nearly knocked each other over inquiring who, exactly, he meant.

"George," he said.

"Great," we responded. George had already been over for a play date, and had impressed us by not only carrying his used dishes to the kitchen counter, but by polishing my shoes and rocking Jamie to sleep.

"Peter."

"Fantastic." The son of one of the professors on campus. A nice kid.

"Gordon."

Dandy. Gordon did archery with Will, and was polite and funny.

"Oliver," Will continued.

Never heard of him. But as long as he cleared the criminal background check, fine.

"Leyton."

"Are you sure?" Ellen responded.

"Thomas."

"I don't know," I said. "I think four is just dandy. Maybe we should stick with four?"

"And Trevor," Will concluded.

Ellen and I glanced at each other.

But what were we supposed to do? These were our kid's friends, after all. And as messed up as some of them might have been, my guess is none of *their* dads plays accordion, keeps a blog, or thinks revising general education will lead to world peace.

So we put the invitations in the mail, strapped bars across the windows, and hired seven security guards to spend the afternoon patrolling the patio.

Just kidding, of course. These days everyone e-mails invitations.

The party began with a treasure hunt. My idea. Will wanted to contain it to our flat, but I had other plans. Borrowing from Mr. Blain, the kids' charismatic but zealous physical education teacher who regularly forced them to practice mini-marathons in the blazing afternoon heat, I was going to run those six boys (Oliver and Peter couldn't make it) all over campus, wearing them down to submissive little lumps of clay.

Herding the gang outside our apartment, I went through the rules:

1. Stick together.
2. Be careful.
3. Collect all the clues so there's no litter.
4. Do the clues in order.
5. No snorkeling.

Blank stares. I felt my face burn.

"What's snorkeling?" asked one of the Chinese boys.

You'd think after four months in this country, I'd know better than to try a joke with a cross-cultural audience. Especially one full of nine-year-old boys.

Then I realized that someone at the back was, well, if not cracking up, at least snickering. "Snorkeling," he said, when everyone turned to look at him. "It's funny. We're not going swimming."

"What's your name?" I asked.

"Trevor." He was handsome, with intelligent eyes and a broad face.

I gave the rest of the gang a significant look. "Trevor," I said, "knows enough to laugh at my jokes. Trevor gets extra cake. Learn from Trevor."

The first clue sent them from our apartment on the eighth floor down to the playground outside the building, where they found a mathematical equation that ran them back up to the third, then the fifth, then the eleventh floors (I'd forbidden using the elevators; I'm sure Mr. Blain would have approved).

For the most part, everything went fine. No one died, no one cried, and everyone worked together. There were some glitches, of course. Pretty much every time they found a clue, Leyton insisted, "We need to go on the roof!" Then he'd begin to scramble up the green railings that rim each floor of our terraced building, and start to make his way to the terra cotta tiles of the floor below. Every time, the rest of the boys called him back and they continued with their hunt.

When, after the eleventh floor, they needed to hustle down to the tennis courts, I figured I was safe, and lagged behind. Five minutes later I arrived outside the courts to find Leyton two-thirds of the way up the chain-link fence protecting the grounds, the rest of the group trying to guide him down.

"Just jump," someone said.

"I can't," said Leyton, fingers locked to the fence.

"Why not?"

"I'm afraid of heights."

After the tennis courts, it was back up to floor six. Then back down to the swimming pool. As they searched the bleachers for the next clue, Trevor threw me a sidelong glance. "I bet we have to go up again after this."

"Clever boy," I said, then sent them back up to twelve. After that, it was down to two, then up to seven. There, sweaty and red-faced, they discovered the last hint sending them back to our flat. Banging through the front door, the whole lot of them insisted they needed water, cake, and a nap, not necessarily in that order.

Lunch was a quiet, albeit surly, affair. Afterward, enough of them woke up to have a rousing balloon fight on the terrace. And they seemed to enjoy the game Ellen had organized for them involving blowtorches, straight razors, and life-sized Gang of Four blow-up dolls.

The part that really got me, though, was when it came to the presents.

To begin with, Trevor brought his gift in a shopping bag. "We weren't able to wrap it," he said, matter-of-factly.

I was about to make some sarcastic crack when I suddenly remembered: Trevor was the one whose mother had cancer. Cancer that was bad enough that she'd flown back to her home country to get treatment. I closed my mouth.

It was a wonderful gift, actually: four historical action figures, all generals of a sort—Jeanne d'Arc, Napoleon, Zhang Fei, and Guan Yu. Plus a professional quality sketchpad and colored pencils. We'd had to leave Will's art supplies in the States when we came over, and I knew he'd missed them. I wasn't sure if Will had mentioned that to his friends or not, but after watching Trevor in action for two hours, I was pretty sure there wasn't much he didn't pick up on.

Then there were the birthday cards. Most of them were handmade, and they were elaborate. Gordon's, for instance, featured hand-drawn pictures on the front and back as well as the inside flap. The note itself, written in precise handwriting in seventeen different colors, said:

Dear Will:

Happy Birthday!!! You one of my best friends at the International School and you are the first classmate to invite me to a birthday party in this school. I'm so happy that you invite me to your birthday party. I'm glad to meet you. I wish you have the best birthday ever.

And then it was signed. And dated.

Sure, there were hitches. Thomas opened his present to Will by himself, then he sat in a corner reading it for ten minutes before reluctantly handing it over. Following that, he spent most of the rest of the party playing with one of Jamie's toy planes, flying it around the room, muttering something about Kim Il-sung and Pyongyang. I still haven't figured out what that was all about. I'm just happy he kept his clothes on and didn't eat anyone.

That night, lying in bed with Will, I asked him what his favorite thing that day was.

"My party," he said.

"What part?"

He paused for a second, then said, "The presents."

"Not the treasure hunt?"

Under the sheets, he punched me. "Dad," he said, turning it into a seven-syllable word. "That treasure hunt sucked."

I laughed. Then I took a deep breath and asked a question that'd been nagging me all day.

"Does Trevor ever talk about his mom?"

Will didn't say anything for a moment. Even though it was dark, I could feel him staring at the ceiling.

"Sometimes."

"Does he ever talk about how she's doing?"

"No."

Now I didn't speak, not sure where to go from there. Will lay silent for a bit, then said, "But we know she's dying."

I looked at him. "How do you know that?"

He named one of the teachers, who'd mentioned it in the context of talking about her own family, a number of whom had died from cancer.

"Are you sure?" I asked. "I mean, about Trevor's mom. Because sometimes things get mixed up when one person tells another, then that person tells someone else."

"No," he said. "I heard it. I was there."

I thought about this for a bit. Then I thought about Trevor, his intelligent eyes, his bright laugh, the way he glanced down for a moment—but only a moment—when confessing his unwrapped gift. And I thought about how, exactly nine years and two days ago, I'd held Will in my arms for the first time, feeling the bend and flex of his ribs as his tiny lungs drew in air and let it out again. And I thought about how, at that moment, these words had entered my head, in no particular order: *Holy crap.* And: *Wow.* And: *I can't believe he's mine.*

And I thought about how it'd never occurred to me that I might possibly not be around to see him play in his first baseball game or register his first sax solo or go to his first prom or wax his first car or fall in love for the first time or walk through the door cradling his own first child.

Or turn ten.

And then, if there's a word that's stronger than "cling," and darker than "fear," and purer than—what? "Fire"? "Water"? "Blood"?—if there's a word that's all these things but even closer still to the bone, then that's how I felt that night with my son, in his room, exactly nine years and two days after he was born.

Part II
Gweilo
Road Trip

CHAPTER 11

SHANGHAI SURPRISED

We're standing in a hotel lobby in Shanghai, having a very People's Republic of China moment.

Ellen and I are at the registration desk, our bags stacked beside us. On the other side of the marble counter, a Chinese woman in her mid-twenties is assiduously ignoring us. The older kids are on a couch behind us. They're behaving, but only just. Will is poking Lucy and Lucy is giggling in that way that's just six inches short of maniacal, maybe twenty seconds away from tears or punches or vengeful fingers in the eye. Jamie is beside them on the floor, also poking and also laughing, but clearly confused about the rules of the game: Is he helping Will or Lucy? Is this fun or mean? And how much longer can he get away with this before his father storms across the lobby and does that yelling thing he does so often, where his face turns the color of a pomegranate and spittle ends up flecking the eyelashes of everyone in the vicinity?

We've been up since 4:00 A.M., have I mentioned that?

"So what you're saying," I ask the woman behind the desk for maybe the fifteenth time, "is that every guest staying here tonight has already registered?"

Her fingers continue to fly over the keyboard of her computer. She doesn't look up, doesn't shrug. Doesn't say a word.

Staying in hotels in Asia can be tricky. For one thing, most rooms consist of two beds, only slightly larger than what we'd call twin beds in the States, not nearly large enough to sleep two people comfortably. Given that we're a family of five, in practical terms what this means is that we need to have two separate chambers. In the States, this would simply mean getting two rooms with an adjoining door—and pretty much every hotel, from a Super 8 to a Hilton, has lots of these.

Not so in Asia. What this means is that we need to get two rooms that are side by side. With that arrangement, we can put the kids down in one room at eight or nine and spend the evening in the adjacent room fighting over who gets which bottle of wine in the mini-bar—leaving the door to the hall open, of course, so that if someone attempts to abduct one of our kids, we'll see and/or hear them, allowing us to provide them with pointers ("Lucy likes her grapes peeled"; "Will hates soft pillows") before sending them merrily on their way.

Once the adult bedtime rolls around we'll transfer one of the (remaining) kids to the second room, then each of us will sleep in a suite, which is one way, or so I've been told, of guaranteeing that our brood doesn't grow any larger.

This approach works just fine, assuming we're able to get rooms that are side by side. The worst-case scenario, though, is when we have two rooms located at opposite ends of the hall. The one time this happened, we nevertheless attempted the kids-in-one-room-us-squabbling-in-the-other model, until, six mini-bottles of chardonnay into the evening, we both confessed to feeling a little nervous that we might find ourselves on the front page of the *New York Post* in one of those "A dingo ate my baby" stories—though in our case, I'm fairly certain the Chinese would take one look at my gut and just assume I'd eaten the little runts myself, leaving nothing for the dogs but bones and a pair of stuffed turtles named Tiny and Dingbutt.

All of which is helpful for understanding what's going on in the lobby of this particular hotel in Shanghai on this particular

Friday afternoon. When we'd first arrived some ten minutes earlier, escorted to the desk by a smart-looking bellman in a long
black coat, Ellen had handed the woman behind the counter our
passports, and, after a formality or two, mentioned that it would
be great if we could have two rooms with an adjoining door, or
at the very least, two rooms that are side by side.

The clerk smiled apologetically. "I'm so sorry. We don't have
any adjoining rooms like this. The hotel is very old."

"How old?" I ask, curious. Shanghai is known for its art
deco, and our accommodations don't disappoint. The lobby is
long and low-ceilinged with marble floors and marble pillars,
twelve-foot-high mirrors trimmed in gold geometrical patterns,
and long, hanging chandeliers made of faux crystal.

The clerk says, "1934," and punches some keys, then shakes
her head. Her hair is short and very professional. "No," she says.
"No adjacent rooms available either. But two rooms on the same
floor is okay."

What this means is that either Ellen and I go to sleep at eight
with the kids, or we hunker down in the bathrooms—separate
bathrooms, mind you, at two opposite ends of a long hall—
reading quietly, hoping the kids won't be kept awake by the
light, the turning of pages, the noise of us shifting uncomfort-
ably because the only seat available is the toilet.

"We requested adjacent rooms," we say to the clerk.

"I am sorry," she says back. "But the hotel is full tonight."

I glance at my watch. It's 4:30.

"So everyone has checked in?"

The clerk keeps her eyes on the computer. "Every room is
booked," she says.

I glance at Ellen. I know what she's thinking. We're Midwesterners, after all, and Lutherans, and Scandinavians. We don't
like conflict, at least not public conflict, where we actually have
to look at the people we're angry at, and have them look back
at us. Normally, in a situation like this, what I'd do is let it go,
assume the high road, take the keys, go upstairs, and bitch about

it for three days until Ellen finally told me to either shut up or find a nice deaf woman to marry.

Not too long ago, though, we were checking into a hotel in Zhuhai alongside our friend David, who's a native Hong Konger, when he ran into a similar problem. The clerk told him that they couldn't accommodate some request regarding room size, or type of bed, or indoor plumbing, or some such thing. Rather than give in, David simply stood his ground, very politely asking the clerk, over and over again, why the request couldn't be met. Eventually the hotel manager came forward and made things work, allowing David to walk away happy.

"That's the way it works around here," he'd explained to us later over dinner. "They've already checked you into the hotel. They don't get paid more for checking you in again. So they just say no and expect you to go away. Eventually, though, they'll push some buttons and give you exactly what you're asking for. It was there the whole time."

Remembering this now, in the lobby in Shanghai, I say to the clerk, "So has everybody checked in for the night?"

"The hotel is completely full," she repeats.

"Yes," I say. "But has everybody checked in?"

"No."

"But there are no rooms—absolutely no rooms left—that are side by side?"

"Sir," she tells me, "the hotel is full tonight."

I feel like a jerk, I have to admit. I really am better at being passive-aggressive, terrifically good at wimping out face-to-face, then walking away and saying to the urinal in the men's room all the things I wish I'd said to the person who's made me so angry. This is a much safer approach to life, you see. There's less risk of getting into a fist fight with a urinal, after all, or of being told you're an ass, or rude, or simply wrong. And because I don't like spilled blood and I don't like being shamed, and I spend an inordinate amount of time in the bathroom, I generally stick with this approach.

Except today. Today I'm tired and I'm hungry and I'm worried about the kids and I've already waded in up to my waist and there's absolutely no point in getting out now, half-wet, and sleeping down the hall from my wife. (I dare you to take that sentence out of context).

I forge on. "So what you're telling me," I say to the clerk, "is that not everyone has checked in tonight, but there are absolutely no rooms left in the entire hotel that are side by side?"

The clerk punches some more keys. The assistant manager comes over, leans over her shoulder, says something in Shanghaiese. This is a dialect that I don't understand, but even so I swear I hear the manager mention something about "bald" and "jerk" and "the room next to the mass murderers from Russia."

But it works. Eventually she hands me two keys for two rooms, side by side. I take them, blushing and apologizing (but only a little) and saying "thank you" extravagantly. We take our bags, head into the elevator. Neither Ellen nor I say anything as we ride up to the fifth floor. When the doors open, we step out, and roll our suitcases down the hall.

"I feel bad about that," I say.

"I know," she says. "I just never know if it's a 'them' thing, or an 'us' thing, or something in between."

"I actually feel a little sick to my stomach." It's true. Guilt is very strong when you're a Lutheran, especially when you haven't really done anything.

She nods. Her forehead is red. I'm guessing mine is as well.

"I just hope," I say, "that she doesn't hold it against us. I'd hate to end up sleeping in the dungeon." I don't mention my theory about knife-wielding Cossacks.

We reach the first of our rooms, key the lock. When the door opens, we stop dead in our tracks.

It's gorgeous. High-ceilinged with ornate crown molding, long brocade curtains, geometric designs on the wallpaper, the pillows, the frames around the many mirrors. Glancing into the bathroom, I note opaque green-and-gold tiles, marble-framed mirrors, a throne-like commode with antique hardware. We don't know it yet, but in the room next door, the bed will be roughly the size of a yacht, so large that I can lie on it with legs and arms extended and not touch either side, so large that all five of us could sleep in it together very comfortably.

Have I mentioned that the bed at our hotel in Shanghai was very, very big?

"Holy crap," I say.
"I know," says Ellen.
"It's beautiful," I say.
"I know," says Ellen.
"I feel terrible," I say.
There's a pause during which Ellen takes a deep breath, then lets it out again.
"I know," she says.

Once you go out a few times, dinner in a foreign country with three *gweilo* kids isn't nearly the adventure you'd imagine. There are some standard things we can get pretty much anywhere that will keep the kids happy: sweet-and-sour pork, for instance, or barbequed beef or chicken, though in Asia the latter's usually steamed and sliced through the bone, providing better access to the marrow (um . . . yum?) but making the whole thing kind of pale and bloody, not really the most appetizing sight in the world as far as kids are concerned.

The beauty of these standard selections, though, is that they free up Ellen and me to explore. Our one evening in Shanghai, for instance, we eschew the relatively safe but boring offerings of the hotel restaurant and ask one of the bellhops if he has a favorite place in the neighborhood. He does, and gives us directions to a seafood restaurant maybe a mile walk from the hotel. Map in hand, we wander out in the fading light, taking a right out the hotel door, then another right two blocks farther. This leads us down a poorly lit street where we pass at least three houses of ill repute—assuming you can call a ground-floor barbershop with a plate-glass window and seventeen scantily clad women sitting on sofas a "house."

Finally, though, we reach 324, the number the bellhop gave us, and are waved in by a Sikh in a gray turban. We're in art deco land again, which is just dandy, because it's fast becoming my favorite design style. The room is brightly lit with high ceilings, half wet market, half hotel lobby. To the left are floor-to-ceiling aquariums filled with brackish water and the night's offerings: grouper, squid, abalone, and cuttlefish, the large eyes and furrowed brows of the latter looking disturbingly wise as we pass the tanks.

To the right is a pair of low-slung settees, their wooden legs and curled arms resplendent with intricate carving. An old-fashioned elevator with a retractable metal gate stands next to a narrow staircase, and the whole place is set off by a huge aquarium framed into the front wall of the building in lieu of a picture window. Goldfish the size of tea saucers muscle through the crowded water.

The maitre d' ushers us into the elevator, where we're shuttled to the second floor at probably half the speed it would have taken us to walk up, even lugging a three-year-old and two surly sub-tweeners.

The restaurant itself occupies a huge room two stories high with a carved balcony surrounding the second, darkened, level. Long opaque lights made of cream-colored strings of glass dangle from the ceiling, and shell-shaped sconces line the walls. Dark wood and ornate mirrors are everywhere—over the bar, by the dessert table—and the effect is rich and warm and wonderfully overwhelming.

The menu is in English, but maybe a dozen pages long and in tiny print designed specifically to tick off forty-four-year-old bald guys with weak eyes.

"Okay?" the waitress, an ageless woman in a blue smock, says to us after we've been seated for all of two minutes.

"Um," we say, "maybe just another minute?"

"Okay?" she says again, five minutes later.

I point to a picture of what looks like a Rubik's Cube coated in breadcrumbs. "What's this?"

She taps it with a pen. "This very good. You want this?"

"Well. Maybe. What is it?"

She nods. "Is very good."

"Very good *what?*"

She nods. "Yes."

Well, okay then. So we order some of that—turns out to be stuffed crab legs, though we never found anything that looked even vaguely crabby, except maybe our waitress after the thirty-second time we asked her to give us another minute to decide.

Finally, we end up pointing to six or seven things that have an Ebert's thumbs up next to them, hoping this symbol indicates a house specialty rather than sautéed digits.

We've barely dug into the first round of dishes when we decide we need to go back to the hotel, find that bellhop, and get his name so that we an write him into our wills.

The stuffed crab legs are essentially deep-fried balls of bread crusts filled with a steamy, tangy sauce. They are crunchy and warm and so flavorful that even Will adores them.

Next up is the "Eight Jewel" dish. Stir-fried and served over rice, it's a collage of diced duck and prawn and chicken and tofu and carrots and—well, at least three other things I can't remember but that taste really good blended in that light sauce. Lucy loves pigeon, and keeps eating dark, chewy chunks of something out of this dish, so maybe pigeon is in there as well.

We also eat chicken and shrimp dumplings, tsui sum (greens cooked lightly in a broth), wrapped cones of abalone in gluttonous rice, and minced crab and cheese baked on the half-shell.

Best of all, though, is the chicken, shrimp, and rice soup. This is blind luck, I admit. At the last second, Ellen pointed to the menu and said to the waitress, "What about this?" It came to the table in a low iron pot, maybe nine inches in diameter, ensconced in a wooden tray over a low candle. The soup is at a rolling boil, bubbles of rice rising to the surface, turning, sinking, and rising again.

And it's good. Man is it good: salty, rich, the shrimp and rice soaking up the flavor of the chicken and the chicken taking on just a touch of the seafood and vegetables. It's the sort of flavor that fills your mouth even when your mouth's not full, touching every corner of your tongue. It's not an exaggeration to say that Ellen and I both have three or four bowls. It's just that good.

Afterward, as is not uncommon in China, a waitress brings plates of fruit to the table, on the house: watermelon, fresh pineapple, cherry tomatoes, Chinese apples that are smaller, harder, and more oblong than the kind Adam ate. We dig in, complaining the whole time that we're too full to take another bite, so stuffed that we hurt, but seduced by the fresh flavors and the sense that the sooner we finish, the sooner we'll have to leave this amazing restaurant, probably never to return.

And eventually we do have to leave. We head to the restrooms with the kids, then go back again with our cameras to get pictures of the amazing wooden trim, the carved leaf trellises lining the edges of the mirrors, the marble floors and countertops and brass-gold fixtures. Then we bundle up the kids and ourselves and roll down the stairs and across the lobby past the fish tanks and out the door held wide by the Sikh doorman.

The streets outside are busier now, long Mercedes with tinted windows creeping past, old men riding bicycles, and serious-looking mothers with groceries in one hand and startled-looking babies in the other. We drift back toward our hotel, charmed by the food, the restaurant, the man selling kebobs from an open grill on the corner, by Shanghai, by our own good fortune at being here and eating this food and seeing this place and walking these streets in the cold dark of a March evening.

The next morning, we waddle down to the hotel restaurant for breakfast. It's on the second floor, at the front of the building, separated from the elevator bank by a flight of stairs. We're greeted by a square-faced woman in a yellow *qi pao*—the traditional, quilted, Chinese dress—who asks our room number. We tell her, and she scans a sheet of paper on the podium in front of her.

"What was the number again?" she asks.

I answer, "511."

"And 512," Ellen adds.

Again she scans the list. One would think they'd put this thing in numerical order, but apparently not. Flipping the sheet over, she runs her pencil down the back as well. Then she looks up.

"Perhaps breakfast was not included?"

I look at Ellen, who frowns. We book our hotels, like our flights, at the last minute, on the web, late at night, while sipping fruity vodka drinks. "It could be," Ellen says. "We used Expedia."

I turn back to the maitre d'ess, or whatever you'd call her. "How much is the breakfast?"

"146."

Renminbi. That's more than $20 U.S.

"Each?" I ask.

The woman nods.

Ellen shifts Jamie on her hip. "Is there a charge for kids?"

"Children under one meter are free. Children under 1.4 meters are half-price."

I look at Ellen again. She's as pale as I feel. Jamie fits under the first measure, and Lucy more or less under the second, depending, literally, on where they draw the line. Even so, though, with Will and the two of us at full price, we're looking at upward of $70 U.S. For breakfast. We'd only paid half that for dinner the night before, and that'd been one of the biggest meals we'd ever eaten. Don't get me wrong: We're willing to pay big bucks for a good meal anytime, but we sort of draw the line at anything organized around toast and jam.

"What about a la carte?" Ellen says.

The woman looks at her, not sure if she's just been called a dirty name.

"The menu," Ellen says. "Can we just order off the menu? You know, one person gets eggs, someone else gets ham."

"Or cereal," I say. "Our kids usually just eat cereal."

The woman frowns, considers for a moment. "Let me ask the chef."

"Oh," says Ellen, realizing what's happening, that what we've asked for isn't standard. "No. You don't have to—"

But the woman is already gone.

She's away for quite a while. A line begins to form behind us: an Asian couple holding hands, maybe on their honeymoon;

an older couple—Eastern European by the look of the woman's colorful headscarf—looking slightly dazed. And behind them . . . I do a double take, then turn and have a good, long look, just to make sure I haven't lost my mind.

"Ola!" I say.

"Ola," they nod back.

The mariachi band is dressed in white, from the tips of their pointy boots to the rims of their sombreros. Extravagant cream-colored trim adorns their shoulders, their cummerbunds, the cuffs of their shirts and jackets. Two or three of them carry slightly off-sized instrument cases, as though made for guitars touched by elephantiasis.

They look—how can I say this?—extravagantly, gorgeously, wonderfully out of place.

The maitre d'amsel is back now, accompanied by a thin young man in a black tuxedo.

"I'm sorry," he says. "What is the question?"

Ellen explains that we wanted to know about ordering from the menu, that we didn't want a full buffet, that we weren't sure why but our rooms hadn't come with breakfast included, but that, now that we know there's no menu, there's no problem and we'll just figure something else out.

The man listens, watching her face, then glances at me. Then he lowers his eyes and surveys our brood: three blond-ish children in a country that fines couples for having more than one baby. His eyes stay on them for a long, long moment, moving from head to head as though doing a math that is both literal and figurative.

Then he looks at the hostess. "The children will count as one," he says.

Ellen and I both begin to protest, but he holds up a hand and lowers his eyes, a Chinese gesture that means the conversation is over. So we herd the kids up the stairs and into the dining room. As we do so, I thank him. "Don't worry," I say. "Usually they just have cereal. And maybe a pancake."

But we're not even at the table before Lucy says, "Daddy, look!"

I turn, glancing at the row of heated silver trays. Dim sum, tomatoes au gratin, ham, bacon, oatmeal, steamed buns. One thing that's great about traveling in Asia is the mix of people you'll find: Asians, yes, but also Europeans, Africans, Australians, and North Americans. And as opposed to, say, France, where what you'll get for breakfast is purely French fare (not that I'm complaining, mind you), every hotel we've been to in Asia has made an attempt to accommodate *every* population that crosses its thresholds, at least with its breakfast buffets. So you'll find blue cheese and salami next to wasabi and sushi; stewed cabbage and corned beef next to kim chi. That *none* of these is a dish I would want to eat for breakfast (I mean, where are the Cocoa Puffs?) is beside the point. It's still pretty cool.

Anyhow, what Lucy has spotted on the way to our table is the serving tray filled to the brim with greasy, fatty, English-style bacon, thick and floppy, more like ham than the crispy stuff we serve back in the States.

Lucy loves this kind of bacon. *Loves* it.

Which explains of course, why, when the manager strolls past our table not ten minutes later, he does a double take, all but stopping in his tracks and staring, horrified.

Fair enough that Ellen and I have loaded up on the waffles and syrup and fresh fruit and ham. We paid for it, after all. But where he'd expected to see a bowl of cornflakes or—what was the phrase? "*Maybe* a pancake"?—rests Lucy's plate, ten inches wide and piled almost to her chin with bacon.

After breakfast, we head back to our room, scrub the grease and pancake syrup off our hands and fingers, pick brie cheese out of our hair (don't ask), and head out the door.

All morning, Ellen and I have been debating about how to spend the day. We know we need to be in Suzhou, an hour away, at 5:00 to have dinner with friends we met in Vietnam. So our time in Shanghai, arguably one of the most interesting cities in Asia, is limited.

One of my Hong Kong colleagues who traveled a lot with her kids when they were younger, once listed to me all the things she'd done with them—all the UNESCO sites they'd visited, all the Buddhist temples, all the cultural events and folk dance performances they'd attended. "And when I ask them now about what they remember from Thailand," she said, "or Bali, or China, you know what they say?"

I shook my head.

She rolled her eyes. "The beach."

So there you have it.

Through all our travels in Asia thus far, we've remembered this story and planned accordingly. Every time we visit a moss-covered temple, we spend some time hiking in the mountains. Every hour we traipse through a museum, we spend an equivalent hour in some park somewhere letting the kids run around screaming "AHHHHHHHHHHHHHHHHHH!"

In Shanghai, though, for some reason, we forget this. The aquarium, with its sharks and stingrays and a special exhibit of the world's most deadly fish, is just across the river from our hotel. The other option we consider is the Yuyuan Garden, one of Shanghai's most famous classical gardens, built in 1577 by some government official who dedicated his life to boring the living crap out of children. Years ago, I'd spent several blissful hours in Yuyuan, scribbling in my journal and taking in the astounding lotus gardens, the small temples, the silence.

Wisely noting how much children love quiet contemplation and journaling, Ellen and I decide that the best way to spend our one day in Shanghai is to stroll down the Bund admiring the architecture before wandering toward Yuyuan where we can spend several hours screaming at our children for acting like (gasp!) *children.*

Don't get me wrong. The Bund is fabulous, even prior to the opening of the 2010 World Expo that Shanghai is hosting, when it's torn up by road crews retooling all the sidewalks with octagonal bricks. For anyone who hasn't seen it, the Bund is essentially a walkway along the Huangpu River separating old Shanghai from new Shanghai. On the old side, you have art deco and colonial architecture so amazing that even the architecturally illiterate (e.g., me) will look at it and go, "Wow." The walkway itself is raised and paved with decorative stones, and though devoid of leafy trees in the winter, it provides a wonderful view of the water with all of Shanghai rolling before it.

Opposite, in new Shanghai, is a potpourri of contemporary office buildings that look like twenty-seven undergraduate architecture students got together, drank a barrel of Everclear, and then had a contest to see who could design the most outrageous structure using plastic straws and candy wrappers. The results are Disney meets acid trip: buildings that curve and twist as they rise, that look like freestanding bottle openers, that resemble semi-crushed tubes of toothpaste. The most prominent of these structures is the Needle (I don't know its official name, and neither does anybody else), which bears an uncomfortable resemblance to a brightly colored enema. The weird thing about the new Shanghai side is that, strange as it is, it too has its charms.

The problem, though, is that absolutely none of this is designed to entertain a nine-, a six-, and a three-year-old, particularly on a day when sandstorms are blowing in from the deserts west of Beijing and the six-year-old woke up at 6:35 in the morning—both events certain to register with satellites circling the globe.

Nonetheless, Ellen and I stick with our plan, strolling beside the wonderful red sandstone buildings, rattling jackhammers, and thousands of other tourists. Lucy and Will have their cameras, and Lucy is taking pictures of the buildings, of the view across the river, of a pair of brass lions outside what surely used to be a bank.

It isn't long though, before Lucy gets bored. When this happens, a serious glint appears in her eye and she wanders over to Jamie and says, "Let me have the umbrella."

"Enh," says Jamie, his face showing displeasure. His grip tightens around the umbrella, one of those small, sheathed affairs that looks like a blackjack.

"Jamie," Lucy says, "It's my turn! Give it to me."

Jamie, though, cued by something—the tone of her voice maybe, or some primitive instinct that will allow him to survive after the apocalypse—refuses.

So, of course, Lucy grabs it.

A tussle ensues, during which Ellen and I chastise both of them, pointing out that sharing is important, but so is using a polite tone of voice, and last but not least, that it's an umbrella for God's sake—and it's not even raining.

But of course it's not about the umbrella. It's about being tired, away from home, about being six, about being the only girl in the family, about getting weird looks when you eat a pile of bacon the size of your head. Any number of objects or incidents, large or small, could just as easily have set her off, leading to a similar scrabble and clawing and moans of "It's not fai-err!"

And indeed, any number of objects and incidents *do* set her off. The rest of our walk down the Bund is accompanied by a melody of whines and moans and petty bickerings, all designed to annoy us and provoke one or both of her brothers into a battle of wills—invitations which, inevitably, they accept.

It doesn't help that the farther we stroll, the more torn up we find the Bund, until finally we're wandering through a dusty building site, looking for road signs, restrooms, a bench to sit down on—anything to give us a break from the cold and the dirty-beige sky and the rattling echo of construction machinery.

Eventually we make it to Yuyuan and discover that in order to enter you have to traverse the world's largest outdoor souvenir mall. There's no end of things to buy, most of them dangerously un-kitschy: woodcarvings, designs cut into lace-thin paper, jade figurines. We're able to avoid most of it, but I do talk Ellen into letting a clever-looking man clip three paper silhouettes of the children. As he does so, he studies their faces earnestly, one at a time, concentrating on the intricacies of their features, the rise and fall of their cheekbones, the particular arch of their eyebrows. Finally finished, he produces with a flourish three red cut-outs: one largish with thick hair combed to the side (Will), one medium-sized with long hair and bangs (Lucy), and one tiny, with crazy hair poking in all directions (Jamie). All three have an incredibly Asian slant to their eyes. They look nothing like our children. We love them.

The gardens are just as beautiful as I'd remembered. Yuyuan was built by Pan Yunduan, who created it for his father, a retired official from the Ming Dynasty, as a peaceful place for the old man to wander. And let me tell you, that old guy must have been a hell of a wanderer, because the gardens are huge, occupying nearly five acres and consisting of dozens and dozens of white stucco temples and homes and studies. The buildings are built in the classical style, with tile roofs that curve out and up at the corners, often decorated with small stone dragons or other elaborate carvings.

Crammed in and among these structures are hundreds of bridges, koi ponds, rock gardens, and "dragon walls" with undulating backs made of gray tiles and ending in reptilian heads. There are willows and elegant bonsai and massive piles of rock climbing out of reflective pools so full of bright orange fish you can see them from thirty yards away. Everywhere you look are intricate carvings and walkways carefully cobbled to create geometric patterns in the shapes of turtles and dragons and other animals.

I try to let Ellen wander alone as much as I can, shepherding the kids from place to place, trying to keep a lid on them by taking silly pictures of them, by pointing out all of the carved dragons, by letting them drift off by themselves every so often to explore some hidden corner.

And for a while they are fine. Rambunctious, yes. Giggly, yes. But within the boundaries of acceptable behavior. The farther we move into the gardens, though, the more the kids seem like springs being wound tighter and tighter. The bursts of laughter get louder, the moments of horseplay rougher, the arguments over who gets what granola bar or who's in the way of whose photograph nastier.

"You guys!" I warn, once, twice, then ten times. "You need to keep it quiet. There are other people around. They're trying to enjoy this place, too."

I gesture toward a crowd of tourists following a Japanese guide with a small green flag and a megaphone wired to a speaker on her waist. Even I, never having spoken a word of Japanese, can tell that her voice is hopelessly garbled by the volume having been cranked up to "11."

One of the great mysteries of our year abroad is whether Ellen's and my insistence that the kids behave in public is for the good of the public, the good of the kids, or our own peace of mind. I'd like to think it's the first, or at worst, the second. Certainly living in a smallish flat with people over, under, and beside us has put some pressure on us to keep the kids quieter—though at times I'm pretty sure our hollering to shut them up is louder than their yapping.

And there are times I wonder, particularly when I look around and see Chinese kids running around in hotel lobbies, or Australian kids climbing on furniture in restaurants, if maybe we worry a bit too much about our kids acting out, if we shouldn't just let them be kids a bit more.

Often, when we've told Will and Lucy 600 times *not* to run around this or that nunnery and *not* to blow raspberries as loud as they can in a restaurant, Ellen will say about herself and her brother, "I just don't remember Brian and me behaving this way."

Then she'll pause for a moment and say, "But of course, we didn't have a Lucy with us."

And it's true: Lucy does seem to be the epicenter of nearly every earthquake, tornado, monsoon, and forest fire that rattles the walls and singes the curtains of our lives in Hong Kong. Part of this, I'm sure, is just her age. At six, she's too old to be constantly dependent on us for entertainment, but not quite old enough to entertain herself by reading a book, getting out the paints, or discovering a new chemical compound (something her brother has been doing since he was four). Consequently, she spends most of her time entertaining herself by bugging the living hell out of Will and Jamie.

Part of it, though, is simply that she's, well . . . *my* daughter. See, unlike Ellen and her oh-so-perfectly-holy older brother, I *can* remember misbehaving when I was a kid. Oh, sure, I may have listened to my mother more than Will and Lucy listen to me—or maybe not—but I had all this energy, all this momentum. During my toddler years, my dad was a pastor at a small Lutheran church in northern Wisconsin. The parsonage was right on the church property, and on Sunday afternoons I'd go out in the yard, get on the play set, and swing so hard I'd lift the legs of that thing right off the ground. My dad tells me there are still parishioners there who remember me running around the vestibule, screaming like Satan's idiot offspring.

When we visit our friends Hilary and Doran and their family in Suzhou the next day, Hilary will comment on how gentle the Chinese are with their children.

"I've been here eighteen months," she'll say, "and I've never—never once—seen one of them yell at their kids."

Maybe this is simply the one child rule: If you're only allowed to have a single kid, you're going to show the little thing as much affection as you can, or risk spending your geriatric years staring out the window and waiting for a knock that never comes.

Or maybe it's just a matter of etiquette, the difference between what you do in public and what you do in private. Regardless, I wish I'd spoken to Hilary sooner, because after nearly two hours at Yuyuan Gardens saying, "Guys, please be quiet!" and "Guys, you need to listen!" and "Guys, there are other people around you! Be careful!" I finally lose it.

It's right before lunch, always an arsenic hour for low-blood-sugar people like yours truly. We're in a quiet corner of the garden, a largish space surrounded by high white walls and off the main lines of traffic. There's a huge pond in the middle, with two large pagodas, one on each side. I'm not sure what sets me off. Maybe it's Will and Lucy sprinting around the outskirts of the water, barely avoiding an elderly man with a cane and a younger couple holding hands. Maybe it's Jamie, stumbling after them on smooth-worn rocks not a foot from the pond. Maybe it's when, after my first, strongly worded and vehemently hissed warning, Lucy and Will started to grin almost before I'm done, and shoot off to continue doing exactly what I'd told them not to. Maybe it's just that I'm an idiot, a bad parent, a control freak.

Or maybe it's just that I'm tired, 1,000 miles away from my home-away-from home, which is 8,000 miles from my actual home. Maybe, in fact, I'm tired of being tired, tired of always being on edge, tired of always turning a corner and not know-ing where I am or what's going to happen next, of having to learn a new geography every other day, of constantly being on the receiving end of the ignoramus stick, of having to order food that's tasty, yes, but unfamiliar and in some ways just plain *weird*, of being surrounded by people who look nothing like me and sound nothing like me and smell nothing like me (not that that's a bad thing) and who very often stare at me all the time.

Whatever it is, I let the kids have it—and I mean *have it*. I don't scream, I don't yell, but the sheer force of my breath—strike that, the sheer force of my *will*—blows the hair off their foreheads, singes their eyebrows, and causes their toes to rise a good six inches off the ground.

"What," I hiss, "did I just tell you? Did you not hear me when I told you not to run? Did you not hear me when I told you it was dangerous, that your brother could fall in the pond and drown, that one of you could slip and crack your skull open?

Did you not understand when I told you to be quiet, that there were other people here, that you needed to respect their rights? Do you think you're the only people in the world? Do you not care about anyone else? Are you so important that nothing and no one else matters?"

And on and on like that, less reasoned and thoughtful than anxious and illogical and angry and—well, you get the point. And when I am done, and I've straightened and Will and Lucy have had a chance to wipe the spittle from their eyebrows, I turn to storm away in self-righteous indignation and find—

Well, no surprise, really. What I find is a small cluster of Chinese tourists: a young man with black-framed glasses, a mother cradling a baby in a knit blanket, an elderly couple barely as high as my elbow and wearing Mao hats. I find this small cluster of Chinese folks and others like them standing near the railing of the pagoda behind me, gazing at us in quiet, confused wonder.

Eventually we need to get our butts to the train station so that we can head to Suzhou to see our friends, the Gringortens. Getting a taxi is more of a problem than we anticipate—not only can't our driver speak English (fair enough), apparently he also can't read the Chinese characters our hotel concierge wrote for us before we left. No worries. Sooner or later we get there, deposited in an underground parking lot where we ride an escalator to a huge fenced-in area outside the station.

It's a madhouse.

Seriously: from the outside it looks less like a train station than a sports arena. It's just that big. And there are that many people, would-be passengers pushing and shoving, negotiating huge, plastic-wrapped bales of clothing and other items from place to place, scurrying around as though there's a bomb about to go off. The overall effect is part performance art, part battle zone, part social experiment. It is, simply put, pushy, energetic, and unpredictable—everything that people who hate China hate about China, and everything that people who love China love about China.

We spend our first twenty minutes there scanning the station for ticket counters. We see plenty of automated ticket kiosks, sure, but where are the flesh-and-blood, face-to-face booths where you can receive personal verbal assurances that you haven't just purchased fifty-four round-trip tickets to Mongolia? Eventually I get in line at one of the kiosks while Ellen takes the kids out for further reconnaissance certain that, somewhere, there's a smiling face just waiting to sell us tickets to Suzhou.

The waiting room/holding pen at the train station in Shanghai.
Amazing how so many people could be so quiet and peaceful.

I'm two bodies from the front of the line when Will comes running. "Mom found the ticket counters!" he says, and we both sprint through the crowds to where Ellen's standing in the doorway of an adjacent building, looking grim.

"False alarm," she says. Then she points at more of the electronic kiosks, each with a bristling line of people. "But at least these ones have English."

And sure enough, there's an LED sign over this bank bearing the legend: "English Users Tickets Machines."

I get in line. And to hedge our bets, so does Ellen at the opposite end of the room. For a long time we stand in our respective lines, not moving. Occasionally we signal each other: "Five people left in this line." "Five left here as well." "No one's moving here. I wonder why?" "I don't know." "This guy's having a hard time. Must be stupid." "No kidding?" "I wish I had a cannoli." "Really? I thought you didn't like ricotta?" "I don't, but what can I say? It's just what I'm craving right now."

Seriously, though, a guy in my line appears more than a little confused. He stands at the kiosk for what seems like ten minutes, shoulders hunched, head down. What the hell is he doing, I wonder, ordering fries?

"Come on," I say out loud. The man behind me, a business-looking dude in a black suit and pink shirt, grunts in affirmation.

Eventually, Mr. Pokey gives up, taking his money and rolling his eyes as he strolls back down the line and out the door. My queue picks up speed after that, and eventually, with only one couple left in front of me, I signal to Ellen that she should leave her line and join me over here.

At which point, of course, the couple in front of me decides that the best way to pay for their 6,000 RMB tickets is by feeding wrinkled twenties into the machine, one after another, looking startled every time the machine spits the bills back out.

Finally, it's my turn.

I step up to the machine, confident in my abilities to read English and push buttons. Sure enough, in a matter of seconds I've booked five tickets to Suzhou, plus five more returns for Monday morning. Pushing the "Approve Purchase" button, I haul out my wallet and feed a 100 RMB bill into the appropriate slot.

Only . . .

It won't take it.

I glance at the bill, then glance at the guide that shows the correct orientation for feeding the machine: Mao facing up, his back to the intake slot.

No problem. I snap my bill once just to remove any wayward wrinkles, and feed Mr. Mao into the machine.

Out it comes.

"Bugger," I mutter. I stuff the bill back into my wallet, pull out another. Again I check the orientation, then slide the paper into the slot.

There's a beat of a full five seconds—then the bill reappears.

"Bugger bugger," I say. I can feel the room getting warm. Pink shirt man is still behind me, I know, probably rolling his eyes in commiseration with those around him.

I try again. And again. And again. I'm not saying "bugger" anymore, having switched to words that will offend not just the English but most residents of San Quentin.

Giving up on that bill, I stuff it into one pocket and grab another. And then another. And another. And another.

None of them works.

"What's wrong?" A young man with spiky hair and glasses has appeared on my right.

"It won't take my money."

"Try another bill."

"It won't take any of them."

"You put it in like this." He points to the orientation indicator below the slot.

"I know," I say. "I've tried that."

Pink shirt is on my left now, looking no-nonsense in his sharp black suit. Without saying a word to me, he feeds one of his own bills into the slot.

There's an unbelievably long pause, during which all three of us hold our breath—then the bill slides out again.

"They're too new," the spiky-haired guy says.

I thumb through my wallet, looking for anything pink and wrinkly. Every bill is sharp enough to cut.

Spiky hair and I both look at pink shirt to see if he has any ideas. He's standing, bill still in his hand, thumb on his chin, gazing at the machine. Then, suddenly, he leans forward, flips the bill over, and feeds it in upside down.

There's a pause, a count of one . . . two . . . three. Then a beep, and the machine takes it.

The three of us sigh, grinning. I hand pink shirt a replacement bill, then slide one, two, three, four more of my own upside down into the machine, smiling each time I hear that beep. Eventually all that's left is to wait for my tickets and my change. These come in short order and I step back from the machine, clasp my hands in front of me, bowing to spiky hair and pink shirt, my head down, thanking them, thanking them, thanking them.

Tickets in hand, we make our way to the entrance of the station where we flash them to the guard and go through security. We're in a high-ceilinged, dingy room with poor lighting and two flights of stairs, one leading to the left, the other to the right. We follow the digitized signs for Suzhou up the stairs to the right and past a large, dining room-looking area. Turning left, we find ourselves in a long hall with a series of waiting rooms on each side. The rooms on the left have the numbers for each train, including ours, and the words "Cars 1–8." The ones on the right have similar signs, with the words "Cars 9–16."

I take out the tickets, finger through them. Then I look at Ellen.

"Guess what?" I say.

"We're in two different cars."

I hand her three tickets. "See you in Suzhou."

She takes Will and Jamie, figuring that the two of them put together are half as much trouble as Lucy, and I lead mini-me in her pink monkey pants and a *Why? Why? Why?* T-shirt across the hall.

"Where's Mommy and Will going?" Lucy asks.

"We're on two different cars."

"Cool."

"Yeah," I say.

I have to admit, I'm still a little pissed off at her about this morning. This isn't quite fair, I know, because both she and Will—and to some extent, even Jamie—were acting like turds, but even so it's the way I feel at this particular moment. Part of it, I think, is that of the three kids, Lucy seems to be the one who has made a consistent, sustained effort to be—well, *bad*. Sure, Will gets into trouble, but then he has all these quiet moments when he sits and reads, or builds something from a science kit. At moments like that, Lucy goes out of her way to poke him or prod him or taunt him, goading him into a reaction that involves yelling or at the very least sustained bickering.

At times she's been so bad that I literally haven't known what to do with her. A month ago, while traveling in Guangxi province, I'd had to haul her out of the rice paddies where the rest of us had been happily hiking and drag her back to our hotel room, because she'd taken such utter pleasure in saying rude things to both of her brothers and getting sassy with Ellen and me.

"Great," I say now, as we stroll into the waiting room. "Do you need to pee?"

Lucy shakes her head. I pick her up, and the two of us survey the room. It's roughly the size of a basketball court, maybe a little bigger, and divided vertically into four rows of seats, each leading to a doorway over which is posted a train number. Ours is on the right-hand side, against a makeshift wall made of bare plywood. Over the top of this, we can see men on scaffolding welding together long sheets of metal. Every so often, big orange sparks float over the top of the wall and drift down into the late afternoon gloom of the waiting room, causing startled screams and laughter from the passengers.

"Right," I say, and put Lucy down. "We go this way. Be sure to stick close, okay?"

She takes my hand and we lace our way through the crowd, angling toward the front, right-hand side of the room. Eventually we make it two-thirds of the way to our gate, at which point Lucy tugs my hand and says, "Daddy?"

I look down at her. Her lower lip is up, as though considering.

"Let me guess," I say. "You have to pee?"

She nods.

We make our way back through the crowd, saying, "Excuse me," and "Sorry," as we shrug around clusters of people, our suitcase inevitably rolling over toes. We find the restrooms way back in a corner, right next to the official smoking area. We trade pee for lung cancer, then weave back to a spot along the plywood sheets, where we can hear the hiss of the arc-welders. It's gray in there, and crowded, and about as gloomy as a story by Poe.

"You hungry?" I say to Lucy.

She nods. I dig through my backpack and come up with an unopened bag of pistachios. Setting my pack on top of the suitcase, I make a table of sorts, laying some nuts on top. We take turns taking one, cracking it, then tossing the shells into a nearby garbage can.

"You want to play mini-mysteries?" I ask.

This is something we started doing in Vietnam, over Christmas, during those dull moments at restaurants between ordering and the arrival of the food—one sentence riddles that can be solved only by asking yes-or-no questions. A man is dead in a room, nothing but a glass of water beside him; what happened? "Was he poisoned?" No. "Did he vote for the healthcare bill?" Yes. And so on. Right now we're on one about a man who takes the elevator down from the twenty-fifth floor on his way to work. Then, on the way back, he takes the elevator all the way up if he's with someone, but gets out at the twelfth floor if he's alone.

Lucy shakes her head, then spits a shell into the garbage can.

"What about twenty questions?" I ask.

"What's that?"

"It's like mini-mysteries, only instead of trying to solve a murder or something, I think of an object and you try to figure out what it is, asking yes-or-no questions."

She considers this for a minute. Then she asks, "Can I go first?"

"Sure."

She grins.

"You have to think of something," I say. "An object or a person. Or maybe a place. And you can't change it once you've decided, okay?"

She nods.

"You have something?"

Again she nods.

"Okay," I say. "Is it alive?"

"Yes," she says.

"Valerie's cats?"

"Uh-huh!"

I expect her to be upset—it's late afternoon, after all, and she's inherited my low-blood-sugar-induced sociopathic tendencies.

But she's unfazed. "Okay," she says, "your turn."

I pick something easy for starters, not wanting to scare her off. She gets it—the pistachios—in maybe twelve questions and we move on to more difficult topics. Pretty soon we've fallen into a rhythm, going back and forth as quick as a couple of ping-pongers. The first question is always "Is it alive?" If the answer is yes, then the next question is "Is he or she in our family?" If no, we ask, "Is it ours?" All around us, the Chinese stand and watch, staring unabashedly at this big white guy and his blond daughter eating pistachios and engaging in a rapid-fire dialogue they don't understand, and probably wouldn't even if they knew English.

In twenty minutes, the guards will open the gate—the wrong one, it turns out, two rows over—and the crowd around us will surge to the left, swelling and falling over the benches like waves in the ocean. In an hour we'll be in Suzhou, rejoined by Ellen and Will and Jamie, hearing their story about not having seats and being escorted up to first class. In two hours we'll be with our friends having dinner in a warm restaurant, watching fireworks over a man-made lake. We'll spend the next day wandering along the wonderful canals and whitewashed buildings of Suzhou, munching dumplings for lunch and stuffing ourselves with Korean barbeque at dinner.

Lucy and me on the train to Suzhou, after our fifty-third game of twenty questions.

In thirty-six hours we'll be back on the train heading into Shanghai, where we'll grab baguettes and brioche in the French Quarter before heading—*finally*—to the aquarium that we should have visited on Saturday. Later that day we'll board a magnetic train that goes 180 miles per hour out to the airport, where we'll get on a plane and fly back to Hong Kong. There, we'll rise the next morning, sending the kids bleary-eyed and groggy off to school. I'll grab a workout, then head into my office to find a dozen nasty e-mails from people who had courses rejected during the recent round of general education submissions.

I'll also discover that I've had basically the largest publication of my life occur while I was away, and find a raft of nasty comments from scholars around the world about that piece. Later that week I'll learn that what we'd thought was minor bullying in Will's class is perhaps more than that, and I'll wonder again what happens to a ten-year-old when the only woman he's ever loved is taken from him by cancer. By Friday, I'll be sitting on a train on the way to Central with Jamie, going to have noodles with friends, crying quietly in my sleeve, it's just been that bad a week.

But none of that matters right now. At this moment, all that matters is that I'm standing in that gloaming train station, orange sparks floating through the air, the eyes of a dozen people I'll never see again fixed on me and my daughter, my 1.4-meters-high Lucy, my eating-pistachios-and-spitting-shells-into-the-garbage Lucy as she says, "Is it Jamie?"

No.

"It is Will?"

No.

"Uncle Brian?"

No.

"But someone we know?"

Yes.

"And someone we love?"

Yes.

Oh Lordy, yes.

Yes.

Yes.

Yes.

CHAPTER 12

HURLING OURSELVES
INTO CHINA

It's 11:30 at night, Thursday, April 1, 2010. I'm lying in a shabby hotel in Lijiang, China, in the Yunnan Province. Jamie is asleep in the bed beside me, and Will is snoring on the floor on the other side of him. I am sweating between the sheets and doing my Lamaze breathing: *he he he he ha ha ha ha he he he he ha ha ha ha.*

I'm doing this not because I am about to have a baby (appearances to the contrary), but because five hours earlier Lucy hurled her guts all over the front steps of a very nice restaurant.

I have to say, she gave us fair warning. When we sat down to dinner and spooned some rice, some chicken, some bacon, and some french fries on her plate, she just looked at it. For a long time. A really long time. Then she said, "I have to go to the bathroom."

We nodded and off she went. We didn't say anything because our mouths were too stuffed with food. This was a fantastic meal, one of the best we'd ever had, Naxi fare from one of the local Chinese minorities (there are more than fifty). The starter was a soup with crunchy greens, noodles, eggs, and lots of salt. Next came chicken, cooked in some sort of flavored oil and pasted with red chili peppers. There was a beef dish, too, and something with pork, either of which would have been the centerpiece of any meal at a Chinese restaurant back in the States, but which, here, paled in comparison to everything else.

And I haven't even mentioned the *piece de résistance:* fermented greens stir-fried with dried bacon. It was crunchy and salty, coated with spicy oil. The bacon was one of the most amazing things I've ever eaten: Maybe a centimeter thick and three inches long, it looked like normal bacon, albeit uncooked. But it wasn't. Normal that is. No, this was uber-bacon, hyper-bacon, bacon magnified to the 45th degree. This bacon was the crispiest and most flavorful bacon I'd ever eaten, like munching on monster bacon bits cooked in bacon grease, flavored with bacon oil, and dusted, ever so lightly, with teeny-tiny crumbs of crushed bacon.

Sure, I ate some of the rice and some of the soup. I tried the beef, avoided the pork, liked the chicken well enough. But that bacon dish? I went to town on that thing, scooping up those greens and the occasional pepper and those dried strips and shoveling them into my mouth, taking breaks only to sip the melon liqueur our guide, Habba, had ordered for Ellen and me. Could life be any better?

Now if this all sounds kind of greedy to you, well that's because it was. But keep in mind there was no resistance from anyone at the table to my gobbling down all the bacon: Ellen's never been a fan of pork. Will won't touch anything that isn't white and the size, shape, and flavor of rice. And Jamie only has a stomach the size of a large grape, and was happily filling it with chicken. Which meant, in effect, that the only person with whom I had to share my favorite dish *ever* was—

"Hey," I said. "Where's Lucy?"

Ellen looked up from her soup and glanced around the room. "Don't know. Still in the bathroom?"

I shrugged. We were the only people in the restaurant except for a French couple. Assuming they hadn't eaten her—and with the French, you never know—Lucy had to still be in the toilet. Her plate of fries and rice and everything else remained untouched. Which was unusual, of course: Of our three children, Lucy is the most adventurous, the least likely by far to leave a plate of tasty morsels just sitting there.

Ellen and I looked at each other. Huh. Then we lowered our heads and dove back into the food.

When Lucy eventually emerged from the bathroom, she crept over to Ellen and whispered in her ear. She didn't feel well. Ellen looked her over carefully. Her face was pale, with olive-green highlights around the jaw.

"Do you want to sit outside?" Ellen asked.

Lucy nodded.

"Don't you want some french fries?" I asked, figuring it couldn't hurt to give it one more try.

But Lucy just shook her head and took a seat in the court-yard outside our window. She laid her head on a wrought-iron table and closed her eyes.

Almost everyone I know who's traveled in China has a story about being sick. China has some potent bugs. Hotels have signs in the bathrooms stating, "Water not for drinking! Water poison! Don't drink water!" Our tour company went even further. "When showering, be sure to turn your back to the spray and keep your mouth shut. Should you have the extreme misfortune to ingest any water—even a drop—gargle immediately with battery acid to increase chances of survival."

We worried now about Lucy, but not overmuch. We'd been in Asia for almost eight months, after all. This was our third trip to the mainland and none of us had ever been sick before. Hell, we'd spent two weeks in Vietnam and had come through unscathed.

By the time we finished dinner, Lucy had a little bit more color in her face and we figured she was fine. Which she was, until we stepped out of the restaurant and she plopped down on the stone steps, spread her knees, and vomited between her red sneakers.

"Oh," I said, ever the helpful parent.

Hong Kong is an amazing place with many wonderful people. But man, it has a lot of rules.

Ellen, of course, pulled Lucy's hair out of the way, wiped her mouth with a tissue, and dabbed the sweat off her forehead. Lucy recovered quickly, at least until we got back to the hotel, where she threw up at least three more times in rapid succession. At one point she was in the bath, splashing around as I moved Will's stuff to my room where he would now sleep in hopes of containing this bug, when she called out to me.

"Daddy!" she said. "I threw up in my hair!"

I leaned against the doorframe. "Really?" I said, keeping my voice light because I wasn't sure exactly what response she was looking for. "That's wonderful, honey."

"Yeah," she said, sitting up. "It got—" and then she paused, rose to her knees while still in the tub, and heaved into the toilet.

Having never toured with the Rolling Stones, this was the first time I'd seen someone sit in the tub and vomit into the john. I fled immediately, knowing that if whatever she had was contagious, Ellen probably already had it, and that I needed to get away so that at least one adult would be functioning the next day.

Except that she didn't. Get it, that is. Ellen. Whatever made Lucy sick.

I did.

I knew this even before Jamie and Will went to bed. Every time I stood up or sat down or blinked, the room seemed to tilt precariously, swashing back and forth like an aquarium on a teeter-totter. So I didn't kiss them good night, and I didn't linger in the hallway outside the room, reading a book by the dim lights. No, I brushed my teeth, went to the bathroom, washed my hands, and put an empty garbage bin next to my bed. And then I crawled between the sheets.

I don't think I slept at all. Whatever it was came with a fever, so by 9:15 I was sweating through my pajamas and mentally arguing about the color of Lucy's socks with my provost who was also Santa Claus and that dwarf from *Fantasy Island*. Which wouldn't have been so bad except that he kept waving a shark in my face and saying, "Just say no to torpedoes, son. Nothing less ethical than a pair of ninetieth-ranked denim trousers."

Even worse were the lucid moments, when I'd lie there holding my stomach, shivering, trying hard not to think about scrambled eggs, or Tibetan yak cheese, or fermented greens with bacon, or any of the other things I'd eaten in the last twenty-four hours. And trying hard not to think about Ellen across the hall, Ellen who'd handled Lucy's vomit-sodden clothes and wiped her vomit-smeared mouth and caressed her vomit-dripping forehead. Because if I was sick and Ellen was sick then damn, we were in trouble.

Which led me into even darker territory. We were in Lijiang, after all, in Yunnan province, a hell of a long way from our home in Hong Kong. We had no insurance so far as I knew, and even if we did, what good would it do in China? Christ, we couldn't even talk to the doctors, assuming we could find a hospital, which was doubtful, because no one in this place spoke English except our guide, Habba, whom we were pretty sure was not above ripping us off by selling us stuff we'd already paid for. In short, if whatever we had was bad, we were dead meat.

Twenty-five years ago, when I was traveling and working in Tanzania with my friend Peter (who has an annoyingly iron stomach), I picked up some sort of bug that landed me in bed with a high fever for three days, sweating my way through dreams about triplanes doing loop-de-loops and a British woman driving me to Milwaukee in a cream-colored Rolls Royce made of Twizzlers. Weeks later, when I went to the U.S. Embassy in Dar es Salaam (the one that was later bombed by Osama bin Laden), the doctor there took one look at my long hair, my scrappy beard, and my protruding ribcage and said, "Now I know what Jesus looked like when he was crucified."

It was scary. I was halfway across the globe, in a third-world country, unable to keep down food or water.

But I was twenty, stupid, and not really aware of what was at stake.

In Lijiang, however, I am forty-four, a father of three, and bone-numbingly terrified that we have gotten ourselves into a situation where one of our kids could end up in a hospital where whatever it is she has will pale in comparison to the things she might catch.

It would have been better had I been able to go to sleep. In my fevered stupor, though, I wouldn't allow myself to do that, convinced that the second I drifted off I'd awake again, vomiting.

And let's face it folks: Vomiting sucks. I don't know anybody who likes to lean over a toilet and hack and gag until he can feel his esophagus rubbing against the roof of his mouth, while having something that tastes like orange juice mixed with chicken broth churn its way up his throat and into his mouth.

That said, we all know the upside of puking. Even Will, who's only nine, said to Lucy after her first hurl outside the restaurant, "Bet you feel better now, right?" Because it's true: If prepuking is horrible, and puking is truth that God hates us, then post-puking is kind of . . . well, peaceful. Our stomachs are calm (for the moment), the sweat on our skin starts to cool us down, and we suddenly feel our bodies drawn blissfully toward sleep. Sure, we know there's a good chance we'll be heaving again in an hour or two—but for the time being, post-puking makes prepuking and actual puking seem kind of worth it.

Kind of.

The problem is, I couldn't get myself past the pre-puking stage. Which means I was trapped forever in the purgatory of anticipatory fear regarding the aforementioned heaving, esophagal-mouthroof rubbing, etc., etc. It didn't help that, over the years, I'd somehow learned to breathe my way through the waves of nausea that would, in a less-control-driven human being, result in the inevitable upsurge, purge, and post-barfing bliss.

It also didn't help that I'm not only a control-freak of a person, but a control-freak of a *writer*. What this means is that, in addition to lying in bed feeling like my lower intestines were about to hurl themselves out of my body and like the world was going to end in a my-family-will-die-from-the-plague kind of way, I was also thinking about how I was going to narrate all this later, when we got back to Hong Kong, for my blog.

You heard me.

In addition to lying in bed trying not to hack my liver out through my nose and worrying about Ellen and tomorrow and our three-hour flight to Beijing and next week and our tour and six more days worth of Chinese food—I was also wondering if I knew enough synonyms for "vomit" to get through an essay on this subject alone.

So there I was, curled up in bed, going "He he he he heave, hurl, gag, ha ha ha ha upchuck, throw up, regurgitate, he he he he," wondering just how the hell long this could go on.

I could, of course, wax poetic for another page or two about all of this, but to be honest I don't have the stomach or the patience for it. So let's just say that I finally gave in and let things reach their natural conclusion. After heaving what felt like a water balloon the size of a brick and tasted like a pound of rancid smoked bacon into the bathroom garbage can, I emptied the can into the toilet, rinsed it in the tub a few times, flushed, washed my face, gargled, and crawled back to bed, where I collapsed into a sweaty but relieved sleep.

The rest of the night passed uneventfully. I wasn't sick again, though when the boys and I woke up, I felt as though Muhammad Ali had been using my abdomen for a speed bag. Across the hall, I could see light streaming beneath Lucy and Ellen's door, and when I tapped, Lucy opened, her face pink, her eyes bright, her hair free of half-digested french fries. Ellen took one look at me and put me in Lucy's bed. Then she and Lucy went across the hall to get dressed. I slept through breakfast and woke mid-morning to find a Sprite on the lamp table. A few sips made me feel better, so I showered and dressed and the five of us went out into the cool morning air to walk along the river to the Black Dragon Pool.

Lijiang, for the record, is an amazingly beautiful place. It rests just below Jade Snow Dragon Mountain, in a lush valley at the easternmost end of the Himalayas. The mountains are astounding: sharp and black, majestic, clouds clinging to the snow-dusted slopes.

Until the mid-1990s, no one in China gave Lijiang a second thought, not even the people who lived there. But then there was an earthquake in 1996, measuring a devastating 7.0 on the Richter scale, and when the rescue teams showed up they were astonished to find so much natural beauty. Since then Lijiang has been rebuilt and has become something of a tourist destination.

The overall effect of the place, particularly in the recently constructed "old town," is something between Disneyland and *Raise the Red Lantern*: red-walled buildings with black-tiled roofs, long canals filled with water so clear you can see the blades of grass wavering around koi and goldfish, elderly ladies and men hired to dress in the traditional costumes—think, Native American with more shades of blue—and do slow, tapping dances as they chant quietly in a circle.

In and among this charming backdrop stand roughly 6,004 overpriced shops selling every variety of crap you can think of: "hand-woven" scarves, "hand-carved" jewelry, yak bells and prayer bowls and painted animal carvings and massive clear jars of herbs purported to increase the libido. It's testimony to the setting and to the dancers and to Lijiang in general that none of this really detracts from the overall pleasure of the place.

Black Dragon Pool is in the opposite direction from the old town, about a twenty-minute walk from our hotel, though Lucy and I are moving so carefully we likely double that time. The pool itself is the main headwater for the Yushui River, and is surrounded by stone walkways, ancient willows, orchids, and songbirds. All of it is very pretty, particularly when the sky is clear and you can see Jade Snow Dragon Mountain in the distance, looking both foreboding and hopelessly beautiful.

Once there, Lucy and I find a bench next to a small garden of bright yellow-and-blue flowers, and spend some time soaking up the morning sun. Then a huge group of Chinese tourists come over, cameras at the ready, saying "Hello! Hello!" We decide to leave.

We wander a bit, find an old temple at the top of a hill. Clasped to the fence surrounding the structure are thousands upon thousands of shiny brass padlocks, knotted over each other, sometimes five or six to a single link in the chain. None of them has a keyhole. Confused, we stare at them for a while, then finally throw a questioning look at a young tour guide standing at a booth beside the stairs.

Prayer locks in Lijiang. I still get nauseated every time I look at this or any other picture from that trip.

"Prayer locks," she says in a short, bored voice—as though she'd answered this question already a hundred times that morning.

Eventually, we make our way to a long white bridge arching to the other side of the lake. Crossing, we gaze at the greenish-gray water, the curving shadows of carp just below the surface. Once or twice a big one drifts to the surface, mouth gaping, an eye peering at us as if to say, "The big one's obviously diseased, but I'll bet that little one is tasty."

One of the real surprises of our year, for me at least, is how I've come to love these decorative fish. You can be anywhere in busy, overpopulated, over-constructed Asia—Central Hong Kong, for instance—and you leave your table at some expensive restaurant, squeezing past waiters and waitresses who make more than you do and customers who could buy and sell your entire hometown, and you wander down a long corridor that leads to the restrooms, and there, in a little stone garden at the back of the building, in the very middle of all the noise and chaos of one of the busiest cities in the world, you'll find a small pool surrounded by a stone wall, with a fountain in the middle. And swimming in it will be seven or eight koi, red, black, orange, and calico. They're gorgeous. At once muscular and graceful, they curve and flow and glide through the water, absolutely taking your breath away.

I've had very few real insights in my life, moments when I've come to understand the world in a completely different way, but one thing I did figure out while living in Hong Kong was that these fish are *good* for you, and I don't mean that they're low in fat or high in fiber. What I mean is, watching them, I can actually sense my heart rate slowing, can actually feel my breathing become calmer, more measured, deeper, more relaxed. It's impossible, I think, to watch these fish— really watch them—and have a bad thought about work, about life, about anything.

Gazing at them now, on that sunny April morning when it is still cool and damp and I can smell the decaying leaves and the fecundity of the soil, I try to tell myself that if pre-puking sucks and post-puking is bliss, then post-post-puking is almost heaven. Certainly, I remember this from my hard-partying college days (all three of them), when I emerged from a night of debauchery of one form or another to a clear spring morning, the buds just beginning to open, the sky a porcelain blue, the chill air making me feel much more full of life. Moments like that, after everything that happened the night before, just enhanced the beauty of being alive, and made me almost glad for the nightmarish darkness.

Standing there, Lucy beside me, I watch the fish, trying to feel moved by their beauty, trying to feel appreciation for the fact that I was alive, that none of us was too sick, that Sprite was plentiful and cheap. Surely, I thought to myself, this is good? Surely I'm grateful for the opportunity to be in this amazing country, to see this amazing beauty—the majestic mountains, the small graceful fish?

But no. If being sick is bad, then being sick on vacation, when you're in a foreign country, when you're away from your own safe bed and a doctor who you know will take care of you and food of the sort that you've been eating since you were born and that's not floating in grease and laced with spices that seem dark and dry to your tongue—if being sick is bad, then being sick under these circumstances just plain sucks. Period.

CHAPTER 13

312 M&M'S LATER

We're in the airport in Lijiang, Yunnan province, waiting for a flight to Beijing. It's the middle of the afternoon, and the kids all have lollipops, which means they're sugared up and squirming like baby rats.

Across from us stands a man, Chinese, maybe in his thirties or early forties. His face is the color of old mustard, his hands broad, as though he's a farmer or a construction worker. He stands between two rows of seats, swaying aimlessly, looking around. One hand is in his pants' pocket; the other is at his side, dangling a digital camera from his wrist. As it swings, I catch a glimpse of the view screen. It's on, flashing images of the waiting area: rows of hard red seats, dim fluorescent lighting, a water cooler, and a kitschy souvenir stand near the exit. I follow the man's face for a moment, watch as he glances this way and that, his eyes darting around the room, snatching a glace at Lucy, staring toward the doors, sneaking a peak at Jamie. I'm tired, not twenty hours from hurling my guts out all over the floor of a skanky hotel bathroom, and here's what I'm thinking:

Give me a break.

And: *For God's sake.*

And: *Just go ahead and do it already.*

The kids get a lot of attention in Asia. This is particularly true of Lucy and Jamie, who both sport hair of spun gold. We'll be walking down the street in Tai Po when a pair of teenage girls in frocks and leggings will turn and point at Jamie on my shoulders. They'll show deep dimples and one of them will chirp "Hello!" To which Jamie will respond by curling his face into his shoulder and grimacing in that charming Hanstedt way.

Or we'll be at the market, watching a butcher scrape the scales off a grouper. I'll raise my camera, eager for a picture of the man, the cleaver, the wooden block as wide as a tree and older than God—and receive a disapproving frown. Lucy, on the other hand, will raise her camera and this same man will stop midswing, grin at her, and heft the half-cleaned fish for better viewing, its exposed air sacks still pulsing.

Or we'll be in Kowloon, going down an escalator. Coming up the other side will be an old woman in a plaid coat, her hair short and white and neatly combed. As we pass, she'll glance at Lucy, those blue eyes, that pug nose. Then she'll reach out one hand, the fingers wrinkled but tipped by long clean nails—and softly brush Lucy's hair.

And then there are the pictures. Most of the time, folks are polite—this is Hong Kong, after all, where to offend someone is, well, offensive. They'll tap Ellen or me on the shoulder and say, "Can I take a picture of your daughter?" Or your son. Or your children. Then they'll kneel next to Lucy, or Jamie, or Will, or all three, and smile for a sister with a camera. Often this will lead to a small scene where more and more people gather around, asking for pictures. Once, at a temple in Vietnam, Will and I were strolling back from a bathroom break when we saw a half-dozen people sprint—*sprint*—across a stretch of green lawn toward something hidden behind a stand of firs. We didn't have to ask what was going on; we both knew Lucy and Jamie had been spotted. One of Ellen's friends who lives on the mainland swears that his kids have attracted large enough crowds that food vendors have rolled their carts over and set up shop.

Every Anglo I know who's experienced this phenomenon— which would be every Anglo with kids in Asia—will eventually, during the course of a conversation, voice out loud a thought I've had a dozen times: What do these folks *do* with these photographs? I mean, I keep picturing the scene eight years from now, when this or that guy with the camera is back in his living room in Huangzhou, sitting on his couch and thumbing through some old snapshots, when a friend points to a shot of a plump-cheeked blond girl and says, "Who's that?"

"Beats me," the photographer will have to say, "Just some kid we saw wandering down the street."

Some day Will's going to get older and wonder why he was so annoyed at having his picture taken with so many attractive Asian women.

I'm trying hard not to be judgmental here, really I am. But this just strikes me as weird. Barring running into Jennifer Aniston at the local Kroger, wearing a tank top and short shorts (her, not me), why would I want a picture of someone I barely know?

Ellen, of course, is more generous: "For a lot of these people, this might be the only blond person they've ever met—or even seen. Who knows? Maybe they grew up in a village somewhere out west and this is their first trip to the city."

Fair enough. One of our guides during a trip to Xi'an (terracotta warrior land, in case you're trying to place it) once mentioned in passing that pretty much no one in China had their own TVs until the mid-1990s—and many still don't. That in mind, seeing a Lucy or a Jamie with their strange white-gold hair flashing in the sun—or even a Will, with his deep-set and greenish-blue eyes—must be like the one time in my life I encountered a real Maasai tribesman while passing through a village in East Africa. He was standing by the side of the road, waiting for the bus, literally head and shoulders above everyone around him, his tightly braided hair powdered with red clay, his skin taut and deep brown-black beneath a plaid robe—details I still remember now, almost thirty years later.

When we told our friend Dat we were going to his home country of Vietnam over Christmas, he made a point of warning us that our children would be doted on.

"They're going to grab them," he said of his countrymen. "Don't take it personally. They just really love children over there."

He wasn't kidding. We'd be walking around Hoan Kiem Lake in Hanoi, and a group of tourists from—Saigon? Bangkok? Tokyo?—would grab Lucy and Jamie, squeezing them in their arms while a friend snapped a photo. One young woman was so physical with Lucy—snatching her up, planting her on her lap, and pinching her cheeks until Lucy squealed—that our guide had to intervene, chastising the woman and carrying Lucy back to our circle.

It was then, I'm afraid, that I began to get a little irritated. Part of it, I'm sure, simply had to do with jealousy on my part—I mean, where were the hoards of skinny Asian women clamoring to stroke *my* cheek and take pictures of *me?*

But more to the point, I didn't like the idea of Lucy thinking she had to oblige every stranger with a camera. I mean seriously:

think about that sentence. And I'm not alone in this feeling. A friend of Ellen's who lives in mainland in China, says almost the first thing he learned to say in Mandarin was, "She's not a toy, she's not a doll, she's a little girl. Put my daughter down."

Bad enough, I figure, that Lucy had no choice but to come to Hong Kong, had no say in what school she was to attend or who her friends would be—now she has to reinforce her lack of agency by being a Kewpie doll for a bunch of people she doesn't even know? Call me ungracious, but I know my gender theory and I know about objectification, and all this was beginning to make me feel more than just a little Judith Butler-y.

Lucy's first encounter with a Chinese groupie. She's smiling, but afterwards she was pretty upset.

More to my liking, actually, is the way Jamie has come to handle all the attention. Back in November when we were visiting the Chi Lin nunnery near Diamond Hill, a monk in a garnet-colored robe approached and began to make goo-goo faces at Jamie. Jamie ducked his chin a little, eyeing the young man, his gracious smile, his shaven head. Then my small son pursed his lips, squinted his eyes—and raised his fists.

The monk grinned, laughed, and raised his hands as though to fend off an attack. And then he went away.

There's a more somber side to all this, of course. Every once in a while when we're traveling on the mainland—waiting at a restaurant, maybe, or in line for a taxi—some slightly worn-looking woman in her late forties will be behind us, weighted down with groceries. Her eyes will be tired, staring off into nothing, almost studiously avoiding everyone and everything around her. But then something will catch her eye—Jamie meowing like a cat maybe, or some movement of Lucy's.

And then her gaze will lower and you can see her struggling for a moment to take it all in. Her eyes will travel from one head, to the other, and then to the other. And then she'll do it again—one head, another, and another. And then she'll just pause, not so much staring or stunned as, I don't know what . . . overwhelmed maybe? Or simply more tired and broken by her life?

Because this is China, after all, where the one-child policy has been in place since 1978. And though some will tell you that the vast majority of the Chinese support the policy, I've yet to meet one person who's expressed that sentiment.

That children hold a special place in the Chinese heart is perhaps the stupidest thing I've ever written—where aren't children loved, after all? But in China, there's something almost tangibly different about this affection. In the States, we love our kids, we pamper our kids, we spoil our kids. In China, though, kids are *revered,* seen almost as tiny vessels carrying a small portion of God in them.

What causes this, exactly, I've yet to figure out. Perhaps it's the emphasis placed on carrying on the family name and the way male children can do this. Or perhaps it's the lack of a good safety net for the elderly, and the way children take on their parents when they grow old.

Of course, we in the West care about family names and the elderly as well, but those things aren't written into our contemporary social fabric the way they are in China. We've become a live-in-the-day culture, less worried about projecting our names into the future than about trading upon that name today to purchase a bigger house, a bigger boat, a newer car.

And we have Social Security, Medicare and Medicaid, and a plethora of nursing homes to chuck Ma and Pa into when they start imitating Doris Day in the pasta aisle or wearing bright purple trousers in public—on their heads. Americans care about family, yes, but we often care just as much or more about careers, about getting ahead, about earning more money.

In contrast, family remains the fundamental social institution in China. Perhaps this is simply because of a longer tradition dating back to sometime before the glaciers retreated; or perhaps it's because of the oppressive and socially isolating nature of an Orwellian government; or maybe it's just because the Chinese are better and more caring people than we are.

One need only think of the riots following the 2008 Sichuan earthquakes, in which dozens of children died because of poorly constructed schools. When's the last time Americans took to the streets because of their children—much less *rioted* because of them? Following the Columbine and Virginia Tech massacres, our sympathy for the parents who lost their kids stopped the moment we started discussing the possibility of redefining gun laws. The American culture as a whole seems to care more about extended clips and keeping gun-show loopholes than about kids.

None of which, of course, is necessarily going through the head of the woman standing in line behind us at the taxi stand, gazing at our three children, whom we're likely to be yelling at and threatening to trade for a really good wheelbarrow if they don't shut up and behave.

What she is thinking, I don't know. But as her dark eyes roll from blond head to blond head to chestnut head, her jaw tightens, slightly, and the line of her mouth draws thin.

By late March, it's becoming clear that even Lucy, recently elected chair of the Hong Kong I'm the Center of the Universe Organization, has gotten sick of all the attention. Flying back from Shanghai, we were stuck in the tail of the plane, right next to the restroom. After the meal trays had been collected, folks started lining up to use the facilities, resting their elbows on our seat backs and chewing toothpicks. I was on one side of the aisle with Lucy and Ellen was on the other, so I'm not entirely sure what happened, but eventually someone pulled out a camera and started snapping photos of Jamie, who was in an unusually cooperative mood. Next thing you know, there's a mob at the back of the plane, maybe fifteen people grinning and waving digital Canons, trying to get pictures of Jamie, with Jamie, or of the back of someone's head who was looking at Jamie.

Jamie flees the grip of some guy we never met.

Lucy was next to me, curled up in the corner, observing all this. She's never been a good flier, Lucy, and she'd had a long weekend playing with her friends and arguing with her brother, so maybe it was that. Or maybe it was something else. But when someone in the crowd finally noticed her—her golden halo shimmering in the light bouncing off the clouds—and raised a camera, smiling, Lucy just frowned and shook her head.

"No," she said.

And that was that.

Which brings us back to Lijiang, and the man with the camera standing in the airport, trying to look nonchalant. Just that morning, we'd been in a restaurant and had bumped into a couple from Virginia who had four kids. They were in China for the long haul—two years down and no end in sight as far as they were concerned. Their youngest two were blond, and as it often does, the conversation turned to this phenomenon of strangers photographing children.

"Our kids were really getting sick of it," the mother said eventually. "Until we started with the M&M's."

"M&M's?" Ellen and I said in unison, wondering if we'd missed a crucial chapter in *Lonely Planet China*.

The woman nodded. "Every time they allow a stranger to take a picture of them, they get an M&M. We tell them they have to smile broadly, though. We consider this our little contribution to greater understanding and world peace."

Later, I was in our hotel room trying to isolate Lucy's and my vomit-soaked clothes from everyone else's clean threads, when Will and Lucy came sprinting in.

"You owe us three M&M's!" they shouted.

"Please don't mention food," I said. "What happened?"

"We got our pictures taken," Will said.

"Three times!" Lucy chimed in.

"We smiled," said Will.

"Like this." Lucy spread her lips from ear to ear, baring her teeth like a jack-o-lantern on methamphetamines.

"And that didn't scare them?"

At which point they both pummeled me with their fists until I threatened to barf all over them.

So now we're in the airport in Lijiang, and farmer man is standing beside us, switched-on camera dangling from his wrist. He's struggling to get up the nerve, I can tell—maybe he's never met Westerners before. Certainly he's never seen one as big and, well, as *green* as me. I know I should help, should nod his way or something, but honestly, my stomach is doing a tango with my large intestine and it's all I can do not to curl up on the floor and moan.

Eventually he's saved. A mildly clownish guy in a dark suit, traveling with his buddies and a tinkling box of Tsingtao, grabs Jamie as he toddles past, propping him on his lap and poking his taut belly, grinning something at him in a dialect I've never heard before. In a matter of minutes a crowd has gathered, mostly men, mostly in their forties, all with cameras, all taking turns posing with my three tooth-flashing children. I count camera flashes and clicks as best I can over the wheezing accordion and stomping heels in my gut, and make it almost to twenty before the furor dies down and we're left, dazed and partially blind, in our formed plastic seats.

The kids are thrilled, of course. They want to know when they'll get their candy, if they'll have their own individual bags or select from a big bag, if they'll have to share with the other kids. I'm still not entirely sure how I feel about this. At one point I swear I catch Lucy glancing desperately about the room, grin pasted to her face, trying to make eye contact with someone, *anyone* with a camera. Ellen and that other Virginia mom can talk all they want about world peace and greater understanding, but where I come from you're not supposed to do things for strangers with candy.

There is one thing, though, that I do like about all this: At almost every one of these mob scenes, if I take the time to step back and look around, inevitably I'll find a stooped old man off by himself, hands behind his back, neck bowed but eyes bright as he surveys the goings-on. Like the woman at the taxi stand, his eyes will do the count, dancing from blond head to blond head to chestnut head—and then he'll do it again, from head to head to head. Eventually he'll look up, hoping to share this joke with someone. Most times he'll catch me watching him, then bend his head toward the kids and raise his eyebrows. *Yours?*

I'll nod.

His lower lip will arch into a pinched smile and he'll do the math again, nodding at each head, then glancing at me as he raises first a pinkie, then a ring finger, then his middle digit. Finally he'll hold them all toward me, pressing his index finger down with his thumb. He'll shake the hand backward at me, questioning: *Three?*

I'll nod. *Yes. Three.*

He'll look again, as though contemplating. Then he'll do the count one more time, starting with Will and Jamie: one, two— and look at me: *Two boys?*

Yes.

And he'll glance at Lucy, nod at Ellen, and look back at me, raising a finger: *And one girl?*

I'll nod.

Then he might, depending on where we are, on what generation he's of, on how much English he knows, say "Happy family" in a thick accent. And I'll nod back. Yes. Two boys, one girl, that's the perfect mix. In China, that's a happy family.

At this point he'll just flat-out grin, gums bare, eyes bright, bobbing his head.

Someone once asked me if I thought this was in approval of my virility, an *hombre a hombre*, "Way to go!" kind of interaction.

I don't think so. There's nothing jarring or creepy about it, no thrust of the hips or leering winks.

Nor is there anger or jealousy, a low-simmering resentment of me or of us or of a government and a policy that leaves parents vulnerable to loneliness and discomfort in their old age. No, it's more like satisfaction: one human being looking at one family, an essentially random selection of chromosomes and split cells and social variables that could, in the worst-case scenario, eventually make us all but strangers to one another. But not now, and not yet, and maybe not ever. No, right now all this old man's eyes and nods and grins show me is this one human being looking at this one family, this one bald man and this one patient woman and these three mildly insane children, and saying, "Yes."

Just "Yes."

And "This is good."

CHAPTER 14

JADE

P art of traveling is, of course, collecting souvenirs, intimate
reminders of the places you've visited. Dim sum aside,
there's perhaps no article so associated with Hong Kong as jade.
You see it everywhere: in temples in the forms of Buddhas and
phoenixes, in shops in the shape of a dragon. Almost everyone
you meet on the street is wearing it in one form or another, usually as a necklace, most often trimmed in gold with a plethora
of flashy diamonds. It's not uncommon for a woman to buy a
pure jade bracelet and have it squeezed onto her wrist, there to
remain ever after. One of the staff in my department has a beautiful pinkish jade bracelet of this sort, so gorgeous I don't think I
ever bumped into her or spoke to her without noticing it circling
her wrist—this perfect, perfectly smooth piece of almost glass-
like jade that glows.

But buying jade can be tricky. There are lots of different
grades, and lots of cheap stuff out there—some of which has
been injected with dye to appear better than it really is. So when,
just before Christmas, a friend of mine offers to introduce me
to "this guy I know," I take him up on it. The two of us take the
26 light bus from our campus into nearby Tai Po and eventually
end up in a shop roughly twice the size of a phone booth. The
walls and ceilings are lined with red silk and the glass cases brim
with jade: necklaces, diamond-rimmed rings, bracelets, earrings.
Most of it is green, but there are other colors too: a light pinkish
lavender; an opaque white; a warm, butterscotchy yellow.

If you can imagine it, you can find it carved in jade.

Behind the counter stands a rather no-nonsense-looking man with thick hair lightly oiled and combed back over a wide forehead. His sleeves are rolled up in exact folds, and, truth be told, he looks less like a jeweler than a midlevel manager for an insurance agency. Everything about him is square: his face, his hands, his shoulders. Even his hair is square.

He nods curtly as we enter. Gavin, my colleague, explains that I'm looking for something for my wife. The problem, Gavin says, is that she doesn't like diamonds.

This is true: Ellen's never been one for bright and shiny things, generally preferring heavier stones and colors with more substance. This distaste for white sparkles is unfortunate, though, because as I've mentioned, jewelry in Hong Kong seems generally to be coated with diamonds.

"Diamonds no problem," the man says. "I give you diamonds."

Having come from a culture where grown men are willing to spend two-year's salary for a chip the size of an ant, I'm not even sure how to respond to this. In the end, I resort to my usual, incredibly articulate, "Huh?"

Square Man comes out from behind the counter and takes us to a display case on the wall. "You spend how much?"

I name a figure so low that Gavin actually laughs. The jeweler, though, doesn't look fazed, obviously used to cheap *gweilos* who don't actually love their wives. Reaching into the case, he pulls out a piece of jade roughly the size of a pinhead's newborn offspring. It's surrounded by rows of diamonds.

"My wife doesn't like diamonds," I say.

"I give you the diamonds," he replies. "No problem."

Clearly he believes I'm clever enough to bargain the price down—and that I have the cold, brass appendages necessary to make such a tactic possible on my part. I turn and face the case he's just opened. There's an interesting necklace there—a teardrop-shaped piece of jade dangling beneath an oval.

"How much is that one?"

He names a figure double what I'd sell any of my children for. I give a small laugh. "Really?"

He neither smiles nor frowns. I must look uncomfortable, though, because he takes pity on me and says, "You like this one?"

I nod, then point to the lone diamond strung between the two pieces of jade. "Except for this. Because my wife—"

"Doesn't like diamonds," he finishes, nodding. He says something to his wife, who's come out from an office in the back and is watching with mild amusement as her husband makes fools of the dumb white guys—admittedly, not that hard to do. She disappears into the back, remerging a moment later with a tiny manila envelope. Upending it on a piece of velvet, she pours out two small pieces of jade—one oval, one teardrop.

Square Man taps them with his fingers, arranging them to imitate the fifty-gadzillion-dollar necklace I'd admired in the case.

"Like this," he says. "I make you necklace."

I look at the stones. They are small, but very pretty. Unlike much of the jade I'd seen, they have layers to them, smoky clouds of darkness beyond darkness. You could fall into these stones, swim in them. I glance at the man. He meets my eyes, unsmiling.

"No diamonds," he says.

After that, there's some paperwork, the exchange of money and receipts. I don't know why, but toward the end of the encounter, Gavin hands the jeweler his card. Square Man examines it politely and nods. And then, again I don't know why, I hand him my card, too. He takes it in both hands, as you're supposed to, and examines it, again politely.

Then he freezes.

He looks at me. At the card again. Then at his wife. She comes to his shoulder, stands on her toes so that she can read it.

She looks at it. Then at me. Then at her husband. He returns her gaze for a long moment, then they both turn to me.

"You work at—" he says finally, naming my host university.

I nod.

"You are"—here he hesitates, pronouncing it carefully—"an *English* professor?"

I nod again. Gavin is watching all this, a mild, questioning look in his eyes.

Square Man almost smiles, but does not. His eyes are softer now, his brow creased.

"I have a daughter . . . " is how he begins. "Right now, she is studying English . . ."

The only problem, of course, is that I have three kids of my own. And a job. And several added consultancy-type things. And, of course, I spend most of my free time exploring Hong

Kong and greater Asia, trying to make the most of my limited stay. I'm busy. Really, really busy.

Plus, I have no idea how to tutor a sixteen-year-old girl for her first level exams. It's just not my audience of choice. Wannabe Hemingways? No problem. Frat boys reeking of urine from last night's bacchanalia? Yep. Self-conscious sorority girls? I can handle it.

But second-language acquisition? High school? High-stakes exam prep? Completely out of my depth.

I try to explain this as gently as I can. Husband and wife watch me with those sincere eyes, those suddenly earnest faces, and the words curl on my tongue. It takes me a while to figure out what's changed, why they appear so different all of a sudden.

But then I get it: They look vulnerable.

Keep in mind that in Hong Kong under the current system, only 33 percent of high school students are allowed to advance to their junior and senior years. And roughly only half of *those* students will be allowed to go on to university.

And keep in mind that in Hong Kong, a university degree is your ticket to any job you want. Because of this, parents in Hong Kong spend tens of thousands of dollars from the time their children are toddlers to prepare them for the exams that determine who will rise to the top and who will not. I once asked a Hong Kong Board of Education director if parents ever pulled their kids out of secondary school early in order to increase the family income.

"Never," he said.

I waited for some explanation, for more detail, for some qualifying "unless"—but he offered none. When he said "Never," what he meant was *never*.

All this flashes through my mind as I try to explain to these folks that I'm just not their man, that I'm not qualified, that I don't have the time. "I just can't do it," I say.

And then I remember the ETAs—the English Teaching Assistants: American university graduates who are given special

Fulbright scholarships to come to Hong Kong and help Chinese university students with their English skills. There are sixteen of them at my host institution.

"But," I say, holding up a finger, "I know someone who can."

Two weeks after Christmas, I bring Laura to the store. Laura is from Wyoming or Montana or some other place where folks wear cowboy boots without irony. She's smart as hell and one of the nicest people I've ever met. When I e-mailed a couple of the ETAs, saying I'd met a guy who had a daughter and this might be a chance to earn some extra traveling money—and oh, by the way, did I mention he's a jeweler?—Laura wrote back and said she was interested. She didn't seem fazed by the jewelry thing—she's not the type to go all gooshy-kneed at the mention of gemstones. Turns out she tutored a lot of immigrant children when she was in college and sees it as a great way to get to know another culture, to form relationships that actually make a difference in the world. So this is right up her alley.

Anyhow, when I show up with Laura and her wide smile and bright face and brain the size and power of a 9030 series John Deere tractor (or whatever the hell it is they drive in Wyoming), Mr. Cheng (for indeed, that is Square Man's real name) calls his daughter back at their flat. In a matter of minutes, she's there, shaking hands with her new tutor. After some small talk, Laura and the daughter begin to discuss what sort of lessons they might have and when a good time to have them might be.

Eventually the daughter asks how much it will cost, and when Laura mentions a price higher than I'd anticipated, I glance at Mr. and Mrs. Cheng. There is a beat. Then the daughter repeats the price, this time in Cantonese. Another beat, smaller this time, before Mr. Cheng nods.

My parents come into town after that, and between them and work and the three kids, I forget all about the Chengs. Then my mother sees Ellen's necklace and we decide it can't hurt to go over and take a look, see if there's anything that catches her eye.

Cheng is lifting the corrugated iron gate covering the entrance as we arrive. When he sees me he gives a quick nod and says hello. Letting us in, he flips on the light and takes off his jacket.

"My parents," I say, gesturing, in case he thought maybe they were random white folks in their sixties whom I'd met roaming the streets of Tai Po. He gives a brief, dry, smile, nods again. Then he looks at me and gestures toward a small velvet-lined box holding six jade discs, each with a hole in the center.

"You like one?" he says.

I lean forward. They're smooth and green, polished to a shine. I've seen discs like this before, worn around the neck on a leather cord.

"They're very pretty," I say.

My mother is glancing around, trying to get her bearings amid all that glass and jade and sparkle.

Cheng nods, gestures again. "Take which one you like."

I straighten. "Oh no. I couldn't."

"Please," he says.

"No," I repeat. "Really. That's very kind, but you don't have to do that."

Just then my mother gestures at something in one of the cases. "Could I see this, please?"

Cheng pulls out his keys and slides back the glass. My dad and I drift toward the wall display where the gadzillion-dollar necklace that inspired Ellen's gift is still on display. I tell my dad about it, letting my eyes drift over the rest of the shelf. Halfway down is a small droplet of jade set in a tasteful bed of flat-cut diamonds. I'd seen it weeks before, but the bling, I knew, would put

Ellen off, so I'd ignored it. My brother though, had e-mailed me
to keep an eye out for something for his wife, so once Cheng is
done helping my mom, I gesture toward the piece.

"How much is this one?"

He comes out from behind the counter. Drawing the piece
out, he shows it to me. "This," he says, "is very good jade."

Setting it on the counter, he rifles through some papers and
pulls out an 8" × 10" photograph. It shows a large piece of rock,
three times the size of a gravestone, veined with white.

"Burmese jade," he tells me, tapping the picture with his
square fingernail.

I hold up the small necklace, then glance at the table of rock.
"This? From that?"

He nods.

I looked at the droplet again. It's very, very pretty—elaborate,
but tasteful. I take my finger and turn over the small tag hanging
from the string.

And nearly fall over.

Its costs even more than the gadzillion-dollar piece—half
again as much, in fact, nearly a month's salary for Ellen and me.

"Oh," I say, and put it down. Quickly.

Cheng sees what's happening and picks it back up again.
"No," he says. He pushes the stone toward me, then picks up
his calculator. Thinking for a minute, he taps out some numbers
and shows them to me.

I look. Then look again. Then flip over the tag to make sure
I'd read it right the first time. Then hold up my hands.

"No," I say. "You can't do that."

"I make it myself," he says. "It okay."

I look at him. He's a very handsome man, his face large with
a fine nose. Small wrinkles crease the browned skin beside his
eyes. This strikes me as odd, because he really doesn't smile
much, though I can see now that change of expression for him
means a glow in the eyes, a twitch of the mouth. He's very much

like my grandmother that way, a woman who never told me she loved me, but whose love I never once doubted.

In Xi'an at a jade market.

"No," I say again. "You can't do that."

"For you," he says, "this is the price."

This, of course, is the line that you hear everywhere when you're traveling in Asia. Peddlers in Vietnam are shameless about using it, all but winking as they say it, letting you know that they know that you know it's a joke—and that they don't mind and you shouldn't either.

Cheng, though, is not joking. The price he's shown me is well under half—*well* under half—of the marked price. Still more than any piece of jewelry I've ever bought before—but even so . . .

"No," I say. "That's very kind of you, but you don't have to do that."

He picks up the stone, raises it to eye level, tilting it so that we can both see into it. "This jade very good. *Very* good. Top quality. But there," he says, pointing. "See there? Little flaw. Tiny."

I peer closely. I can see what he's talking about—a small, darkish speck, like a gnat caught in green amber.

He takes his hand down. Looks at me. "Is very beautiful."

He isn't kidding. If I'd thought the necklace was pretty before, now, after looking into it and seeing that universe of green with one small planet floating—now, I think the piece is gorgeous.

I have, as anyone who's met me for more than five minutes undoubtedly knows, an unlimited capacity for screwing up a good thing. The tools in my arsenal are varied and well maintained, honed, oiled, locked, and loaded. I can say the wrong thing, sigh so that it sounds like a snort, roll my eyes in a bizarre attempt to express gratitude, crack an ill-timed joke, or freeze my brain by overanalyzing.

Of all these, the one I'm closest to at this particular moment is the last. Standing there, looking at Cheng, looking at that necklace, looking at that ridiculously low price flashing on the calculator, all I can think is *I don't deserve this.* If anything, this is a gift that should be going to Laura. After all, she's the one who is tutoring his daughter because I couldn't be bothered. Geez, the guy is rewarding me for being too arrogant and too busy and too preoccupied to help with the education of a sixteen-year-old girl.

Somehow, though, this time I have the cognitive wiring necessary to recognize a gesture of genuine—if not friendship—at least kindness. Just this once, I find the intelligence to accept the offering of a man who is honest enough to show me the one flaw in a perfect stone—and then to reassure me that, indeed, this makes it just that much more perfect.

I look at Cheng, then at the jade tear.

"It's very beautiful," I say.

He nods.

"Thank you," I say. "You're a very good man."

His chin lowers slightly, and the skin stirs around the corner of his eyes. For a moment there—just a moment—he may even smile.

CHAPTER 15

GRIEF AND
THE VILLAGE

We didn't know there was a problem until Will told us Thomas had left school.

"What?" said Ellen, from Lucy's bed. It was late in the evening, and we were kissing our two eldest good night.

"He went to the Japanese school," said Will.

Ellen and I contemplated this for a moment. We'd been in Hong Kong for six months and had thought the little international school we sent the kids to was pretty much perfect. And we liked Thomas. He was a little weird, yes, with an IQ somewhere in the low 900s and shockingly white-blond hair. He'd once spent an entire afternoon at our house buzzing a toy plane around the living room, pretending it was carrying Kim Jong-Il—but he was sweet, and we were sorry we wouldn't see him anymore.

"Why did he leave?" Ellen asked.

"I don't know."

Our daughter piped up. "Because Trevor and George were picking on him."

"Really?"

From Ellen's inflection I could tell she was thinking the same thing I was: Just how bad does "picking on" have to be to drive a kid to another school?

We found out soon enough.

Ellen was coming home with Will on the 26 light bus one afternoon when Will mentioned that Trevor and George were teasing him.

"What about?" said Ellen.

"Reading books."

"Why do they tease you about that?"

"I don't know."

"What do they say?"

"Well, Trevor will say, 'Will, what would you do if you couldn't read?'"

"That doesn't sound so bad."

"He says it over and over again—like, one hundred times."

When Ellen told me about this, I went to Will with a simple solution: "Next time he does that," I said, "ask him what he would do if he couldn't ask the same stupid question over and over again."

Will laughed. He was doing his homework, sitting at the dining room table, tapping his pencil. But then he stopped laughing, and as he looked back down at his work, his lips stayed fixed in a smile longer than they should have.

Now there are two things you should know.

First, there was a day, maybe seven years ago, when I was standing knee-deep in the public swimming pool in our hometown back in the States. Will was three, a little bit of a scaredy cat, and he was moving cautiously into waist-deep water. And there was another boy, maybe a year older, who was pushing Will, or taking a toy from him, or splashing him, or something that was making him cry.

And I was wishing I had a thick wooden plank.

I don't mean to say that, had I actually been holding a two-by-four in my hands, I would have belted the other kid. I wouldn't have. I haven't hit anyone since I was in the fifth grade, and I didn't enjoy it much then. What I'm saying is that right then, at that moment standing in that swimming pool, I really wanted to hurt this kid, really wanted to inflict on him whatever pain I could to stop him from making my own kid cry, and holding that plank would have made me feel a heck of a lot better, even if I wasn't allowed to use it.

"Wow," I said to Ellen that night after we'd put the kids to bed. "Being a parent is a powerful thing."

She gave me a quizzical look. Ellen has always been very clear about how much she loves our children. She puts it this way: "Someone comes up to you and says, 'We can either cut off your arm or hurt your kid,' you say, 'Here's my arm.' Someone comes up to you and says, 'We can either cut off your arm or hurt your spouse,' and you say (insert long pause): 'What exactly do you mean by *hurt*?'"

"It changes you," I said to her. I considered adding, "Today I thought about belting a four-year-old with a plank," but decided against it, figuring if I wanted to be institutionalized, there were much more enjoyable ways of going about it.

"You're just figuring this out?"

"Hey," I said. "I knew it changed you; I just hadn't realized it *changed* you."

The second thing you should know is that Trevor used to be homeschooled by his mother, a lovely and kind Malaysian woman. His father, who's originally from England, had a high-pressure job and couldn't be at home very much. The arrangement worked well for them. They had a nice family, Trevor, his two sisters, their mom, their dad.

Then last spring Trevor's mom was diagnosed with cancer. And Trevor and his sisters were sent to school.

Trevor struggled some. He was smart, but not necessarily school smart. He was good-looking and charismatic. And sometimes it's hard for a ten-year-old boy to know how to handle all that attention.

In the fall his mom went to Malaysia for treatment. And then she came home. Trevor attended Will's birthday party on the fifth of December carrying that unwrapped present: a professional-quality sketchpad and colored pencils.

Three weeks later, just after Christmas, Trevor's mom died.

At first we didn't worry much about the teasing. This is what kids do, after all, and Will was just being his father's son: simultaneously thin-skinned and mildly self-righteous. At one point I suggested that maybe it wouldn't be the worst thing in the world if he spent a few recesses outside developing his social skills, but other than that, we just assumed all of this would go away.

Then one night Ellen received an e-mail from Will's teacher. "There was an incident at school today," she'd written. "Will got a little teary-eyed."

I glanced up from Ellen's laptop. "Did you know about this?"

She shook her head. "He mentioned something about having a bad day but didn't go into any detail."

I went back to the e-mail. "It seems the kids are playing 'excluding games,'" it read. "This is not unusual for kids this age. I'll keep an eye on it, and I've been praying about it."

I straightened. Ellen and I looked at each other. We were quiet for a good two minutes.

"Those bastards," I said.

Ellen rolled her eyes. "They're just kids."

"You're right," I said. "Little kid bastards." I looked back at the e-mail. "Praying?"

"I know."

"How about instead of praying, you throw the little creeps out of school?"

Some people, I sometimes fear, just have "mock me" carved into their genes. Along with "I'm desperate to fit in," "I'll never be as cool as you," and "I won't fight back." Other kids seem to wear cool like a leather jacket: They can afford it, they look good in it, and they know it.

I was not one of the latter. And although it's true that I did my fair share of picking on kids who were further down the ladder than I was (sorry, Ron—and I really mean that), I spent most of my childhood on the receiving end of the "kick me" sign. There was Jim Thorn in seventh grade who pinned me down under his dad's pool table and poured a bottle of breath freshener down my throat, then told me I couldn't sit with my friends at the basketball game. There was Bill Travis, the quarterback of the football team, who walked past me in the halls imitating my speech impediment: "There goeth Paul Hanthtedt!" There was Todd Bodner who was my best friend all summer and who then, after one particularly brutal football game, spent most of the ride home leading a variation on that old chant "Yee-i-yee-i-yee-i-yo!"—to which the rest of the bus full of fifteen-year-olds replied "Yee-i-yee-i-yee-i-yo!" I don't remember what the next line was supposed to be, but Todd—who'd spent a week with my family at our cabin that summer—changed it to, "Hanstedt is a homo!"

I considered explaining to him that the rhythm of that line was all off, that it needed another syllable, an "e" perhaps, or even just a long pause. Not surprisingly, though, I found this difficult to do with my face fiercely red and something—not shame, or embarrassment, but closer to confusion and sadness—dripping from every cell of my body.

I suppose it's also worth noting that in addition to having a lisp (or, as Bill would say, "Lithp"), I was a pastor's kid and a major-league smartass. I like to think that it was the first two that garnered me so much harassment, but the fact is, it was probably my sharp tongue that got me so many atomic wedgies and the occasional black eye. No matter how hard I tried, I just couldn't resist telling the biggest kid in class that he was dumber than most warts on a toad's ass.

Seriously: I'd be lying on my back in the locker room after football practice, getting my brains drummed out by a fullback who thought I'd given him a late hit, and I'd find myself thinking: *Most. That's pretty good; he was dumb, yes, but smarter than some warts. Just not all.*

Making everything worse for Will was the fact that Trevor wasn't the only one picking on him. George was, too. George, who'd been to our flat for play dates, who'd shared his toys, who was otherwise a smart, kind, well-behaved kid. George, whose mother hadn't actually died, giving him an excuse to be a prick. George, who'd been Will's friend, not just his acquaintance.

This same George was now in the habit of telling Will that he was annoying. Every time Will would come up to him on the playground, or try to talk to him during class, George would say to my son, "Will, you're so annoying. Why are you so annoying?"

Complicating matters was the fact that looming on the horizon was the school trip to Beijing: twenty-nine ten- and eleven-year-olds together nonstop for five days, on buses, at meals, in hotel rooms.

"Maybe he shouldn't go," I said to Ellen one night.

She paused over the dishes. I waited, but she didn't speak.

"It's one thing," I said, "when he can come home after school and tell us what happened. At least then, we can talk about it and hug him. It's another thing when he's stuck with those little jerks twenty-four hours a day."

Ellen shook her head. "Let's just wait. Let's see what happens."

Things kept getting worse. There was the day at school when all the kids were in groups creating ad campaigns for well-known products. Will's group picked Adidas, and Will ended up being the spokesman. He'd barely opened his mouth, though, when Trevor and George started shouting, "Adidas sucks! Nike is better!"

"I tried to tell them I knew that," Will (who couldn't care less about shoes) said to me later. "I tried to tell them I didn't pick Adidas, but they wouldn't listen."

Then there was the day in Mandarin class when they were waiting for the teacher, and Trevor said, "I hate Mandarin. Who here likes it?" Will was the only one who raised his hand—as Trevor knew he would.

There were some good days, of course. Will came home one Monday afternoon with an invitation to George's party.

"That's great!" we said.

He grinned. "I know."

"We need to get him a present," Ellen said. "When is it?"

Will flipped the invitation over, looked at the date. "Friday."

"This Friday?" Ellen said. She gave me a look.

Will nodded. He was still grinning.

When the bullying did persist, I have to admit, it involved some pretty low-level stuff—no physical violence or lunch-money shakedowns. But day after day after day at a small school where there are only fifteen kids in each class and you're away from your best friends in the States ("My real friends," Will had taken to calling them), and when you're only nine—well, in a situation like that, low-level and high-level is a moot distinction.

Eventually it all built up to the point where, one day on the bus ride home from school, I felt obliged to ask Will if he wanted to skip the Beijing trip.

He didn't look at me at first, just kept his eyes straight ahead, his lashes fluttering with concentration. Then he stole a glance at me and said simply, "Yes."

We raised all this with his teacher a few days later, after a meeting with all the parents to discuss the trip. She tried to reassure us, mentioning the low student-to-faculty ratio, how they'd all keep an eye on Trevor. He'd been in trouble lately, she said, and there'd been talk of putting him in a room with a chaperone. We left feeling somewhat better, but still nagged by doubts.

Outside, we ran into George's mom.

"Thanks for inviting Will to George's party," Ellen said. "He's really excited about it."

"Sorry it was so late," George's mom said. "I asked George a couple of times if he wanted to invite him, but he kept saying he wasn't sure Will would enjoy those kinds of activities."

"What activities?" I asked.

"Nerf gun wars."

I looked at my shoes, dug one toe into the earth. Will loved Nerf guns.

"He's fine with that stuff," Ellen said. "It'll be great. He's really excited."

That night, at home, I said, "We have to call her."

George's mom was smart and caring and insightful in the ways of the human heart. When the stuff with Thomas had started going on months ago, she'd understood it all. "What Trevor is doing is textbook grieving," she'd told Ellen. "He's pushing everyone away as hard as he can, trying to see who'll leave next."

"She would want us to tell her," I said to Ellen now. "She'd be horrified if she knew what was going on."

"I know. I'll do it tomorrow."

She didn't have to. At 9:30 the next morning, Ellen's cell phone rang.

"I'm so sorry," George's mom said. "When you said Will loved Nerf, I started to wonder, and then Louise"—her daughter—"mentioned that some kids had been picking on Will, and it all clicked. We've already talked to George. He feels terrible about the way he and Trevor have been treating Will and he's really, really sorry."

We were so relieved.

I picked Will up after the birthday party. "How was it?" I asked as we strolled down to the taxi stand.

He made an indefinite sound. "It was okay."

I looked at him. That thing below my ribs that tightens up at moments like this tightened up hard.

"What happened?"

"They played soccer."

I waited.

"George and Trevor divided us into two teams: 'popular' and 'unpopular.'"

My brother Mark avoided a lot of the bullying that I encountered. Two years older, quiet, and with a better sense of who he was, he kept a lower profile and generally stayed out of trouble.

Then one day when I was thirteen, John O'Hare—a kid in my grade—was goaded by his friends to pick a fight with Mark. John was small and wiry, and though he didn't have that mythic Irish temper, he certainly did have the ability to turn his fury on and off like a spigot. By noon the next day, everyone I knew was talking about how John would beat my brother to a pulp. By the end of seventh period, the buzz in the halls was so loud it actually rattled the fire alarms.

When the 3:15 bell rang, everyone raced to their lockers, grabbed jackets, and poured outside. In minutes, there was a circle of maybe a hundred people in the street beside the school. In the middle were John—small, dark-haired, thrilled to show how tough he was—and my brother, bespectacled, pale, and freckled, clad in the Toughskins our mom made us wear until we were in high school.

"What are you looking at, Four Eyes?" John asked my brother, even though what Mark was looking at was obvious: this weirdly angry, weirdly cocky thirteen-year-old standing in front of him unable to think up a better insult than "Four Eyes."

"Take those damn glasses off," John said.

Mark just stared. He's smart as hell, but like the rest of my family, only good at insults two hours later and out of the presence of the person we want to cut down.

Then John punched him. In the face. Mark's glasses went skidding across the pavement.

"What are you going to do now? Huh?" John asked my brother. So Mark hit him.

Hard.

John took a step back. Then he came in swinging from both sides. Mark took the blows, flinched some, but began moving closer and closer, hitting John in the head over and over again. Hard. Very hard.

I don't remember how long it went on—maybe forty seconds, maybe less—but I do remember how it ended: with John in a fetal position on his knees in the slush, face in his hands, crying. With Mark walking over to his glasses and picking them up. With me walking home maybe a hundred yards behind my brother, not quite sure what to think.

It was the first time I'd seen anyone actually fight back—and win.

Riding to the airport with Will before the Beijing trip, I felt sick to my stomach, as if I were tossing him into a pit of lions. No, as if I were pouring steak sauce on him, loosening his joints, rubbing herbs and spices under his skin, and *then* tossing him in.

The teachers had given us more reassurances, of course. They would keep an eye on everyone, they said. Really they would. But when we got to the airport, I saw how futile this was. Trevor and George were sitting on their suitcases, surrounded by a gang of fawning nine- and ten-year-olds. You could regulate them, yes, but only so much.

Will approached the group, hands in his pockets, shoulders stiff.

"Hey, George," he said. "Hey, Trevor."

George gave him a glance. Then he turned to Trevor and said something quietly. Trevor laughed, and the two of them fell into conversation.

To be nine, and to go to Beijing without your parents!

Will just stood there.

I'd like to say my emotions at that moment were complex: fear, anger, anxiety, confusion all rolling together. But that would be a lie. My feelings right then were pure as spring water and boiling hot. Had I been holding that proverbial two-by-four, a dozen security guards would have had to tackle me and hold me down to keep me from using it. The jerks. The morons. The little shits.

I watched as the room assignments were read. When Trevor realized what'd happened, that he'd been segregated from George, from all his friends, from, well, *everyone,* he laughed a dry, sarcastic cough that said he didn't care.

His dad, though, was also there, also watching. He was a handsome man with thinning hair, an athletic frame draped in a pinstriped suit. His hands were in his pockets as he watched his son, a smile fixed on his face—though it was hard to tell how much of it was a smile, and how much was fixed. He listened as the assignments were read off. Watched his son laugh carelessly. Watched as Trevor and George leaned toward one another and began to whisper.

I got distracted then, I'm not sure by what—perhaps my own anger—but when I looked up, Trevor and his father had walked off by themselves. The father's hand was on the boy's shoulder, the boy's hands in his pockets, echoing exactly his father's posture from a moment ago.

I watched as the father leaned in, spoke to his son. I saw Trevor nod, saw his shoulders hunch, then fall. His father patted him on the back, lightly. Trevor nodded again.

Standing there in the airport, watching the two of them huddled together, I suddenly thought of a news story I'd seen not long after Will was born. There'd been an outbreak of violence in the West Bank and there was footage of a father and son cowering in a corner of cement below a stoop, bullets ringing around them. The dad was on the inside, his son beneath his arm as the two of them cringed at the rattle of weapons fire.

In the next shot, the boy's body was limp, draped over his father's knee. The man's face was ragged with grief, his mouth watery and wide, his eyes torn with loss. Watching him, I kept wondering, *Why? Why didn't he pull his son to the inside, shelter him with his body?*

It's meaningless, I know, what we'd do for our children. Yes, we'd cut off our arms. Yes, we'd throw ourselves in front of freight trains. Yes, we'd suffer, willingly, a thousand slow, nail-pulling tortures. But it wouldn't matter. Bullets fly. We can't see them coming. We can't predict the angles. We can't stop them.

Watching Trevor stroll back to his friends, I found myself struggling, my head still fire-hot, but my insides melting, wishing I could—wishing I were capable of—saying something, anything, to make it better, to put all the pieces back into a whole. But what do you say to a kid for whom all metaphors fail—whose heart is more than broken, whose world is more than turned upside down? What do you say to a ten-year-old who's stood before a coffin staring at the woman who is—who was—his mother, a woman who three days earlier was living and breathing and told him she loved him? Who six months ago hugged him in the dark and kissed his forehead and said it was going to be all right, that they would beat this thing? Who a year ago pulled him into her arms after she opened her Christmas gift, laughing into his ear that she loved it, that she loved him, her hair tickling his cheek as he inhaled the nylon scent of her new sweater, never thinking—not ever, not even once—that he wouldn't hug her this same way the next Christmas, and the Christmas after that, and the Christmas after that.

What do you say?

You say I'm sorry.

You say it's okay.

You say anything you can. And you keep saying it.

CHAPTER 16

LOK SAY

I'm walking across campus with Will and Lucy when they point to a long black poster set between two buildings. They say something I don't catch.

"Huh?" I'm tired and hot. It's late May and the mild spring is beginning to give way to the sort of weather that glues your shirt to your body the second you walk out the door. All I want to do is get back to the flat, crank the AC, and lie on the couch with a remote control in one hand and something cold and wet in the other.

"It's a six," Lucy says. She points to a large Chinese character in white paint. Then she moves her finger. "And a four."

"Yeah," says Will. "A six and a four. But just them. It doesn't mean anything."

"Maybe it's sixty-four," I say, leaning my body in the direction of home, hoping they'll get the hint. But they stand their ground.

"No," says Will. "Then it would be six-ten-four."

"It doesn't make any sense," Lucy says, echoing her brother.

But it does, of course. Earlier that same month, the members of my faculty office were planning a meeting to coordinate a number of task force working groups. In total, fifteen people would need to be invited, and it was turning out to be difficult to find a day and time that worked for everyone.

"What about the second week of June?" said K.S., the acting director of my program.

"I have a two-day workshop," I told him. "How about the first week?"

We all looked at our planners.

"The first?" said William.

"I have a practicum," K.S. said.

"The second?"

I shook my head. "At a conference at Poly. What about the fourth? My book is blank on that day."

William's head shot up. He stared at me. K.S. actually laughed. "You can come that day," he said, "but I won't be here."

Twenty-one years ago I was in England, winding down the second year of my stint as a rock star in the nearly-almost-but-not-quite-even-semi-famous alternative rock quartet, Don't Kick the Baby. My high school friend Steve was visiting that spring, and he and I were having a grand old time, going up to St. Aidan's College to flirt with English girls and drink beer, then stumbling down to the city center in the wee hours to stuff our faces with greasy kebabs and raw onions.

Evenings, we'd sit in front of the TV watching the news and eating take-out Chinese. The Ayatollah Khomeini died at the end of May that year, and I remember Steve and I leaping up and actually slapping high fives, sort of a bizarre response for two would-be hippie peace freaks.

And there was this thing in China, these students protesting in this square we'd never heard of before. They'd been there for more than a month already, and every night the crowds were getting bigger, the speeches more fiery. And the government wasn't doing anything about it.

It was, I have to say, magical to watch. There was this sense, very tangible, that something big was going to happen, that the government was about to cave, that everything in China would change. This was the period of Glasnost, after all, when Gorbachev was rewriting the rules in the

Soviet Union. And there was Lech Walesa in Poland, and the
Solidarity movement. Quietly, but steadily, the world was
changing—oppressive regimes were coming down. The world
was becoming a better place.

Early during our stay in Hong Kong, our neighbors Anita
and Colin took us to Victoria Park, down on Hong Kong Island,
to celebrate the Mid-autumn Festival. Glowing red lanterns
hung everywhere and families wandered from stage to stage,
taking in the Peking Opera, the shadow puppets, the traditional
dance shows. We ate popcorn, the first we'd had since coming to
Asia, slightly burned and sticky with sugar.

"We do this in the fall," Anita said. "And then in June we
bring you back."

We grinned. "Bring us back? Why? What's in June?"

Anita, who usually smiles, stopped. She looked at us closely.
"For June Fourth." She didn't actually say the words, but her
voice implied *of course.*

We must have stared for a moment too long.

Her voice dropped in pitch, but not in volume. "Tiananmen
Square," she said. "Tiananmen Square."

So on June 4, 2010, our family piles into Anita's car, along
with her husband Colin and their two kids, to head back
down to Victoria Park. We'd told our kids about the massacre,
explaining that the students were unarmed, that they were protesting for more open communication with the government,
for freedoms that we don't even think about in the United
States—like, for instance, the right to sit around the dinner
table and talk about the government. We tell them that this is
a somber event, that they should take it very seriously, that we
won't tolerate any acting up.

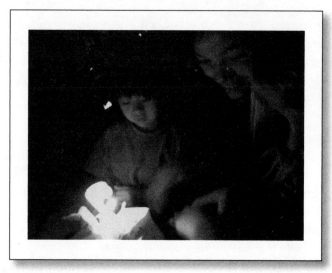

There are very few situations in which I'm not inclined to make
a joke. This is one of them: lighting candles in commemoration
of Tiananmen Square.

On the drive to the Island, Anita talks about the original vigil,
twenty-one years ago, about how nearly 20 percent of Hong
Kong's population showed up, spontaneously, the night after the
massacre, protesting the slaughter of students by soldiers of their
own country. Anita is not one to show emotion, and she does
not get choked up as she speaks of these events. Rather, you can
tell that she's proud of Hong Kong, of how this tiny region that
would soon be co-opted by China refused to ignore this blatant
act of unjustified violence.

Indeed, defiance seems to be the mood *du jour*. When we
get to the park, there's Canto-rock blasting from a huge pair
of speakers. We're directed into a roped-off area in a slightly
damp field. Over the trees and in every direction you can see
that famous Hong Kong skyline, Lego-block apartment buildings stretching up like fingers, flickering with the blue lights of
hundreds of televisions. Opposite them stand dozens of glass-
and-steel bank buildings and corporate offices, many of them
trimmed with flashing neon lights.

"Where are we?" I ask Anita. There's no stage, no microphones, no video screen—just grass and people and a lot of speakers. "Is this the main venue?"

She shakes her head. "Overflow," she says. We arrived too late. The main event is off to the right, in front of us, near a stadium. "There," she tells me, "there's a stage and microphones and huge screens."

I'm about to ask her another question when there's a shift in the music blaring from the loudspeakers. The pounding bass and grinding guitars pull back a little, and over them, digitally mixed, we hear the rapid fire of machine guns, the grind of tank engines, the whine of sirens. It's a sampling, of course, and the song is a protest song—of course. Once that tune finishes, another begins, less bass-and-drum heavy, but its to-hell-with-you tone is evident even for people like me who can't understand the words.

And then the speakers begin. It's all in Cantonese and Putonghua, the Beijing dialect of Mandarin, which seems funny to me— why use the language of the oppressors? But Anita tells me that mainlanders come down to Hong Kong for the commemoration each year, that remembering the massacre in the People's Republic isn't so much illegal as just not done. This matches something one of my colleagues from the mainland had told me earlier in the day as we were strolling past those black banners on campus.

"Does anyone up there discuss what happened?" I'd asked.

The words weren't even out of my mouth before Anna cut in. "We do not talk about this. No one talks about this." She paused, staring straight ahead as we walked. Then she said, "At Peking University, every year people show up on campus around this time to see who is discussing it. No one does."

That very morning, the *South China Morning Post* had carried a story about witnesses to the massacre. It described how, over the years, they'd struggled to cope with what they'd seen—legs crushed by tanks, brains splattered onto the hands and clothes of university classmates—having no outlet to express their anger. Many, the newspaper said, protested by pulling on the same black shirts they'd worn that night in 1989; others simply wore white, the traditional color of mourning in China.

Now, tonight, we sit on a sheet of narrow plastic Anita brought to protect us from the damp ground and listen to the mother of one of those killed as she tells her story. Her voice is elastic—not quite lively, but gentle and rounded, restrained but full of emotion. Behind her plays a single *erhu*, the traditional two-stringed instrument that can sound like an Appalachian fiddle or a mournful ghost calling from the salt marshes. During this year, I've come to appreciate the *erhu*, but listening to it now, bending its way behind this woman's voice, I can feel moisture gathering beneath my eyelids, and I realize I love this instrument, and will probably never hear it again without thinking of this place, this murmuring crowd, the glowing skyscrapers around the park.

The woman finishes, and then there's another protest song, more mainstream pop this time, with a rousing chorus that, each time it occurs, seems to swell the collective chest of the crowd. There's a photographer in front of us, a lanky kid with long hair and an oversized T-shirt, and as he focuses his massive lens on the goings on, I can see his mouth stretch with each rounded "O" and pull wide with every "E" sound. All around us, we can hear people singing heartily, lustily, almost joyfully—voices filled with that same note of pride that Anita's held in the car.

They pass out candles. Our kids are fascinated. They drip wax onto their fingers, into the grass, onto the plastic, trying to build wrinkled castles out of the melt. The next speaker is the wife of a dissident who was jailed for railing against the government after a recent round of earthquakes and collapsed buildings in China. After her, someone younger speaks earnestly and eloquently for a while, then breaks into a call and response, shouting phrases to the crowd, who holler back 60,000 times louder. Every time this occurs, in the bare second between the shouts of the crowd and the next call of the speaker, we can hear the booming echo off the buildings around the park, all those voices rolling off glass and steel, sounding not quite human, but unquestionably holy.

A sea of candles at Victoria Park. I don't think Hong Kong will ever forget Tiananmen Square.

It has to be hard to be a Hong Konger when it comes to China. On the one hand, being linked to the PRC is like being the prom date of the coolest guy on campus. Everyone knows China is rising. Everyone knows what's coming will almost undoubtedly be China's century. It has the resources, it has the labor, it has a strong centralized government that can keep businesses in line and the economy under control, and that seems to be making the right decisions, at least for the moment, as you can see from the fact that China's economy has grown between 6 and 10 percent every year for the last decade. For the most part it was unscathed by the banking crisis of 2008 and 2009. And it only knows the concept of trade imbalance from the grip end of the pistol.

Who wouldn't want to dance with that guy?

But then there is Tiananmen Square. Maybe it would be different if the Chinese government demonstrated some regret for what, in the People's Republic, is simply referred to (if it is referred to at all) as "the 1989 incident." Almost immediately after the death of Mao, for example, the Cultural Revolution was declared an unconditional failure, and Mao's wife and her cronies were prosecuted for its execution. Twenty-plus years after Tiananmen, however, there's no move to revise history, no attempt on the part of the government to redeem itself by admitting overzealousness in attacking unarmed students with tanks, crushing them into the pavement as they attempted to flee on their bicycles. Indeed, almost the opposite seems true. Consider the recently published diaries of Li Peng, the premier during Tiananmen, in which he says, repeatedly, that he was prepared to die in order to stop the protesters.

Statistics are always difficult to read, particularly when you're trying to discern motive, but it's worth noting that between 1990 and 1994, the number of people emigrating from Hong Kong never dropped below 50,000 per annum. This is almost ten times higher than the rate prior to 1989. That said, it should also be mentioned that there are those in Hong Kong who are unapologetic about their big brother to the north. In an attempt during the spring of 2010 to embarrass the PRC into allowing Hong Kong full democracy, a number of liberal politicians resigned from their posts, forcing midterm election as a *de facto* referendum on one person, one vote. Turnout for the maneuver was so low that even democracy-leaning supporters declared it a fiasco.

There's more music. The organizers have passed out programs with words to all the songs and translations of everything that's in Putonghua. A beloved dissident, dying now of cancer, speaks; the crowd roars its approval (albeit in a reserved, Hong Kong kind of way).

Then a student from Chinese University steps up to the microphone.

The Chinese University of Hong Kong, founded in 1949 by scholars and thinkers kicked out of the mainland by the Red Army, is one of the top three universities in Hong Kong, ranked seventieth, more or less, internationally. It's a beautiful place, nestled on and around a range of mountains overlooking Tolo Harbour, in the northeastern territories. The students there are smart and engaged. Strolling across campus even on a Friday night you'll see clusters of them walking arm in arm, laughing in the dark.

And the students there—like the founding fathers of the university—are politically active. Earlier in the week they had asked the university council to place the Goddess of Democracy—a twenty-foot statue commemorating the sacrifice of the Tiananmen students—on campus following tonight's vigil. The council, led by a university president who is largely seen as pro-Beijing, declined.

"The University," he argued, "should not align itself with actions or activities which project a political position that would compromise the university's principle of political neutrality."

Besides being one butt-ugly sentence, this declaration is patently absurd: Disallowing political activity is itself a political action. And the crowd knows it. When the young man from Chinese U repeats these words at the vigil, tens of thousands of voices roar with laughter.

Between speeches and songs, the announcers keep telling everyone how big the crowd has grown: 60,000 people, 90,000 people, 100,000 people. The police have now closed down streets to allow the overflow. The police started to turn people away, but have changed their minds. The police now estimate 150,000 people!

It is a night of numbers. I realize, for instance, that the protesters who were killed were the same age as Steve and I were that spring in England, that had they lived they might now be stockbrokers and literature professors and proud parents of their own children. How this could have eluded me at the time is bizarre. Perhaps because China was so remote from Northern England. Perhaps because what they were doing was so much braver than anything I would have considered, have considered, or likely will ever consider.

Amidst all the Cantonese, I recognize a few words, but only a few: "*Lok say*," for instance, both words low in tone, the second sharp and short. Six. Four. Of course. The numbers Lucy and Will saw and couldn't decipher: June 4, the sixth month, the fourth day.

And there's this: *yi sup yut li*. Twenty-one years. Twenty-one years ago.

And this: 2047, the year China takes over Hong Kong for good. It's a number I don't hear mentioned, but one I don't doubt is on everyone's mind, even if at the back, lingering like an uninvited guest. I'm sure, too, that there's a quiet calculus that's occurred in the minds of the parents in the crowd, the people who, like us, have children in their laps playing with the softened wax of their candles. This calculus begins with the child's age, then adds thirty-seven, the number of years until the handover. By this math, Enya, in Anita's lap, will be forty-three when Hong Kong becomes fully a part of the PRC, exactly Ellen's age now. And Angus, Enya's brother, will not even be forty.

Then the math continues, adding thirty-seven to the ages of the parents. Thus, I would be eighty-one, likely not around, and Anita, younger than me, would be in her late seventies. And, of course, this second calculus has less to do with self-preservation than with the desire, projected forty years out, to protect the wee ones sitting now in their laps, holding their fingers above the flames, trying not to get burned, trying to keep safe, as a nation remembers the night when its own leaders sent tanks to spill the blood of young men and women whose only fault was to ask for a better life.

CHAPTER 17

BLOG WIDOW

It's April and we're at Jade Dragon Snow Mountain, just outside Lijiang in southwestern China. Jade Dragon is at the very eastern tip of the Himalayas, and it looks like it: stark black rock dusted with snow, alternately hidden by clouds and glaring in bright sunlight. Even from a distance, it's foreboding.

But we're not looking at it from a distance. No. We're up on the mountain, all five of us, in the clouds, shivering in our fleece as we hike through pine woods to a clearing where we should—if the clouds lift—be able to get a close-up look at the rocky peaks. It's snowing, which is something of a shock after a year in Hong Kong—but it's also gloriously refreshing. The air on Jade Dragon Snow Mountain is as pure as water, the smell of pine just strong enough to clear your head, the snowflakes just heavy enough that you can hear them pat-pat as they hit the ground. Ellen and I are loving it.

The kids, on the other hand . . .

The annoying thing is that we chose this activity from a list of possible ways to spend the day specifically because we thought the kids would enjoy it. Two months earlier, we'd visited Ping'an in the Guangxi province, and as we'd hiked through the terraced rice paddies rising up the karst mountains, Will had turned to me and said, "You know what, Dad? This is the best thing we've done this whole year."

Well, okay then. If it worked in February, why not in April? "Take a cable car to a mountain meadow to see locals performing regional dances," is what the brochure said. What could be better?

Well, a lot. Or so it appears. Almost from the moment we start walking, Will complains about the cold. Jamie wants to be held. And Lucy is—well, not her usual chipper self (turned out this would be the evening—already described—when the two of us would be up all night puking, but we didn't know that, then).

"Come on, you guys!" Ellen or I call every eleven seconds or so, like speed-smoking cheerleaders. "Isn't this great? Isn't it beautiful?"

Lucy on Jade Snow Dragon Mountain: T minus four hours to throw-up time . . .

"Ehh," Will says.

"Carry me!" Jamie demands.

"Urp," Lucy, um, urps.

"Little turds," I say to Ellen.

"Maybe it's the altitude."

"More like the attitude."

But she's probably right. Lijiang itself is well over 1,000 feet, and we've climbed at least twice that, first in the bus and then in the cable car.

But never mind. We trudge on. Eventually we see a clear-ing through the trees and feel a fresh breeze blowing across our foreheads. To the right are numerous small buildings—a food kiosk, restrooms, and a long wooden walkway made of pine beams stripped of bark. Hanging from every square centimeter of this last structure are woven prayer tokens—bell-shaped bas-kets with wooden tags dangling below, inscribed with the wishes of the person who'd bought it and hung it there. Dongba, the script of the Naxi people, is one of the last hieroglyphic lan-guages still in use, and many of the tokens are inscribed with simple characters: water, sun, children.

"Is this a natural meadow?" I ask our guide.

He's a young man, a Pumi, with a nose like a dorsal fin, and he blushes slightly when I ask this question.

"No," he says. "It used to be a lake. But they drained it."

"Really? Why?"

A bit of a smile, a bit of a shrug. "It used to be for suicide. Couples would come here, you know—when they were forbid-den to marry? And they would throw themselves in."

Oh.

I glance at Ellen. Neither of us says anything for a minute as we walk on, dragging the kids along. Then I see her shoulders begin to shake, just a little bit. And then mine shake too, just tremors at first, but in a matter of seconds I'm trying so hard not to laugh that I actually hiccup.

We make a lap around the meadow. A couple dressed in traditional Western wedding attire are there, having their pic-tures taken in the middle of the field. The boy is heavy, mildly spoiled looking in that one-child-policy way you often see in male youths. The girl is gorgeous: tall, with black-blue hair and a regal air that intimidates me, even a moment later when, as she lifts her skirts to trek through the muddy grass, I catch a glimpse of Nike trainers.

The kids race ahead, anxious to complete the circuit, get back to the cable cars, get the heck out of here.

Ellen and I, though, we linger. Above us, a broad face of the mountain, deep and black as water, keeps flashing its sharp features our way, taunting us, promising to show us something really spectacular if only we'll stick around long enough for the clouds to lift.

Arguably the only twelve seconds of our trip to Jade Snow Dragon Mountain that Will actually enjoyed.

So we drag our feet. Enjoying the crisp cold, the wet air that seems to promise more snow, the sense of being someplace we'll never be again, someplace that most Westerners never get to see—or at least, most Westerners hailing from semirural Virginia. At one point we stop, lean our shoulders together, hold a camera at arm's length, snap a photo of the two of us laughing. I can smell Ellen's hair in the cool air, the sharp scent of her shampoo, the slight smell of incense from a museum we'd visited earlier that day. It's nice, and I squeeze her a bit closer, feeling her presence through the layers of fleece.

This is not like us. In no way is this like us. We don't usually take those kinds of cuddly pictures—hell, we don't usually cuddle, period. And we don't usually laugh and linger and get all smoochy-faced when our kids are tired and grumpy, racing on ahead and threatening to disappear into the woods where we might never see them again.

I can't emphasize this enough: We don't do this. We have never, that I can think of in the ten years we've had children, placed our own pleasures as a couple ahead of their desires.

Never.

On Jade Snow Dragon Mountain: not a typical photo of Ellen and me.

Back when I was a kid, my parents used to drag me along to confirmation retreats for ninth-grade students. This is a concept, I know, that may be unfamiliar to some of you, so allow me to

explain. Twice each year—once in October and once in March—
my Lutheran minister dad and several of his church staff drove
a busload of fifteen-year-olds to a Bible camp in northern Wisconsin where there was a huge retreat center. We'd spend the
whole weekend there, my brother and I and the other staff brats,
playing ping-pong in the cinderblock basement, stealing Cokes
when our moms weren't looking, and hiking down to the lake
to skip stones.

The ninth-graders would have discussions and mini Bible
studies and sing camp songs and pop popcorn and play Frisbee
and sled down the hill and go on treasure hunts and listen to
records and munch Cheetos and watch whatever crappy movie
the staff had rented for the weekend (I remember, and I'm not
making this up, at least one showing of *The Corpse Grinders,*
detailing the exploits of a cat-food company that took corpses
and . . . well, I'm sure you can fill in the rest).

For some of you, I know, this sounds like pure hell, and fair
enough—there are plenty of churches and plenty of religions
that can turn a warm, fun, community-building weekend in an
amazing rural setting into a nightmare. My sense, though, from
my ten years as a tag-along and my two stints when I was myself
a ninth-grader, was that these were pretty amazing weekends.
Up north and in the woods, everyone got away from the usual
middle-school cliques, the posturing, the constant low-grade
bullying that goes on most of the time when folks are in that not-
quite-kids-but-not-quite-adults stage. I remember very clearly
coming away from those weekends feeling both better about
myself and my place in the world, and about my classmates, even
the ones who usually drove me nuts.

The problem, of course, was that it only took a few hours
wandering the halls of Woodrow Wilson Junior High to make
this feeling go away. My father called this phenomenon as
"Coming down from the mountain." He was referring, I've no
doubt, to some biblical thing—Moses or the Easter Bunny or
some such business—but even if I didn't fully get the allusion,

I understood what he meant. It's like in the movie *The Breakfast Club* (my generation's *The Graduate*) when the geeky guy played by Anthony Michael Hall gets all snotty-faced and teary-eyed, asking his newfound friends what'll happen on Monday—will they acknowledge him at all, or just walk on by? (Hmmm . . . that sounds vaguely like a song . . .)

Molly Ringwald's character is blunt in her reply, directed mainly at Emilio Estevez: "If Ryan came walking up to you in the hall on Monday, what would you do? I mean, picture this, you're there with all the sports . . . you know exactly what you'd do. You'd say 'hi' to him, and when he left you'd cut him up so that your friends didn't think that you really liked him."

In other words, it's one thing to be on the mountain, up there with God or Buddha or Ally Sheedy before she got kind of freaky—on the mountain, everything is holy, everything is pure, and we're all at our best, our most divine.

Coming down from the mountain, on the other hand . . .

Ellen and I have had some rough moments in our relationship. Not a lot of them, mind you, but some.

A little background: We met in 1989, on the first day of TA training in the English MA program at Iowa State. We spent two years in glorious Ames, Iowa, struggling daily not to kill ourselves from sheer boredom, then moved together to Columbus, Ohio—another dazzling Midwestern city—where I started a PhD program.

That last bit is important: where *I* started a PhD program. Ellen liked grad school well enough. She wasn't crazy about the teaching part, but thrived on the ideas part. But five to seven years more of grad school, followed by a career in academia? It just wasn't part of her long-term plan.

So *she* followed *me*. This is key. Because five years later, newly minted PhD in hand, I was offered a job in sexy Salem, Virginia, home of, well . . . nothing really, other than a minor-league baseball team, a handful of pizza joints, and the college that hired me.

And a funny thing happened. Given the choice between following me yet again to yet another amazingly nondescript place that definitely wasn't Paris, and . . . well, *not* following me to not-Paris, Ellen chose the latter. She decided to go to New York and work for a large university press there. Part of her decision was purely practical. She's a university press editor, and there weren't any university presses in Roanoke, so why move someplace where she couldn't work?

Part of her decision was romantic, in the non-lovey-dovey sense of the word. I mean, who *wouldn't* want to live in New York City, given the chance?

And part of it was principle. She'd already followed me once to a city where she knew no one. She hadn't been raised by adventurous parents, gone to an extremely progressive college, studied feminist theory and literature and drama so that she could become the sort of person who just followed someone else from place to place for absolutely no reason.

Which is fair enough.

I know that.

Know. Meaning, "to be cognizant or aware of a fact or a specific piece of information."

Which, of course, if different from *understand*, which means, "to comprehend the nature and significance of." Not to mention different from *feel*, meaning, "undergo an emotional sensation or be in a particular state of mind."

I'm going to gloss over this next part, because: a) it wasn't really the best part of our relationship; b) it really wasn't the best part of my life; and c) it's really none of your business.

Suffice to say it sucked. Oh sure, it was cool in some ways. We got to roam the streets of New York together every sixth week or so, alternating with visits to the Blue Ridge Mountains. But basically? Seriously? It sucked.

For me, at least.

I can't remember if it's something I read somewhere or something someone told me or just something I've always intuited, but pretty much from the day I was born I've known that, frankly and despite all the Hollywood stereotypes to the contrary, women are often happier—and arguably better off—not being stuck in some house with some man.

Men, on the other hand—at least in my experience and again contrary to societal impressions—are really pretty dependent upon other people. Simply put, we just don't like being alone. We're too stupid, too shallow, and too scared of our own thoughts to be comfortable with an empty house and nothing to distract us.

Ellen and I were married by a man named Lowell Erdahl, who, years before, had confirmed Ellen and is one of the few clergy she trusts, which is kind of funny given that both her father and mine are ordained ministers. Lowell wanted to spend some time with us before the wedding, so one rainy day in the fall of 1992 we traipsed into his office in St. Paul and sat down for a conversation. One of the things I remember from that meeting was Lowell's theory that there isn't a single honeymoon—that, to the contrary, marriages wax and wane. There are lots of okay times, yeah, and lots of bad times, but there are also times in a marriage—even, say, eighteen years into it—when a couple will almost be back in that giddy, happy, just-fresh-off-the-haywagon kind of love.

Why do I mention this?

Not because Hong Kong was one long honeymoon. It wasn't. It was great, yes, and adventurous, yes, and scintillating on an hourly basis, yes. But it was also *hard*. Besides the basic logistical things—getting the kids to school, shopping for groceries, wading chin deep through a language that's way too complicated—there were emotional things: short-tempered moments, intense negotiations about who gets to exercise when, or who gets to go out and wander while the other stays home with Jamie, or who should do the dishes.

And I'll be honest with you: I wasn't the best partner a lot of the time. This was partly work related. Hong Kong faculty members are government employees. What this means, in practical terms, is that the government keeps very careful track of your hours. On the left side of my institutional home page was a small meter telling me exactly how many personal days I'd accumulated since the beginning of the year. Halfway through the year, my institution asked me to take on additional, non-consultative responsibilities, essentially becoming an employee of the university. Once I did that, I felt obliged to act like a real employee, being more careful about my hours—going in earlier, staying longer, taking fewer days off.

Additionally, though, I wasn't the best partner because I spent a lot of time writing. A *lot* of time. Every night after the kids went to bed—and this includes many Fridays and Saturdays—I poured myself a glass of wine, grabbed a handful of chocolates, and sat on the couch with my laptop. And wrote. And wrote. And wrote—sometimes as many as nine or ten pages in a single evening. Writing was my way of coping with everything that was going on around me, with all the new experiences, with the challenges at work, with the fact that every time I walked out the door—*every single time*—I saw something or did something or ate something that was completely new and unexpected. Writing helped me make sense of all this, helped me keep my head on more or less straight.

Ellen, meanwhile, slogged away at the family blog, posting the hundreds of pictures that she'd taken to let our families know what we were up to. And she did the laundry (something, in my defense, that she refuses to let me help with), and the dishes. This last was the worst. We only had six bowls, six plates, six forks, and six knives. So if we wanted to eat breakfast the next day, one of us had to wash and dry dishes every night. I intended to help with this, really I did. But sometimes I offered, then got caught in a particularly difficult passage and didn't get around to it soon enough, so Ellen just did it. Other times I'd wash the dishes, then get distracted with some idea and rush into the living room to write it down before I forgot—and Ellen just dried the damn things.

We have a "Birthday Club" in Virginia, a group of four couples who celebrate all our birthdays, going out for dinner and giving each other gifts. One of our number is a genius at finding or having made T-shirts that capture perfectly our personalities (one of mine says "Just shut the hell up!"). When we got back, we all gathered for a belated celebration of Ellen's and my birthdays. Ellen's gift from Ross? A black T-shirt with the white logo "Blog Widow."

But, of course, there were amazing times as well. And one of the amazing times was up on that mountain, cold flakes brushing our cheeks, that black wet face of rock towering over us, that feeling of being somewhere special, of seeing something amazing, of just—I don't know—being alive.

And there was this: Early in June, a Fulbright colleague at another university mentioned to me that a German university outside of Hamburg was looking for an experienced general education coordinator.

"Really?" I said.

He nodded. "And it looks good. They seem to know what they're talking about."

That next morning, back at the flat, I logged into the Chronicle of Higher Education and punched in "Germany" and "General Education."

And there it was: XYZ university in northern Europe had received a grant from the European Union to experiment with an alternative to Germany's fairly strict, career-oriented educational system. And yes, they were hiring. In fact, not only did they need someone to oversee the GE program—something I'd been doing for years—they also needed someone to work with writing and general education—bringing my area of specialty into play.

Now I don't want you to think this was a slam-dunk decision for me, one of those easy "But of course!" moments. Just *applying* for a job like this would mean a ton of work at the very time we were trying to relish our last days in Hong Kong. And if I got an offer (and in the end, I didn't, not even close) then moving to Germany would mean giving up a lot of security, tenure, and a good job and good friends in one of the nicest small towns in America.

But even so . . . Germany!

"Ellen?" I called, my voice cracking. "Can you come here for a second?"

I heard her coming down the hall, talking to Lucy as she passed the kids' bedroom. Outside the office, she paused for a second, peering in at me. The last time I'd called her to my computer, my voice wavering, it was to announce that her father had died.

"Yes?" she said.

"Look at this."

She came to the desk, glanced over my shoulder.

"Holy crap," she said after a second.

I looked at her. She leaned in closer, peering at the screen. Then she bent over, fingers clicking on the keyboard. Opening a new tab, she Googled the town, then hit image. Pictures of an old-style German city cluttered the screen: narrow cobblestone streets with Tudor-style homes leaning over walkways; an open square surrounded by brick-arched buildings and narrow turrets with flags flapping overhead; a strange kind of castle-looking thing with two fat towers, one on each side.

"Wow," she said.

"I know." I was actually shaking. "What do you think?"

She read the ad again. "It fits you perfectly."

"Yes."

Straightening, she gave me a look. "It would devastate the kids."

I nodded. It was true. They were more than ready to get back to Virginia, more than ready to be back in their own rooms, to play with their own friends.

Neither of us spoke for a long moment. Then I said again, "What do you think?"

"We have to try."

"Really?"

"Absolutely. A chance like this—you can't let it go by."

I looked back at the computer, considered, nodded my head.

"Right?" she said.

"Absolutely."

"Okay then!" She gave me a quick pat on the shoulder, then a little squeeze, a ripple of electricity passing through my shirt. "Hop to it, buddy! You've got a lot of work to do."

I grunted, swung my chair back to the computer, reached for a pen. She gave me that little squeeze again, then left the room, calling to Jamie as she went back down the hall.

God I love her.

CHAPTER 18

ASSURANCES

It's the sort of conversation you avoid as long as you can. Finally, though, Ellen and I choose a night, put Jamie to bed early, and lead Lucy and Will into the living room. Once they've settled in, we take their hands and tell them we love Jamie more than them.

They both frown.

"Are you sure?" Will says. "Because I thought you loved Lucy best."

"Yeah," his sister pipes up. "You always said I was your favorite."

"That's right," Ellen says to Lucy as I stroke Will's hair (being the first child is always so bittersweet). "We used to love you best. But now we love Jamie more."

"But why?"

"He's squoodgier."

Will's frown deepens. "That's not even a word."

"Yes it is," I say.

He squints for a moment, thinking. "No it's not."

Ellen cuts in. "Honey, it may not be a real word, but it's a real emotion."

"What does it mean, then?"

Ellen and I exchange glances. I shrug.

"It means we like to hug him more," Ellen says. "That he's so cute, you just want to pick him up and smoosh him against you as hard as you can."

"I can be smoodgy," Lucy says.

"Squoodgy," I say.

"Whatever."

"And no you can't," I tell her, "at least not like Jamie."

Will has returned to his book. I poke him with a stick. "Pay attention, son," I say. "This is important."

"I don't get it," Lucy says. Her forehead is red. "You always said that I was the cutest."

Ellen leans in and gives her a kiss on those fat little lips. "That was before, sweetie. Things change."

"Why?"

"Evolution."

"That's right," I say. "Survival of the fittest. Just like Darwin said."

"I hate Darwin," says Lucy.

"That's because you didn't read him carefully enough."

"Jamie's just so cute," I say. "With his little butt. Have you seen him in his pajamas? I mean, have you really *looked* at him in his little pajamas?"

"Follow him down the hall sometime," Ellen says. "He's just the sweetest little thing. He walks on his toes."

"Isn't that a sign of Asperger's?" Will doesn't even look up from his book. I crane my neck to glance at the title. *Das Kapital.* Huh. Don't remember giving him *that* for Christmas.

"And he can't talk," Lucy says. "He says 'ladder' instead of 'water.'"

"And you used to call your polar bear 'dapple' because you couldn't pronounce it."

"Until you lost him."

"Hey," I say. "You were twenty months old. Plenty mature enough to take care of your own stuff."

"Jamie poops in his pants," Will says.

"Now see," Ellen says, "that's exactly the kind of comment that loses you first place in your parents' hearts!"

"But he does," says Lucy. "He knows how to do it in the potty, but instead he'll go out on the patio, poo in his

underpants, then walk around the house with his butt dragging down."

"It's actually pretty funny," Will says. "He waddles."

"Jamie's just really really cute," Ellen says, squeezing
Lucy's hand.

"Says who?"

"About 7 million Hong Kongers. Haven't you seen how
much they like to pick him up?"

"And get their pictures taken with him?" Ellen adds.

"They like to get their pictures taken with me, too," Lucy says.

Ellen frowns. "That's because they think you're Lindsay
Lohan."

"Who's Lindsay Lohan?"

"A girl who lost her underpants."

"And her mind," adds Ellen.

"Does this mean we have to stay in Hong Kong when you
guys leave?" Will asks.

I glance at my wife. "We're not sure."

"It depends on the tickets," Ellen says. "We don't have a lot
of money left."

There's a pause during which all of us consider the implica-
tions of this. Then Lucy sits straight up in her chair.

"If we had to stay here, where would we live?"

"Excuse me?"

"If you left us here," Lucy says, "would we get to stay with
Valerie and Chris?"

I frown. "Um. We hadn't thought about it. Why?"

Lucy's face is brightening now. "I think I want to stay."

"What?" says Ellen.

Will's caught on now and is also grinning. "Yeah! Me too! I
want to stay with Valerie and Chris."

I look at Ellen and she looks at me, and I can tell we're both
thinking the same thing.

"Ouch," I say. "Now that's just mean!"

Okay, so none of that happened.

It could have, though. That our year in Hong Kong was a real gift is obvious. That one of the most important ways it's been a gift is by providing us with another son perhaps requires a bit more explanation.

Jamie wasn't quite three-and-a-half when we left China. Nevertheless, my guess is he will remember this moment for the rest of his life.

Part of what I'm talking about is simply age-related. Jamie was thirty-two months old when we arrived in Hong Kong. He could walk, and talk, and, well—that's pretty much it. And frankly the whole talking thing wasn't really his specialty. Personality-wise, he was cute and funny, but essentially an animated thirty-pound bag of sugar. During our time in Hong Kong, though, he passed from baby to toddler, shifting from object to subject: There is a real human being in there, and watching him emerge was a blast.

So that's part of what I mean when I say that being in Hong Kong gave us another son. But there's this other part, too: I was forty-one when James was born. Ellen was nearly forty. In educational terms, he was what might be referred to as an "unintended outcome," which is to say that he happened, yes, even if we hadn't necessarily, um, *planned* for him to happen.

This is not to say that his "out coming," so to speak, was necessarily a bad thing. On the contrary, unintended outcomes are often the things that instructors most enjoy about their classes— they are the surprises, the moments when students step forward and put new and interesting light on a topic. I'm only mentioning this to point out that we're neither Catholic nor gluttons for punishment nor getting any younger or more energetic. We are, on the contrary, incredibly lazy and incredibly practical when it comes to things like, oh, being able to sleep at night, not having more kids than we can afford to feed, and not attending high school graduations at an age when, as we're heading out of the house, one of us asks the other, "Did you bring the extra batteries for your pacemaker?"

But these things happen. And of course, within a year or two after Jamie's birth, we decided we might as well give up pretending he didn't exist and actually love him.

Just kidding. Seriously.

In actuality, we were smitten the minute Jamie emerged from the womb, pink and gooey and looking vaguely miffed. Nonetheless, it's worth pointing out that, for some portion of his first few years, we occasionally forgot he existed. This isn't to say to say we were horrible parents. We never left him in the car at the end of a long day of running errands; we fed and clothed him; we cuddled with him before putting him to bed; he's the only one of our three children to whom we sang lullabies every night, something for which he will likely never forgive us.

But the reality of our lives was that we already had two children. And they kept us very busy. Particularly since one of them was a Lucy.

You heard me: When faced with Jamie's fascination with the bubbles coming out of his nose, Will's math homework, and Lucy's crawling onto the kitchen counter to get the butcher knife so that she can use the handle to knock a box of matches down from the refrigerator, we knew where we needed to put our attention.

Turns out ignoring Jamie seems to have been a pretty good parenting technique. The fact is, he is the most independent of our kids, insisting at the age of three that he can brush his own teeth, that he can make his own PB&J sandwiches. He already knows how to turn on the DVR, where to find the spring water in the fridge, and how to make a nice *roux* for the Thanksgiving gravy. The day he disassembled our malfunctioning vacuum cleaner and reassembled it perfectly—with an added time-traveling feature—Ellen and I looked at each other, wondering why we hadn't been smart enough to ignore the other kids as well.

So beyond getting to know the little human being Jamie is becoming, our year in Hong Kong allowed us to know the little human we'd been ignoring. This was particularly true for Ellen, who spent roughly 167.5 out of 168 hours per week in Jamie's company. He came with her to the bus stop to meet Lucy and Will, to the grocery store to get mango juice, to the malls in Sha Tin and Kowloon Tong to pick up clothes, or good bread, or cheese, to the temple to—well, you get the point. They went to the playground together almost daily, always ate lunch together, had whole hours in a single day just strolling to and from bus stops.

I, meanwhile, got whole days trolling around Hong Kong, chatting to the little blond head in the stroller below me, listening to his questions phrased in that peculiar Jamie way: "Can we take a taxi, can we?" "Why can't we take a taxi, why?" "Can I have a snack, can I?" That I never had this kind of opportunity with the other two kids goes without saying. When I'm in the States, I occasionally will avoid my one-hour commute by working at

home, but then I'm forced by a tight teaching schedule to actually *work*, rather than searching for a great dumpling restaurant
or a new playground. In Hong Kong, on the other hand, I had
ample opportunity to watch as my little sack of sugar developed
a personality.

And what a personality. If Will is the kid most likely to marry
a fundamentalist Christian who won't let us see our grandchil-
dren, and Lucy is most likely to get a tattoo before the age of
ten, Jamie is most likely to become a professional surfer who
accidentally invents a machine that makes him a trillion dollars,
which he will then blow on throwing a party for his friends.
Jamie goes with the flow. Sure, every once in a while he gets a
little huffy with his sister (like, for instance, after she pokes him
in the face six times for no reason), but even on the rare occasion when his eyes become rimmed with red and he unbuckles
those huge lungs of his, bellowing until the mortar crumbles
from between the bricks of our building, within a minute or two
he's over it and has moved on to the next thing.

And he's funny. Maybe a month before we left Hong Kong,
Jamie discovered Lucy in the bathroom, attending to private
business. He was, at that point, in the middle of a good streak
in the midst of a bad year regarding potty behavior. Just that day,
he'd received lots of praise and a handful of M&M's in the vain
hope that these would induce him toward a repeat performance
for the next—well, for the rest of his life.

Discovering Lucy on the toilet, the door open, he shouted
down the hall, "Lucy's pooing!"

He glanced at her, appraising the situation carefully, then
provided another update: "It's really amazing!"

Which leads us to a peculiar and rather telling detail in
terms of understanding Jamie, his year in Hong Kong, and how
he felt about returning to the States. Three months after this
moment with Lucy, we got on a plane in China and flew back to
the American Midwest, where we spent a week visiting family
before making the dawn-to-dusk drive back to Virginia. Arriving

at our home well after the kids' bedtimes, we threw ourselves
into unloading suitcases, snapping sheets on beds, and trying to
calm them all down as they raced from room to room, thrilled to
be back in their old home.

All except for Jamie. He didn't know where his room was.
He didn't know where the stairs were to get upstairs. He had no
idea where the light switches were, or what room mommy and
daddy slept in. Which is fair enough. After all, he'd only had a
two-and-a-half-year-old brain when he'd left, barely capable of
remembering his own name, much less the floor plan of an old
Queen Anne house with a million nooks and crannies.

But then, twenty minutes after he arrived, Jamie said, "I
need to poo."

And then he went into the bathroom, dropped his pants,
climbed onto the toilet, and went poo.

And he's never had an accident since.

How weird is that?

Back in the fall when the school sent home sign-up sheets
for afternoon activities, Will decided he wanted to do archery.
We were okay with this, even though it meant tromping across
town every Sunday and sitting in the hot sun while he learned
the finer points of hitching an arrow and adjusting sights.

He loved it. This makes sense if you know Will: It's a
sport that requires concentration, a fair bit of intelligence, and
very little sweating, which, as you know, has never been Will's
favorite thing. The first few times he came home ecstatic, talking about how many bull's-eyes he got, what his scores were,
what he had to do before they'd advance him to another level
and move the target back.

Then, maybe a month into it, he came over to where I was
working on my laptop during practice and said, "I don't feel good."

I looked up. His face was pale with dark red circles around
his eyes. I could see sweat forming in his bangs.

"You're probably just hot," I said. It was October, but still steamy and mildly suffocating. "Sit in the shade for a bit."

So he did. And then he went back to his bow and arrows and shot a few more rounds.

I was lost in my computer again when he reappeared.

"I really don't feel good."

"You think you're going to throw up?"

He nodded.

I took him to a shady spot beside the fence, plopped him down on a stool, and made him put his head between his knees.

"Did you feel okay walking up?" I asked. It's a good mile from the bus stop, with not much shade.

He shook his head a little. Then nodded a little. Then shrugged, his face still between his knees.

We waited for a few minutes until he started to feel better. I got him some water and that seemed to help. Some.

"You want to stay a bit?" I asked.

He didn't say anything for a while. I saw his eyes glance from the bow to the target to the arrows. Then he shook his head. And we went.

Which wasn't really a big deal.

But then it happened the next time, too. One minute, he was happily shooting away, the next he was standing beside me, pale as a sheet, forehead dewy with sweat.

"The heat again?" I said.

He nodded.

The next week, we didn't even make it out of the apartment.

"I don't feel good," he said when I strolled into the living room, laptop satchelled on my shoulder.

I stopped where I was. Something below my lungs gave a twist. I looked at Ellen, who was sitting on the couch downloading pictures on her computer. She met my glance. Ellen and I aren't very often on the same page (or even in the same book), and we're arguably the worst parents ever (why else would we eat our kids' M&M's when they're not looking?), but every once in a while we get it right, and we get it right together.

This was one of those times.

What we did was sit Will down and talk to him about archery, about his stomachaches, about what was going on. He couldn't give us a clear answer about why he was so anxious. He said he loved archery, and we believed him. Who knows? Maybe he was putting too much pressure on himself, comparing his numbers to Gordon's, the little dynamo whiz kid he shared a target with. Or maybe, standing there, bow raised, one eye closed, focusing on the target—maybe he just felt the heat swell through his body, felt something huge and unmanageable crushing his lungs.

Regardless, we talked to him about trying to relax, about enjoying himself. We talked to him about moving forward, driving through his fears rather than allowing them to dominate his life. We talked to him about how once you start something, you should stick with it, even when it gets difficult.

He went to archery that day. And he had fun. And he went every week after that except for the ones when we had something else we needed to do—and on those days he complained vehemently about having to miss.

I know a couple faculty at my college who, a few years back, decided to take a group of students to Africa. In order to prepare them for the unpredictable nature of traveling in an emerging nation, my colleagues planned an outing while still in the States.

"Be on the bus at exactly 5:30," they told the students. "Anyone not on the bus will be left behind!"

The students all showed up, and the bus roared off, supposedly to visit a museum of African history and then to have a group dinner at a local restaurant.

Only that's not what happened. Instead, my colleagues quietly instructed the bus driver to head out into the country and pretend to get hopelessly lost. And then, once the bus seemed to be on track again, the driver was to act as though the vehicle was suffering engine trouble, and pull over to the side of the road.

Three hours later, the bus returned to the college, its occupants dazed, bored, annoyed, and hungry. They never made it the museum. They never made it to dinner.

"This," the instructors told their frustrated, soon-to-be-world travelers, "is your first lesson about Africa. Sometimes things don't go as planned. Get used to it."

I'm not sure Will ever learned to go with the flow during our time abroad. And certainly, that was one of our goals for taking the kids to Hong Kong: to get them used to the idea that things sometimes don't go as planned, and help them understand that—most of the time, at least—it doesn't really matter. Sure, we were hoping to get to the HK Space Museum and ended up playing in the park for too long, but is that the end of the world? And no, they don't have chicken wings to eat here, but they have lots of other good stuff, so maybe you should try some of that.

Of all our children, Will is the most cautious, slower to try new things, slower to embrace new things even after he's tried them. Which isn't really a problem, of course. That sort of attitude will serve him well when he's faced with the inevitable temptations of drugs, alcohol, and slutty coeds with STDs (not that I'm speaking from experience, or anything). But even so, I think we were hoping the year would help him lighten up a bit.

Which I'm sure it did. In some ways.

But he didn't have an easy time of it. Besides the usual stresses of being overseas and away from his friends and his room and his backyard and his school, there was, of course, the whole bullying thing. Stretching out and exploring and feeling confident becomes a lot more complicated when you're in an environment where the most popular kid in Year Four has decided to spend most of the school day explaining to you why you're "annoying."

And as if that weren't bad enough, then he was faced with the prospect of going to Beijing for five days and spending twenty-four hours a day with this guy.

Which leads to this story: It's about two weeks before the trip. Will and his mom are in the kitchen. She's just asked him if he'd rather stay home than go to Beijing. And after a long moment's silence, Will has said yes.

The thing is, as much as Ellen and I don't really want him to go, don't really want him to be in that situation, we also know that—like the archery thing—he probably needs to do it. I hate clichés, but there's one about a horse and falling off and—well, you know the rest.

So Ellen basically tells him that we think he needs to do it. There's a long silence. I'm lying on the couch in the living room, trying to read a book and failing miserably. Even from that distance, I can feel the resignation in the air, the utter loss, a hopelessness so hopeless it can't even get up the energy to protest or argue.

After a few minutes, Ellen comes out of the kitchen and starts doing something on her computer. Will comes out too, and sits down, pencil in hand. His homework lies on the table, untouched. He's just staring at it, not moving.

"Hey, Will?" I say from my spot on the couch.

He looks up.

"Come here."

So he clumps over, kicks off his shoes. Then he lies down on top of me. When he does that, his body stretches all the way from my chin to my ankles. He's heavy, too, but not enough so that I can't breathe.

He doesn't say anything. And I don't either.

And he doesn't cry. And I don't either, though I'd understand if either of us did.

Instead, I stroke his hair, his chestnut-brown, slightly greasy hair, with my thumb.

And we stay there for fifteen minutes: me on the couch, stroking his hair, him on top of me, face down, melting into me.

And he goes to Beijing, of course. And he comes back, happy and exhausted and mildly intoxicated with a sense of his own adventurousness—to be only nine and to go off to China by yourself! Stuffed in his backpack are four small boxes, the kind you get in China whenever you buy a souvenir, with an old-fashioned pattern on the outside and red velvet on the inside.

And in each of these boxes is a small *cloisonné* figurine: a bird for Ellen, a bracelet for Lucy, a turtle for Jamie, and a small owl for me. I don't know if Will knows how much I like owls—my grandmother loved them, and they're the only birds that don't give me the heebie-jeebies—but when I tell him this, he shrugs a little. He's not smiling, but his lips are pressed together and I can see from the way his cheeks puff that he's about to.

Which is very sweet. And significant too, especially for a kid who spends so much time in his head that he can tend to be a little self-absorbed.

But what finally gives me hope is this: For Mother's Day, Will made a pop-up card for Ellen. The outside is plain brown, maybe with a little picture or something. The inside, though, is a row of cutout palm trees that stand straight up when you open the card. Below them is a treasure chest with a sliding bolt and a key. Open it, and you find the word "Mother" spelled out vertically, so that each student can provide a phrase describing his or her mother for each letter. Here is what Will wrote:

M—Made of molecules
O—One of a kind
T—Takes me to school
H—Happy and kind
E—Editor
R—Reassuring

While thinking about writing this chapter, I'd planned on focusing on "Made of molecules." I mean, who doesn't love a kid who comes up with a line like that? Especially when you know that he and his friend Alden laughed their asses off when he wrote it.

Yet one more "first" for Will and Lucy to remember: taking pictures of a statue of, um, a demon or god or something with a really long tongue, holding a naked woman. Clearly one of those travel moments that we never quite anticipated.

Typing this now, though, what I find myself focusing on is "Reassuring." I know this word should scare me. "Reassuring" implies the need for assurance, the presence of fear and anxiety in his world—things caused by school, yes, but also by his mom and dad deciding when he was eight to take him away from Mayberry, USA, and drop him in one of the world's biggest and loudest cities, where the food smells funny and the people talk funny and the caterpillars are so poisonous that you're not supposed to touch them.

So I know this word should scare me. But it doesn't. We can't protect our kids, finally. Eventually they'll leave us, moving out into the universe on their own—and who knows what they'll find there, how often their hearts will be broken, the various forms of bullying they'll meet? But what "Reassuring" tells me is that I have a smart boy, a boy who knows what's good for him, and who's good for him, and where to go when it all gets to be too much.

This might have been a skill Will had before we left. I don't know. I don't care. All I know—and all I care about—is that he has it now.

We're at the Hong Kong Science Museum, in the basement playing with these funky machines. Some blow so hard they can hold a ball up in the air; others look like upside-down trashcans and are miked so that when you hit them with small hammers you get all sorts of different sounds, depending upon where you strike the blow. It's Sunday, and the museum is packed. Will has invited two friends along and the three of them pull us from one exhibit to the next at pinball speed. Eventually the mechanics of air and light cease to charm, and one of the boys says, "What next?" And another shouts, "The electricity display!"

And off they go, Lucy in tow.

Only when Ellen and I and our 200-pound three-year-old finally make it up the escalator and to the electricity display, Lucy isn't there.

I search out Will by one of the circuit conductors. "Where's your sister?"

He looks up, looks around. Shakes his head.

I find the other boys. "Where's Lucy?"

They both shrug.

I feel the momentary urge to gather all three boys together and wire them to one of the neon electrodes flashing all around the room, but a mild and rising panic pushes that idea aside. Sliding back and forth among the throngs of children, I search for my daughter. It shouldn't be that hard: This is China, after all, and her hair is the color of honey mixed with sunlight. But I can feel my eyes shuttling quickly, too quickly, the same way they do when I'm in a hurry and I can't find my keys. Where's my daughter?

I see Ellen and sprint-walk toward her. "Have you seen Lucy?"

She frowns for an instant, then realizes what I'm implying. "Oh my God," she says.

I sprint back to the escalators, the ones that lead down into the massive underground display with its fifteen or sixteen rooms and seven or eight hundred kids and parents and grandparents looking at the display of how the eye works or laughing at their reflections in the house of mirrors. I don't even know where to begin.

But then she's there.

I'm halfway down the escalator, swearing at the old lady blocking the left-hand side, when I spot Lucy strolling down the hall in my direction. Then she starts to skip. *Skip.*

What happens next, I'm not sure I understand. She's skipping across the red museum carpet, her feet off the floor at the same time, her hair flying out behind her, arms swinging back and forth. She spots me and changes the angle of her gait, flouncing toward the escalator.

And just when she reaches the bottom, she bursts into tears.

I grab her, of course, her chest wracked with sobs, snot flowing from her nose, mouth a watery grimace. And I hold her, of course, and tell her it's okay, and press her against me as hard as I can, and tell her again it's okay as we go up the escalator. Her mother's at the top, and takes her from me (if, by "takes" we mean "rips from my arms"), but Lucy continues to cry, huge gasping sobs that make my ribs ache just watching her.

I'd always thought that Lucy was fearless.

This is the girl, after all, who learned to swim when she was two-and-a-half, who jumped off a thirty-foot junk and into Ha Long Bay along with her dad, who loves to climb the tree in our front yard, never mind the cars whizzing by three feet away.

This is *my* little girl, the kid who, the first time we sat down for lunch with my Hong Kong colleagues—while Ellen was back in the States and we were all still jet-lagged and grief-lagged and just plain messed up—looked at the roasted chicken they'd ordered for their American guests, and asked, "Can I eat the head?"

This is the girl who loves Singaporean noodles and Peking duck and pulling the eyeballs out of the roast pigeon and tearing apart its skull to see what's inside. I'm sure of very few things, but one thing I am certain about is that I'm the only one of my Facebook friends who's had to tell his six-year-old daughter "No honey, we're not taking the brains home tonight."

This is *my* Lucy, the skinny whelp who likes to play rugby with the older boys, who's never been scared of any book or movie we've ever read or seen (unlike, ahem, some of my other children who *still* won't read Harry Potter).

Parenting brings with it many dangers. Not the least of these is interpreting our children in terms of our own pasts. Thus, the vivacious daughter becomes "Just like old Auntie Elaine," who used to perform in a questionable Vaudeville act involving bubbles, a feather boa, and little else. The slightly surly son who spends all his time alone in the woods becomes just like your drunken cousin who loves to hunt and downloads clips of *Extreme Game*—when he isn't in prison for smuggling automatic weapons into the state.

And, of course, we read into our children what we see in ourselves: our sense of humor, our anxieties, our love of books.

Or maybe what we *want* to see in ourselves, the selves we some-times have but wish we had more often—our best selves, our imagined selves, our desired selves.

So I loved that Lucy was fearless. Loved that she seldom seemed intimidated by new situations or new friends, that she could walk into a room full of people she'd never met and just *shine*.

Needless to say, it was something of a shock to see that this wasn't necessarily the case. Standing in that classroom back in September, listening to Lucy's teacher explain that my daugh-ter just didn't seem happy . . . well, frankly, "shock" doesn't really describe my reaction. What that did to me went way beyond some simple stunning of the nerves, the creation of chaos in the brain. It struck straight at the core of my bones, burning through my marrow and leaving me weak and gutted, frightened and powerless.

What I found difficult was that this newfound realization of Lucy's vulnerability never went away. Although she seemed to adjust relatively well to school, she never really found friends of the sort that last for a lifetime, never mind how young they are. And although she seemed better than Will at going with the flow, there were moments throughout the year when she'd explode into vague and unexplainable anger, or provoke her siblings for absolutely no reason.

And then there was stuff like this: It's a Thursday night in June, and Ellen and Lucy have been down to the pool. As they're coming back, Lucy reaches up and grabs a berry from one of these odd, palm-like trees we have right beside the stairs of our building. I'm not sure why she does this or what she's thinking, because I'm not there with her. What I am sure of is that when she starts screaming, I can hear her from two stories up, halfway down the hall, in our flat, with the air conditioner on full blast.

Apparently she popped the berry. And apparently the berry contained some sort of juice or resin that stings and itches—instant poison ivy in a can, with added heat.

Into the flat the two of them tumble, Lucy roaring: "Oooow-wwww! It hurts! It hurts! Oooowwwww!"

The resin has gotten all over her arms, her legs, and parts of her neck. Nothing we say, nothing we do, helps. Hell, nothing we say or do can get her to shut up, calm down, to come down from whatever mountain or bad acid trip or hallucination of damnation she's on. She's screaming and ranting and kicking her legs and crying and pulling at her skin. Ellen tries to wash her down with a cold cloth, but that doesn't seem to help. So Ellen turns to the tub and begins filling it with water.

"Owww!" Lucy screams. "It huuuuuuuurrrrrrrrrrrts! Owwwww! Owwwww!" It's a horrible, bellowing, bullying howl she's got going, and Ellen and I aren't sure whether to hug her or duct tape her mouth shut.

The water doesn't help, or the soap that Ellen employs. Eventually, some emergency in the living room forces Ellen to head there, leaving me alone with Lucy in a tile bathroom that turns piercing whines into sonic shrieks that threaten to pop my eardrums. I stick two huge wads of toilet paper in my ears and kneel by the edge of the tub.

"It still hurts?" I ask.

Lucy says, "Oooooooooooooooooooooooooooooowwwwwww-wwwwwwwww—"

"Are you sure?"

"—ooooooooooooooooooooooowwwwwwwwwwwwwww-www—"

I reach into the tub, search for the washcloth. The water is freezing cold.

"—ooooooooooooooooooooooowwwwwwwwwwwwwww-www—"

"Ellen?" I holler down the hall.

"—ooooooooooooooooooooooowwwwwwwwwwwwwww-www—"

"Ellen?" I holler louder.

"—oooooooooooooooooooooooowwwwwwwwwwwww-www—"

"Screw it," I say, and go back to the tub. I reach in. Pull out the plug. The water starts to drain.

"—ooooooooooooooooooooooowwwwwwwwwwwww-www—"

"Breathe," I say.

"—ooooooooooooooooooooooowwwwwwwwwwwww-www—"

"Breathe."

She stops. Looks at me.

"You need to breathe," I say. "With your lungs. Remember?"

She nods, inhales, then goes, "Oooooowwwwwwwwww—"

I put the plug back in, then turn on the hot water.

"—ooooooooooooooooooooooowwwwwwwwwwwww-www—"

As the water rises, the screaming increases in volume. The hot water makes it worse, she hollers, the itching is becoming itchier, the burning is becoming burnier.

"This will help," I say.

"No it won't!"

"Yes it will. The hot water will cut through the resin."

She stops. "The huh?"

"The resin. Those seeds or whatever you popped were filled with oils that irritate your skin. Once we get rid of the oil, you won't hurt anymore."

She looks at her leg. "I don't see any oil."

"It's invisible."

She looks more closely. "Really?"

"You need hot water to cut through the oil. It dissolves it. And then we can scrub it off with soap, and you won't hurt anymore."

"Why does it dissolve it?"

I'm not a chemist, but I had a crush on one in college, so I give it a shot. "Hot water heats up the oil, making it more difficult for oil particles to bond. And when the particles are split up, it's easier to scrub them away with detergents. Plus," I add, just to make sure she doesn't end up one of those serious scientificky girls who breaks the hearts of boy English majors, "everyone knows oil fairies hate hot water fairies, and will run away if they see more than one at a time, especially if they're eating pomegranates."

She gives me a look, then says, "How do you know?"

"I used to get poison ivy. Hot water and soap was the only thing that helped."

"Mommy used cold water."

"Mommy didn't used to get poison ivy."

She watches as I scrub one leg, then the other. This, I realize, is the other side of Lucy—or more accurately, another way of looking at the same side. She's less fearless than curious, wanting to know what's inside the skull of that duck, wanting to know what makes that berry so shiny, wanting to know what Daddy's new colleagues will say if she asks to eat the head of the chicken.

And if fearlessness has its downsides—Evel Knievel was fearless after all, and so were all those people who died trying to climb Everest—then curious has its upsides. For one, it's the sign of a good brain. And this is easy to forget about Lucy: She has a good brain. There's so much sound and fury, sound and humor, sound and—well, just *sound,* whenever she comes in the room that you forget there's a smart kid behind those bright blue eyes and that mischievous grin. This is a kid who learned to read in a foreign country, away from all her best friends, largely away from her own language. This is a kid who, when we return to the States, will start playing piano without lessons, just because she wants to. This is a kid who will hold her seventh birthday party at a nearby creek so that she and her friends can chase after crawdads and minnows with butterfly nets.

I finish wiping her legs. "Better?"

She nods. She holds up her arms. I scrub them, too. Then she pulls her blond mane to one side and leans her head away from me, stretching her neck so that I can apply the soap. It's an indescribably beautiful gesture. Her hair is mouse-brown at the base, but honey-highlighted everywhere else. Her neck is confident and graceful, the line of her jaw cutting at just the right angle. This is a motion I've seen Lucy make a thousand times: at the pool in Virginia with her friends, sitting on her grandma's lap listening to a story, stepping out of the tub and drying herself with a thick towel.

Yes, it was a hell of a year, both good and bad, full of fears and crying and silly jokes and quiet walks. I don't understand, finally, who Lucy is—or at least not *entirely* who Lucy is.

But even so? This is the Lucy I know.

CHAPTER 19

MOST HOLY

When you're traveling abroad, sometimes you have moments like this: We're sitting in a restaurant in Kuala Lumpur, Malaysia. No, actually, it's not a restaurant: it's a *bistro*, which means that the booths are high and wooden, the floors are tiled, the bar is elaborate with mirrored shelves lines with shiny bottles of Tanqueray, Citroen Vodka, and seven different brands of single-malt scotch. Bing Crosby, Frank Sinatra, and other well-known Malaysian jazz singers blast from a phalanx of speakers at the far end of the room.

Our year in Hong Kong ended a few days ago. Before returning to the States, though, we've decided to spend a few weeks traveling through Southeast Asia, trying to see as much as we can while travel is still cheap and relatively easy. We're in KL for exactly half a day, en route from Sabah to Bali, and we'd set out to find the "Little China" and "Little India" sections of the city, hoping to get a taste of what makes this city at the crossroads of Asia so fascinating. Somehow, though, we'd been waylaid by an indoor market hawking overpriced dragon kites and scorpions set in glow-in-the-dark plastic key chains, stumbling out ninety minutes later tired and hungry and bordering on the sort of desperation you feel when you're with three smallish kids who are also tired and hungry. We made a half-hearted attempt to find one of the restaurants lauded in *Lonely Planet*, but quickly gave up. So now we're sitting in a bistro on our only night in Kuala Lumpur, trying to avoid eye contact with a bartender anxious to make us cosmopolitans, and being blasted by Lena Horn singing something about books and writing and the way we look.

Oh well.

"At least they serve real Malaysian food," Ellen says, just after Lena ends and right before someone else starts to croon "All of Me."

Except that—well, I hate to say this, but there's a reason you don't find thousands of Malaysian restaurants in cities around the world. Imagine Thai food, with less spice, less lime, more sugar, more peanuts, and more, I don't know, sort of an over-cooked potato taste, though with nary a potato in sight—and that's your basic Malaysian dish.

Which makes it all the more the pity that we couldn't find Little India, with its notoriously fabulous cuisine. And all the more frustrating, albeit in an exhausted kind of way, that we're sitting here at our marble-topped table, sipping Sprites, listening to Ella croon about how she don't get around much anymore.

And there are moments like this: After dinner, we make a restroom run. Our bistro is, not surprisingly, attached to an upscale mall, so we straggle in, searching for the usual blue-and-red man-and-woman signs. We find them and go down a narrow hallway between (no kidding) an Irish deli and an international grocery store. After attending to business, we walk into the latter, searching for bottled water and maybe some fresh fruit for the next day's flight.

We wander. We've been traveling for ten days at this point, stayed in three different hotels, and spent maybe twelve hours in the air. We're tired, and bored, and a little depressed, all the more so because we realize this is our last gasp in Asia. Slogging past cans of squid and chili-pepper-flavored Pringles and beef-flavored Doritos, we blink dully. Then we turn a corner and Will says, "Hey."

We stop. He points. On the second shelf down right in front of us stands a row of white Quaker Oats boxes, the little dude in the blue hat and coat, wearing a fluffy ascot.

"Quaker Chewy Granola Bars," Will says. The listlessness has left his face. "I've been missing those ever since we left America."

I'd like to think I understand my son. Really, I would.

I look at Ellen. She nods. Traveling in Asia, we've learned to pack our own snacks, filling half a suitcase—seriously—with granola bars and Go Aheads, an orange-flavored Garibaldi rip-off that the kids used to like—the operative term being "used." I know this sound strange, but after probably a cumulative six weeks on the road over the course of the year, gnawing their way through forty-three packages of Go Aheads, apparently the kids have become sick of them. Go figure.

I grab two boxes of granola bars from the shelf. I start to reach for another, then stop, check with Ellen. She nods again. I get two more and she grabs a fifth, and we make our way to the checkout counter, lighter of foot and freer of spirit.

And then there are moments like this: We're at the Bayon temple in Angkor Thom, outside of Siem Reap, Cambodia. It's four in the afternoon. The sun is already low behind the surrounding jungle, and the temple has an almost reddish glow to it. Bayon is amazing. Imagine a child's castle, built on the beach by dribbling layer upon layer of wet sand until a rough-textured tower rises up. Then imagine a number of these pebbly structures all clustered around a single, central heap rising nearly five stories into the sky. Now imagine courtyards and walkways worn smooth by 800 years of bare feet, long hallways stretching into darkness and wonderfully musky with damp. And as if that isn't enough, now imagine that all this—the towers, the hallways, the dark and damp of half-a-dozen centuries—is carved with hundred and hundreds of massive, serenely smiling Buddha faces.

Bayon temple is the perfect place for a nine-year-old boy, something straight out of an Indiana Jones film. Climbing the sunken stairs, ducking under the low arches, every racist stereotype of an Angelina Jolie–style adventure movie springs to mind: natives with blowpipes ducking behind crumbling walls, scarred and sneering Nazi commanders ordering shoot to kill. The place almost feels like a movie set, it's just that unbelievable, just that exotic, just that perfect. Every corner you turn, there's a stone face six feet tall and six feet wide, a smooth-eyed Buddha with a broad nose, wide lips, and a calm, silent, peaceful smile. It's paradise. Really it is.

Only Will's having none of it.

"What's the matter?" I say after we've climbed the steps and explored a little bit. Lucy and Valerie—doppelgangers, separated by thirty years—are running in and out of tunnels, taking photos of each other, laughing.

Will sighs the sigh of an old man. "I'm just hot," he says, squeezing out his words.

Cambodia: one of the places where everything just blows you away.

Fair enough. It *is* hot, smotheringly so, the kind of hot that pulls all the air out of your lungs the moment you walk outside. Every time we get back on our little mini tour bus, Vulthy, our guide, reaches into a cooler and passes out freezing cold towels scented with jasmine. Rubbing them over your face, along the back of your neck, with the bus's cranked-up AC drowning out the surrounding voices, is better than sex.

"I know," I say, and give Will a little hug, against which he squirms, resisting my body heat, maybe more. "You just have to give in to it. Just accept that you're going to be hot, that you're going to be sweaty—then go have fun."

He won't even meet my eyes, just sighs and wipes his hair away from his forehead.

It's been a long year. I don't know what else to say. We arrived in Hong Kong and it was hot, we settled in, we sweated, we saw the sights. Winter came and it was freezing cold in our unheated flat, and so damp that mold grew on the inside walls. We traveled to Vietnam, to the mainland, to Beijing, to Xi'an, to Shanghai and Cheng Du and Ping'an and Yangshuo. Lucy and I counted up all the trips we've taken and got to twenty.

Will at Banyan temple in Cambodia, looking/ feeling/being miserable.

In some ways that was the easy part. The harder part, for Will at least, was when we were at home, when his friends turned on him, when his illusions about being able to go to the other side of the world and feel happy were rattled. Since the middle of May he's been ready to go home, quietly curling into himself and keeping himself numb until he's back in Virginia, back with Maria and Charlie and the other kids he loves—and who love him.

But no, first we have to drag him to Cambodia, first we have to haul him to six or seven different temples in the smothering wet heat, driving past semi-squalid shacks and over dusty roads, the van surrounded by women and girls trying to sell postcards and scarves and bracelets every time we stop.

For what it's worth, Cambodia is a delight. The people (even these saleswomen) are gracious, the food is a mix of Thai and Vietnamese, the massages are cheap (and appropriate), and the countryside is beautiful: red-brown soil and palm trees, huts on stilts, and dogs barking in the warm evening glow. We spend an entire evening at the top of one small temple, watching the sun set over an endless green forest, towering thunderheads twenty miles away bending the light into shades of yellow and gold, blue and purple.

None of which matters to a nine-year-old—or at least not our nine-year-old. Will has spent much of the trip thus far reading books. He brings one down to breakfast with him, scooping dry cornflakes into his mouth without lifting his eyes from the page. When the rest of us go out to the hotel's saltwater pool to cool off, he sprawls on the bed in his room and smirks over some joke in one of his *Disgusting Science* books. He spent most of the time during the previous evening's dinner showcase of Cambodian folk dance and music lying on a sofa at the back of our balcony area, sighing loudly.

At the temple I try to appease him, offering him a granola bar and some water, assuring him these will boost his energy and cool him off. He accepts both as though I'm handing him dry bread and poison.

I try to engage him, asking him how to set the black-and-white feature on my camera, how to create images with a higher intensity of blue and red the way he did on his. He shows me the settings, hands the camera back to me, and doesn't say another word.

I try to ignore him, snapping pictures of the various rock faces, the jungle spreading out beyond the temple walls, Lucy and Jamie pretending to pick the Buddha's nose.

I try to use his passive-aggressiveness to my advantage, snapping a few poetic images of him slumped on a wall, his back to me, the distant smiling face of a Buddha just visible over his shoulder.

But none of these works. Will trudges along behind us, slumping when we stop, all but rolling his eyes when we continue forward, every angle of his body determined to convey his utter dissatisfaction with the heat and his parents and this place and one more stupid several-hundred-year-old temple. At one point, Vulthy suggests we pose for a family picture, and Will sighs so loudly and so deliberately that I want to strangle him.

"Get a grip!" I say. "We're here for a whole forty-five minutes. Just relax and enjoy yourself!"

This is all of us at Bayon Temple in Cambodia with our good friends, Chris and Valerie.

My voice has more edge than I intend—or maybe not. Maybe it's just the exact amount of anger I'm feeling right now, anger at the way he's behaving, anger at the fact that I put him in this situation, anger that I can't do anything to help him now, anger at my own anger.

We wander a bit more. I'm still tinkering with the settings on my camera, trying to make myself feel better by getting some good photos of what I'm beginning to realize is probably my favorite temple. Eventually I glance around and realize that everyone else has moved on. Picking up my pace, I dart past stone walls older than anything I've seen or touched before. I stumble up a small flight of stairs, into a darkened cloister. To my left everything is blocked off, collapsed stone walls and broken pillars barely visible in the gloom. To my right is a series of old planks laid out over an uneven stone floor. I go right. The trail takes me straight, then left, then straight again, ducking beneath ad hoc scaffolding built to support the low roof. I keep moving, still trying to figure out my camera, not quite sure where everyone is. Then, at a juncture, I hear "Daddy!" and I look to the right.

A corridor stretches that way, pitch black in the blackest way possible, the sort of darkness you only find buried under forty feet of earth or in an ancient temple made of stones upon stones. At the far end, I can see a golden light, small figures moving back and forth in front of it. I turn, stumble forward.

I arrive in a small enclosure, maybe 6 × 8 feet, open on all four sides to more low, dark corridors that seem to stretch for hundreds of yards. The only light comes from a small wax lantern next to a statue of a seated Buddha. Someone has erected a faded canopy over the Buddha, probably to protect him from dripping rain, and a glowing golden sash of silk has been draped over his shoulders.

Next to this, on the ground, squat two men with bare feet and worn trousers, holding out wands of incense between clasped palms. Several dozen of the sticks smolder in a sand-filled urn beside them.

Of our group, only Vulthy and Ellen remain in the chamber, the dancing light drawing shadows over their eyes. I glance at our guide. He nods, gives me not so much a smile as a warming look.

"This," he says, "is the most holy place." And he bends back his head, looks straight up.

I attempt to follow his lead, but can't because I'm toward the side and under a low arch. It is at this moment, however, that I realize we must be in the center of the temple, under the tallest tower, at the very heart of the very heart of this heap of stone. As Vulthy nods to the two men and departs, Ellen and I linger, taking in the small, festive canopy, the silken yellow sash, the stone walls that look coal-black in the flickering light.

Standing there, I feel a deepening of the air, as though it's grown darker, cooler, as though the temple is somehow sinking into itself, sliding into the earth. The air is musky and smells of soil and joss and old water, all of it edged, not unpleasantly, by the slightly acrid scent of the two men and my own sweaty shirt.

I glance at Ellen. She looks back, raising her eyebrows just a touch, showing the hint of a smile. I say, "Wow."

She nods. "I know."

I look at the two men. One of them holds out the incense, gestures with it. I nod and reach for my wallet.

Years ago, when I was finishing grad school and Ellen was beginning to wonder if being married to a high-strung, task-oriented, obsessive-compulsive man with a PhD was really her idea of fun, the two of us took a trip to France to visit an old friend. We did the usual sightseeing things, ate as best we could on a grad-school budget, spent a lot of time hanging out in parks and cafés, sipping beer and talking about our college years. One evening we ended up having dinner on the hill near Sacré Coeur, and on a whim decided to visit the church.

It was a windy night, especially that high up on the hill, and stepping into the cathedral was like entering another world: The lights were dim, the only sounds were the murmur of docents and the dull rattle of the wind outside. An overwhelming sense of the sacred reigned, a sense of a still place protected from the chaos without.

We did the usual tourist circuit, gazing at the vaulted ceilings, the massive pillars, the huge white altar with the fresco of Jesus with his arms spread over it. At one point we split up, wandering on our own, enjoying the peaceful silence, and eventually I found myself standing in front of a bank of candles glowing in red-glass jars. The smell of hot wax was strong, and above the sound of the wind I could hear the sputtering of wicks. I'm Lutheran, mind you, was born and raised that way, and don't really believe candles have much to do with prayers being answered, anymore than, say, eating ice cream or mowing the lawn. But things with Ellen were so rough at that time and this place was so clearly holy that I figured, not a little ironically, *What the hell?* I put down a few francs and lit a candle for Ellen, for our marriage, for her thinning patience.

Sixteen years later, here we are in Cambodia, and she's still standing next to me. Her patience, if not stronger, is at least worn thin as often by our kids as by my sense of humor, and on occasion she's actually been known to admit that, frankly, being married to me isn't the worst thing that's happened to her.

The way I see it, if a French, Catholic god is willing to help a Lutheran boy from the upper-Midwest, then maybe a Buddhist god could see fit to as well. Pulling out a 5,000 *riel* note, I hand it to the man with the incense, holding up three fingers, one for each of our children—though at this moment, my thoughts are particularly on Will.

The man takes the money, lights the sticks, and hands them to me. I hold them upright between flattened palms, close my eyes, and bow silently, three times, in the Chinese way. Then I open my eyes and breathe in the incense. Squatting on the cool stone, I nestle the sticks into the sand-filled urn.

But it appears I gave the man too much money, because he hands Ellen three sticks as well. She, too, closes her eyes, bows silently three times, and places them in the sand. I don't even think to ask what she prays for; I don't have to.

And then I feel a gentle tug on my hand. The second man has my palm between his fingers, and is pulling it toward him. I watch as he takes a piece of red yarn—I later realize it's a thin, tightly woven bracelet—and wraps it around my wrist. He attempts to knot it. But I'm too big. He says something to the first man, who laughs quietly and selects another piece of yarn from a sheath. Again the guy attempts to tie it around my wrist, but again it seems too short.

"Here," I say, and show him, rolling it off the bones of my wrist to the narrower part just above, where the bracelet fits nicely.

The other man is tying one around Ellen's arm, and as they proceed the two men break into a murmuring prayer, warm and low and gentle as—I don't know—water over smooth stones? A breeze beneath a shade tree? Leaves rustling on the warmest night of the year? We stand there, Ellen and I, these two men on their haunches in the ancient dark, whispering to us, for us, to some ancient power. And we feel immensely blessed.

And then it's done. They release us and we nod our thanks and step away from the lantern and the shrine and into the darkest black that surrounds everything. We're moving toward the passageway when I stop, remembering Vulthy in this same spot. I look up.

I don't know how to explain what happens next. Maybe it's just fatigue. It's been a long day, after all, and a long week, and a long year—an *exhausting* year, every day filled with unexpected stresses and new mysteries to solve.

Or maybe it's the kids—Will with his weariness, his resignation, his unwillingness even to try to have fun. And my sense, every time I see him this way, that somehow I've failed him by dragging him to stranger and stranger places that have nothing to do with who he is and what he wants, by not teaching him how to relax and enjoy the unexpected experiences that life has to offer.

Or maybe it's a sudden, tangible awareness of how lucky we are, of what a gift this year is, despite Will's surliness and the constant low-thrumming stress of living abroad.

Or maybe it's religion, a remote Buddhist god reaching down and tapping some part of my ribcage that hasn't been prodded for a long time. I'm a Protestant boy in a strange land, after all, and even when we're home in Virginia I only make it to church once or twice a quarter—and that's a generous estimate.

Or maybe it's just the age of it all, this 800-year-old tower rising above me, these stones set in place by men and women so long dead that their dust may well be part of my own bones. Gone, for an instant, is the world of cell phones and digital cameras and tourist minibuses with ice-cold wet towels. Gone are oil spills and computer viruses and the 200,000-plus landmines still buried in Cambodian soil. Gone is the Tea Party and health care reform and political vipers who are only as relevant as their last snide comment.

What I see, when I look up, is a light. A small square of sky, dim and gray, maybe 200 yards distant. I see outcroppings of stone, some near, some far, all jumbled, and all rubbing up against this light. I see the occasional flash of wings, the rustle of feathers against rock. We're a thousand years ago, in this temple, in the middle of a jungle filled with vines rambling over trees as tall as skyscrapers, a jungle that stretches for hundreds of miles in every direction beneath a sky that is blue and wide and over soil that is red dirt and gray rock.

And looking up, taking all this in, Ellen beside me, air catches in my lungs, my shoulders rise and fall—and out of my throat comes a single, broken, sob.

EPILOGUE

It's Christmas Eve, 2010. We're back in our Virginia home, curved around the Christmas tree in the front window. The floor is carpeted with wrapping paper, ribbons are flying through the air, our ears are ringing from the various shrieks—"Oh! It's a robotic arm!" "Oh, it's a . . . sweater." "Oh! Oh! It's a, a, a—what is it?" This last usually comes from Jamie, who's taking his cues on this, his first full-fledged, overindulgent, American-style Christmas, from his brother and sister.

Ellen's mom is there, and both of my parents. It's the first time we've ever done this—gathered all the in-laws at once—and with Ellen's dad absent, it's a simultaneously rich and quietly melancholy experience. Ellen's mom sits on the couch, hands in her lap, trying to help Jamie when he'll let her, murmuring approval when Lucy holds up a gift she really likes. My mom has her camera out, and glows, a smile plastered to her face. My dad just laughs.

The kids are tearing through their presents. We try not to let them do this, always starting the evening with the best of intentions, insisting that we each take turns opening a gift, one at a time so that everyone can see what everyone got, so that everyone will know what everyone else gave, so that each present can be celebrated as its own unique expression of—well, whatever it is that you call that peculiar intersection between thoughtful offerings and unabashed greed.

Every year, though, the gift-opening slides into a free-for-all, an eruption of tape and bows and paper and those peculiar wiry ties used to lock action figures against a sheet of cardboard. Ellen and I frantically take notes, trying to keep track of who gave who what so that the thank you notes won't express gratitude to Aunt Barb for the life-sized, professionally weighted medieval mace that came from Uncle Mark. Jamie brings gift after gift to Will, asking who it's for. Lucy rips open everything with her name on it, intent on finding the gumball machine she *insists* Santa will bring for her, despite Ellen's repeated assurances in the preceding months that Santa, like Mommy, hates gum chewing.

It's exhausting.

Then around nine o'clock, there's a lull in the action. Ellen seizes the moment, giving me the signal, and we present each of the kids with a pair of photo albums from their year in Hong Kong. For Will and Lucy, these pictures were culled from the 3,000 or so they each took over the course of the year. Jamie's albums are drawn from Ellen's snapshots. All three gifts cover the entire year, from the night we arrived in a jet-lagged haze all the way through our last dinner with Chris and Valerie in Kowloon Tong on our way back from Indonesia.

This picture pretty much says it all: in Cambodia, in the middle of nowhere, all of us just wandering. Perfect.

Everything stops. Will's and Lucy's heads are down, their eyes scanning as they flip the pages: spiders the size of tea saucers, squid at the wet markets, tea eggs, pig heads, Victoria Harbour, crickets in bags at the bird market, dragons at the New Year's parade, the Big Buddha, shimmering storefronts full of brass gods in Vietnam, the Bird's Nest in Beijing, old women doing tai chi, friends from school, sunsets over Cambodia.

Occasionally they shout, "Will, remember this?" The jellyfish at Ocean Park. "Lucy, look! Remember?" The orange sails of a junk on the harbor. "Remember?" Speckled moths that almost disappear against the concrete walls of the dorms we used to pass every day. "Remember?" A sign with a red circle and line showing a man urinating and missing the toilet, bearing the legend *Please Be Considerated.* "Remember?" Panda bears. "Remember?" Our bare-walled flat.

It goes on for twenty minutes, the other gifts forgotten, the packages under the tree ignored. They haven't talked much about Hong Kong in the time we've been back, throwing themselves into their old lives, relishing old friendships and old rituals and the ease of living in a place where everything smells familiar, where the food wrappers are in a language they understand, where it isn't so damn hot. But now it's an outpouring of memory, pointing and laughing and saying *Remember this? Remember this? Remember?*

Here's what I remember: It's February and we're in Yangshuo, in the Guangxi Province, in southwestern China. Yangshuo is a fairyland. Everywhere you look, karst mountains rise out of the earth, skyscraper-tall formations that climb and fall, climb and fall in individual, graceful waves. If you've ever seen a Chinese calligraphic painting depicting steep rounded mountains with clouds floating over their tips, that's Yangshuo. And chances are, if you've ever seen those paintings, you've thought, *Dang! I want to go there!*

And you're right: You do.

Anyhow, it's our last day in Guangxi, and we're hiking a back route to Moon Mountain, a nearby peak with a massive sphere cut through its center by centuries of rain and wind. We're way out in the middle of nowhere, on dirt paths, cutting through palm groves and patches of garden where you can still smell the charcoal fumes from when they burned the ground cover at the end of the growing season.

We're not entirely sure where we are. The instructions we received from our hotel said something about a fork in the path, and we haven't found any such thing. Eventually we stumble into a small village. There's a basketball court there, and small red hens running around pecking grain from the tarmac. On a flat stone wall outside one house, someone has laid out a head of lettuce from gate to gate, a leaf at a time, each glistening with water.

We move on through the village, passing mud-brick houses washed with yellow paint. We see a small canteen to our left, where a girl in a pink raincoat and black boots chats on a rhinestone-covered cell phone; behind her, four men play cards on a plastic table, their faces shriveled and brown.

Will and Lucy are ahead of us. They're running. Past the mustard-colored houses, past the girl in the raincoat, past a pair of roosters eyeing each other near a water pump. The path we're following is cobblestone and as old as God, the rocks uneven and slippery even when dry.

Our instructions tell us to take a left between two watering holes. We're not sure what that means. Were the pumps watering holes? Or those cisterns? Eventually we come to a bend in the road that passes between two large, muddy hollows and we think, *Ah yes, this is it.* So we turn left and continue on.

Will and Lucy are still ahead of us. Each carries a stick, and both are marching through this place that is as foreign as anywhere they'll ever be, conspiring together, plotting out forts and surprise attacks on chickens and parents and their little brother. It might be they don't even see the watering holes, the mud-brick buildings, the low gray sky, the water buffaloes in the barns, those crazy peaked mountains bursting out of the earth all around us. It might be they're so locked in their heads, in whatever game it is they're imagining, that they see none of this.

This is near Yangshuo, Guangxi Province. If it looks like it's too good to be true, that's what we thought, too.

But I do. And Ellen does, too. And what we see as well is our family, deep in rural China, wandering through a village in the middle of nowhere. We see our children, kids raised in Virginia and watched like hawks by their parents and their day-caregivers and their preschool teachers, watched so carefully they didn't learn to ride bikes until they were eight and five. We see our kids, moving beneath that sky, past those ragged palms, toward those glorious mountains—we see our kids running along, hair tousled, shirts gritty with dust, heads full of adventure, the whole world open before them.

INDEX

ABOUT THE AUTHOR

Paul Hanstedt left his home in Wisconsin at the age of twenty and flew to Tanzania, East Africa where he promptly got lost. He's been getting lost ever since having traveled to nearly thirty countries, often dragging his family along. The product of a Midwestern Lutheran upbringing, Hanstedt graduated from Luther College, and is now a professor of English at Roanoke College where he also edits the *Roanoke Review*. His writing has appeared in numerous literary journals, as well as MLA's *The Profession*; *The Chronicle of Higher Education*; and *Brain, Child*. When not traveling or teaching, he consults on matters of general education and curricular revision, is a staple on Virginia Public Radio, and blogs at *www.whiteboyfromwisconsin.blogspot.com* and *www.nochickenpatties.blogspot.com*, his website for harried parents who are sick of bad food. He is also the author of *General Education Essentials: A Guide for College Faculty*. Hanstedt and his family live in Virginia.